INCEPTION POINT

The Use of Learning and Development
to Reform the Singapore Public Service

James Low
Civil Service College, Singapore

INCEPTION POINT

The Use of Learning and Development
to Reform the Singapore Public Service

World Scientific

NEW JERSEY · LONDON · SINGAPORE · BEIJING · SHANGHAI · HONG KONG · TAIPEI · CHENNAI · TOKYO

Published by

World Scientific Publishing Co. Pte. Ltd.

5 Toh Tuck Link, Singapore 596224

USA office: 27 Warren Street, Suite 401-402, Hackensack, NJ 07601

UK office: 57 Shelton Street, Covent Garden, London WC2H 9HE

Library of Congress Cataloging-in-Publication Data

Names: Low, James (Civil servant), author.

Title: Inception point : the use of learning and development to reform the
    Singapore Public Service / James Low.

Description: New Jersey : World Scientific, [2018] | Includes bibliographical
    references and index.

Identifiers: LCCN 2017049050 | ISBN 9789813235069 (hardcover)

Subjects: LCSH: Singapore--Officials and employees--In-service training. |
    Singapore--Officials and employees--Training of. | Civil
    service--Singapore--History. | Civil service reform--Singapore--History.

Classification: LCC JQ1063.A69 L96 2018 | DDC 362.6/3095957--dc23

LC record available at https://lccn.loc.gov/2017049050

British Library Cataloguing-in-Publication Data

A catalogue record for this book is available from the British Library.

For any available supplementary material, please visit
http://www.worldscientific.com/worldscibooks/10.1142/10850#t=suppl

Desk Editor: Karimah Samsudin

Typeset by Stallion Press
Email: enquire@stallionpress.com

Printed in Singapore

Contents

Preface

I was on a consultancy in a Southeast Asian country in 2003 when a local civil servant told me, "If only we had Lee Kuan Yew, we will be as successful as Singapore."

Conversations with foreign officials since did span beyond a single leader in explaining Singapore's transformation — effective governance, economic strategies, the early embrace of infocommunication technologies (ICT), and so on. Reforming the bureaucracy was an engaging topic too, from growing policy-making capacities to using case studies for realistic training. However, reforming the bureaucracy rarely featured as a factor in modernising developing countries in these discussions.

In 2007, these ruminations intersected with insights arising from the history of the Singapore Public Service I was researching for the book *Pioneers Once More*. The course from colonial bureaucracy to high-performing Public Service, framed against the rapid modernisation of Singapore, raised to the fore themes of constant reforms and the use of training as an agent of change. The story of learning and executive development as an inception point through which reforms were introduced into the Singapore Public Service, began to emerge.

However, it was only in 2010 when Professor John Wanna (Australian National University) and Professor Evert Lindquist (University of Victoria, British Columbia) encouraged me to develop this story fully as a PhD research. For their patience in guiding me, germinating and shaping the ideas into this book over the next four years, I will always be grateful.

This is also the story of the men and women who pioneered the Singapore Public Service and Civil Service College (CSC). I am deeply appreciative to all of them whose recollections allowed me to flesh out this book: Mr Lim Siong Guan, Mr Peter Ong, Mr Herman Hochstadt, Mr Ngiam Tong Dow, Professor Kishore Mahbubani, Ms Lim Soo Hoon, Ms Lim Hsiu Mei, Mr Tan Boon Huat, Mr Yam Ah Mee, Mr Kirpa Ram Vij, Dr Tan Thiam Soon, Ms Teo Hee Lian, Mr John Ewing-Chow, Mr David Ma, Ms Patricia Lam, Mr Roger Tan, Mr Lim Ang Yong, Dr Ang Chin Tong, Ms Jaimie Teong, Ms Tina Tan, Mr M. Logendran, Ms Michelle Wong, Ms Ngiam Su Wei, and Dr Rinkoo Ghosh.

I was not spared the challenges of archival research, encountered by not a few scholars studying Singapore. I am thus beholden to many people, some of whom wish to remain anonymous, who helped me access useful records, from the CSC, National Archives of Singapore and National Library, to the ANU Library, National Archives of Australia, National Library of Australia, and Hong Kong Public Records Office. Professor Rodney Lowe and Mr Tim Yap Fuan, in particular, helped me navigate The National Archives, Britain, and National University of Singapore Library respectively.

I am grateful to the Dean and management of CSC for their strong support.[1] Thanks to my colleagues and friends whose assistance and encouragement spurred me on: Donald, Aaron, June, Boon Kwan, Felina, Sheila, Karin, Su Fern, Naomi, Huey Bing, Richard, Joseph, and many more. I am indebted to Wendy for designing the cover art.

Sandhya, Karimah, and World Scientific were wonderful in the production process.

Professor Tan Tai Yong and Dr Albert Lau have been instrumental in inspiring my academic pursuits all these years, and my special gratitude to Prof Tan for writing the foreword.

Above all, I thank God, for blessing me with Esther, Ethan, and Joye, whose love inspired me and accompanied my journey.

November 2017
Singapore

---

[1]All views in this book are the author's and do not in any way represent the Civil Service College or Singapore Public Service.

Foreword

The pivotal role played by the public service in Singapore's growth and development as a nation-state cannot be overstated. Singapore's founding Prime Minister, the late Lee Kuan Yew, had attributed the success of the Singapore model to a strong political leadership working hand in glove with a politically attuned and highly efficient civil service on many occasions. He pointed out that the political leadership was able to deliver the goods because of a "neutral, efficient, honest civil service...that shared the same nation-building philosophy and development goals of the political leaders".[1] Prime Minister Lee Hsien Loong reaffirmed this by pointing out that Singapore had taken the important political decision to build "a high-quality civil service with a strong ethos of service, that appreciates our national context and that civil servants are proud to be part of."[2]

The political side of the Singapore Story is well-known, and there is certainly no dearth of detailed studies on the political system built by Lee Kuan Yew and the People's Action Party (PAP) from 1959. However, the other side of the coin, the politics and processes of policy-making and the evolution of the public service in response to the shifting circumstances of state and nation building since 1965, had not received the scholarly attention that is commensurate with its obvious significance in the Singapore story. Indeed, beyond Chua Mui Hoong's *Pioneers Once*

---

[1]Speech by Lee Kuan Yew, Senior Minister, for the Africa Leadership Forum, 8 November 1993.

[2]Speech by PM Lee Hsien Loong at the Administrative Service Dinner and Promotion Ceremony, 26 April 2016.

More: The Singapore Public Service 1959–2009, published in 2010, an insightful volume that captured the experiences of the public service through extensive interviews with a wide range of civil servants, the extant literature on the character and function of the public service in Singapore is inexplicable sparse.

James Low's new book, *Inception Point: The Use of Learning and Development to Reform the Singapore Public Service*, will fill an important gap. The volume is not a mere chronicle of the growth and development of the civil service in Singapore, nor of key policies that had been designed and executed since 1965. It focuses, instead, on the internal change and reforms in the civil service, explaining how training and education were used to develop the public service as a responsive institution that kept constantly relevant with the context of the ever-changing Singapore. The chapters in this book offer useful insights on the changing contexts that shaped public service thinking, and the training and education that were developed in response to the evolving challenges of a new state. The publication of this volume is both timely and important, and a much-needed addition to the history of contemporary Singapore.

I am personally delighted that James has written this book. Over the many years that I have known him, he has constantly demonstrated his ability as a thoughtful and careful scholar. He is indeed well placed to execute this task, given his training as an historian and his perch as a senior staff in the Civil Service College, where he has developed a good feel of the public service ethos, as well as the necessary insights that an outsider might not be able to offer.

Professor Tan Tai Yong
President, Yale-NUS College

Abbreviations

AA	Administrative Assistant
ADB	Asian Development Bank
ADS	Administrative and Diplomatic Service, Malaysia
ANZSOG	The Australia and New Zealand School of Government, Australia
AS	Assistant Secretary
ASEAN	Association of Southeast Asian Nations
ASTD	American Society of Training and Development, US
BMA	British Military Administration, Malaya
CAPAM	Commonwealth Association of Public Administration and Management
CEO	Chief Executive Officer
CO	Colonial Office, Britain
COE	Certificate of Entitlement
COSEC	Core Skills for Effectiveness and Change
CSC	Civil Service College
CSCG	Civil Service Consulting Group
CSCI	Civil Service College International
CSI	Civil Service Institute
CSPS	Canada School of Public Service, Canada
CSSDI	Civil Service Staff Development Institute
CSTDI	Civil Service Training and Development Institute, Hong Kong
CSTI	Civil Service Training Institute, Hong Kong
DPM	Deputy Prime Minister

DS	Deputy Secretary
EIC	East India Company, Britain
ENA	École Nationale d'Administration, France
EO	Executive Officer
ESCAP	Economic and Social Commission for the Asia and the Pacific, United Nations
Excel	Excellence through Continuous Enterprise and Learning
FC	Foundation Course
FY	Financial Year
GDP	Gross Domestic Product
HEO	Higher Executive Officer
IDC	Inter-Departmental Charging
INSEAD	Institut Européen d'Administration des Affaires, France
INTAN	Institut Tadbiran Awam Negara, Malaysia
IPAM	Institute of Public Administration and Management
IPD	Institute of Policy Development
LAP	Leaders in Administration Programme
MCS	Malayan Civil Service, Malaya
MFE	Managing for Excellence
MBA	Degree of Masters in Business Administration
MNCs	Multi-national corporations
MOF	Ministry of Finance
MPA	Degree of Masters in Public Administration
NAS	National Archives of Singapore
NIC	Newly Industrialising Countries
PAB	Personnel Administration Bureau
PAP	People's Action Party
PAS	Principal Assistant Secretary
PGU	Personnel Guidance Unit
PhD	Degree of Doctor of Philosophy
PM	Prime Minister
PMO	Prime Minister's Office
PPPS	Public Policy Perspectives Seminar

PS	Permanent Secretary
PS21	Public Service for the 21st Century
PSC	Public Service Commission
PSD	Public Service Division
PSO	PS21 Office
PWD	Public Works Department
SAF	Singapore Armed Forces
SAR	Singapore Annual Report
SASC	Singapore Administrative Staff College
SEO	Senior Executive Officer
SESL	Singapore Establishment Staff List
SLAD	Report of the Singapore Legislative Assembly Debates
SMP	Senior Management Programme
stat board	Statutory board
STI	Staff Training Institute
TAC	Training Advisory Council
TNA	The National Archives, Britain
UK	United Kingdom
UN	United Nations
UNDP	United Nations Development Programme
WITS	Work Improvement Teams

A Timeline of Key Events

1819   East India Company claimed Singapore, beginning British administration of Singapore.

1826   Singapore merged with Malacca and Penang to form Straits Settlements.

1867   Singapore and Straits Settlements administered by Colonial Office.

1869   Straits Settlements Civil Service established as dedicated administrative scheme of service; renamed Malayan Civil Service in 1904 following British consolidation of control over whole Malaya.

1942   Singapore under Japanese Occupation.

1945   British Military Administration over Singapore and Malaya after World War 2 (WWII).

1946   Singapore separated from Malaya upon return to civil rule.

1947   Trusted Commission standardised civil service into four divisions.

1951   Public Service Commission set up in Singapore.

1954   Staff Training School set up as first administrative training facility in Singapore.

1955   Limited self-government; adoption of ministerial system of government.

1956   Localisation of bureaucracy (Malayanisation).

1959   Self-government, People's Action Party won elections to form government; Political Study Centre set up, Staff Training Centre renamed from Staff Training School.

1963   Singapore merged with Malaya and British Borneo
        Territories to form Malaysia.

1965   Singapore separated from Malaysia to become independent.

1968   British announced early withdrawal from Singapore; amidst
        economic uncertainty from UK withdrawal, PAP called for
        general elections in which PAP won all parliamentary seats
        and 84% popular vote.

1969   Political Study Centre closed.

1971   Staff Training Institute set up; Singapore economy powered
        by state-led development continued to grow, recording 17.5%.

1975   Civil Service Staff Development Institute renamed from STI,
        moved to Heng Mui Keng Terrace.

1979   Civil Service Institute renamed from CSSDI; PAP won 78%
        popular vote and retained monopoly of parliamentary seats
        at general election.

1980s   CSI played key role in nation-wide Productivity Movement
        and Computerisation Programme; PAP share of popular vote
        reduced to 63% (1984 general elections) and 62% (1988
        general elections).

1991   PAP lost four parliamentary seats and witnessed worst ever
        61% popular vote at general elections; Deputy Prime
        Minister: "inculcate greater political sensitivity
        amongst. . .civil servants."

1993   Civil Service College set up.

1995   Public Service for the 21st Century reforms launched.

1996   New Civil Service College set up, consolidating CSI
        (renamed Institute of Public Administration and
        Management) and Civil Service College (renamed Institute
        of Policy Development).

2001   CSC became a self-financing statutory board by act of
        Parliament.

Introduction

Training and executive development in the Singapore Public Service is rarely associated with the modernisation of Singapore. Yet, training and development, by professionalising and reforming the bureaucracy, rendered the Public Service an instrumental institution in transforming Singapore into a successful city-state. This role played by the Public Service in Singapore's modernisation, and the reform of the bureaucracy through training and development, is absent in current discourse.

Singapore's transformation is traditionally attributed to the strategic foresight and political will of founding Prime Minister Lee Kuan Yew and his colleagues of the People's Action Party (PAP).[1] When Lee and his newly-elected government assumed power in 1959, Singapore after 140 years of colonial rule, had a Gross Domestic Product (GDP) of S$2.1 billion, per capita GDP of S$1,306 among the 1.5 million population, and literacy rate was 523 per 1,000 persons.[2] Lee and the PAP were typically

---

[1]See for example, C. M. Turnbull, *A History of Modern Singapore, 1819–2005* (Singapore: National University of Singapore Press, 2009); *A history of Singapore*, eds. Ernest Chew and Edwin Lee (Singapore: Oxford University Press (OUP), 1991); John Drysdale, *Singapore: Struggle for success* (Singapore: Times Books International, 1984); Dennis Bloodworth, *The Tiger and the Trojan Horse* (Singapore: Times Books International, 1984); *Lee's Lieutenants: Singapore's Old Guard* eds. Lam Peng Er and Kevin Y.L. Tan (Australia: Allen & Unwin, 1999); Tan Siok Sun, *Goh Keng Swee: A portrait* (Singapore: Editions Didier Millet, 2007); Irene Ng, *The Singapore Lion: A biography of S. Rajaratnam* (Singapore: Institute of South East Asian Studies (ISEAS), 2010); Asad Latif, *Lim Kim San: A builder of Singapore* (Singapore: ISEAS, 2009).
[2]Singapore Department of Statistics (DOS), *Economic and Social Statistics: Singapore 1960–1982* (Singapore: DOS, 1983) 10–13.

credited for turning the small island, devoid of any natural resources, into one of the most vibrant city-states; the GDP today is S$410 billion (US$290 billion), per capita GDP S$73,167 (US$51,744), even when the population grew to 5.6 million, unemployment 3%; and literacy 97%.[3] Its multiracial population — ethnic Chinese majority, and substantial Indian and Malay communities — live in relative harmony and crime rate is low. This stability and modern amenities rank Singapore among the most liveable cities in the world.[4] Even critics of Lee, the PAP, and the Singapore political system acknowledged, explicitly or implicitly, the central role played by Lee and his PAP colleagues in Singapore's modernisation.[5]

Even so, surely the vision of the political elite depended on the bureaucracy to be translated into policies, and then implemented. The Public Service shouldered the heavy work of state-building, from attracting foreign investment and building industrial estates to create employment, to erecting public housing to replace slums, to ramping up education to provide skilled labour for the economy. When Singapore became fully independent in 1965, the bureaucracy's list of nation-building priorities expanded to include raising a defence force and setting up from scratch agencies of a sovereign state. The ultimate realisation of the political leadership's grand vision rested on the shoulders of teachers, nurses, postmen, and other civil servants to be translated into actual public policies and programmes.

The Singapore Public Service in 1959, re-inaugurated from the colonial bureaucracy when the island became a self-governing state,

---

[3]DOS, "Latest Data," Web, 23 March 2017, http://www.singstat.gov.sg/statistics/latest-data#1.

[4]Singapore consistently tops Asia in Mercer's survey of most liveable cities. Mercer, "2017 Quality of Living Rankings," Web, 23 March 2017, https://www.imercer.com/content/mobility/quality-of-living-city-rankings.html#list.

[5]See for example, Garry Rodan, "The Growth of Singapore's Middle Class and its Political Significance," *Singapore Changes Guard: Social, Political and Economic Directions in the 1990s*, ed. Garry Rodan (New York: St. Martin's Press, 1993) 52–53; Ross Worthington, *Governance in Singapore* (London: Routledge Curzon, 2003) 1–3; Carl Trocki, *Singapore: Wealth, Power and the Culture of Control* (Routledge, 2006), 124ff; Thomas J. Bellows, "Meritocracy and the Singapore Political System," *Asian Journal of Political Science*, 17(1), April 2009: 24–25.

did not inspire confidence. The PAP government found senior officers disconnected from the population they were supposed to serve.[6] Conditioned to ruling by colonial *fiat*, these bureaucrats were mostly sequestered in the comforts of their offices and unaware of their operating milieu. Frontline civil servants were known among the population to be overbearing and corrupt: "[P]eople had to grease palms to obtain licenses, permits, immigration papers, public housing and coveted places in schools."[7]

Today, however, the Singapore Public Service is regarded as 'one of the most efficient and honest in the world'.[8] Unlike its counterparts in some post-colonial states, Singapore's bureaucracy has never interfered in the political arena. Unique even to civil services of developed countries, the Singapore Public Service has gone beyond efficiency to 'anticipate, welcome and execute change'.[9] High-performing, clean, and faceless behind the political masters, the Singapore Public Service is quintessentially 'professional' by Westminster standards.

How did the Singapore Public Service professionalise itself? How did it adjust itself to the wide range of priorities through different phases of state- and nation-building? How did the Singapore bureaucracy remain relevant through the decades?

This book suggests that training and executive development was the medium through which change was introduced into the Singapore Public Service, professionalising and reforming the Public Service. It proposes

---

[6]Lee Kuan Yew, *The Singapore Story: Memoirs of Lee Kuan Yew* (Singapore: Singapore Press Holdings and Times Editions, 1998) 319.

[7]Sonny Yap, Richard Lim and Leong Weng Kam, *Men in White: The untold story of Singapore's ruling political party* (Singapore: Singapore Press Holdings, 2009) 555.

[8]"Singapore's public institutions (2nd behind Finland) are transparent and highly efficient (1st on public sector performance)," consistently ranking first or second in "Institutions" since 1999 in World Economic Forum's *Global Competitiveness Report*, Web, 27 March 2017, http://www3.weforum.org/docs/GCR2016-2017/05FullReport/ TheGlobalCompetitivenessReport2016-2017_FINAL.pdf, 26, 318–319. Singapore topped a 2013 survey of attitudes towards 12 Asian bureaucracies, Political and Economic Risk Consultancy Ltd, "Bureaucracy: Asia's Best and Worst," *Asian Intelligence*, No. 885, 16 October 2013: 3; N. C. Saxena, *Virtuous cycles: The Singapore Public Service and national development* (Singapore: UN Development Programme, 2011) 2.

[9]Singapore Public Service Division (PSD), "Organisation Chart," Web, 4 August 2011, http://www.psd.gov.sg/AboutUs/OrganisationChart/.

that this professionalisation and constant reforms allowed the Public Service to be in the position to carry out the policies and programmes to modernise Singapore.

This use of training and executive development to successfully change, reform and professionalise a bureaucracy is not seen in any other jurisdiction. As this has not been featured in academic literature, this postulation introduces into public administration the use of training as a medium of reforms and offers a reference for other jurisdictions seeking to reform and professionalise their bureaucracies.

Filling a Literature Gap, Theoretical Significance, and Policy Implications

Despite its significance, the role played by the Singapore Public Service has not been fully explored in literature on Singapore's modernisation. Most accounts, even when acknowledging the contribution of the bureaucracy, used it as a foil to accentuate the vision and political will of Lee Kuan Yew and the PAP leaders.[10] One analyst, for example, argued that civil servants were so firmly under the control of the political leaders that they had 'lost their sense of mission and identity'.[11] When complimenting the Public Service as 'competent', political scientist Henri Ghesquiere attributed its 'creation' to the foresight and determination of the political leadership.[12] The crucial role played by the Public Service towards Singapore's success became diminished when the part of the political leadership was magnified.

On the other hand, Chan Heng Chee coined the phrase 'administrative state' to assert a pervasive role by the bureaucracy in the state's developmental activities.[13] To be sure, these arguments were not

---

[10]See notes 1 and 5.

[11]Ho Khai Leong, *The politics of policy-making in Singapore* (Singapore: OUP, 2000) 149.

[12]Henri Ghesquiere, *Singapore's success: engineering economic growth* (Singapore: Thomson Learning, 2007) 102.

[13]Chan Heng Chee, "Politics in an administrative state: Where had the politics gone?" *Trends in Singapore*, ed. C. M. Seah (Singapore: ISEAS, 1975) 68. Also Seah Chee Meow, "The Administrative State: Quo Vadis?" *Singapore towards a developed status*, ed. Linda Low (Singapore: OUP, 1999) 253.

alleging that bureaucrats were impervious to the authority of the political leadership. Rather, they were positing that the Public Service had served as the recruiting ground for the state's leaders across both political and economic spheres, and thus become part of the national elite without being subjected to any systemic oversight. The bureaucracy, it was argued, was exerting an inordinate amount of unchecked influence over the country and had developed a symbiotic relationship with the political leadership.

However, even these 'administrative state' arguments were premised upon the bureaucracy being part of the PAP's grand design. By default, they acknowledged the centrality of the political leadership in transforming Singapore. In focusing on the political leadership's primacy in developing Singapore, the existing literature has omitted the role of the Public Service in Singapore's modernisation.

To be fair, there is a discrete body of literature on the Singapore Public Service, although much of it is concentrated on specific aspects of the bureaucracy. Jon Quah wrote extensively on its management of personnel, particularly through the Public Service Commission and the fight against corruption.[14] He studied the bureaucracy's ability to implement policies formulated by the political leadership, contrasting this effectiveness with the difficulties faced in other developing countries.[15] Lee Boon Hiok led the study of statutory boards in the country's

---

[14]Jon S.T. Quah, "The Public Service Commission in Singapore: a comparative study of its evolution and its recruitment and selection procedures *vis-à-vis* the Public Service Commissions in Ceylon, India and Malaysia," M.Soc.Sci. Thesis, Department of Political Science, University of Singapore, 1971; Jon S.T. Quah, "Decentralizing public personnel management: the case of the public sector in Singapore," *New Trends in Public Administration for the Asia-Pacific Region: Decentralization*, eds. Susumu Kurosawa, Toshihiro Fujiwara and Mila A. Reforma (Tokyo: Local Autonomy College, Ministry of Home Affairs, 1996) 492–506; Jon S.T. Quah, *Administrative and Legal Measures for Combating Bureaucratic Corruption in Singapore* (Singapore: Chopmen, 1978); Jon S.T. Quah, "Singapore's Anti-Corruption," *Corruption and Governance in Asia*, eds. Susumu Kurosawa, Toshihiro Fujiwara and Mila A. Reforma, (Basingstoke: Palgrave Macmillan, 2003) 180–197.
[15]Jon S.T. Quah, "Public bureaucracy and policy implementation in Singapore," *Southeast Asian Journal of Social Science*, 15(2)1987: 77–95.

development.[16] Recent works dwelt on administrative reforms in the bureaucracy.[17]

The existing literature overlooks two important aspects relating to the Singapore bureaucracy. There is no dedicated history of the Singapore Public Service apart from two outdated accounts by Seah Chee Meow and Lee Book Hiok.[18] Quah's *Public Administration Singapore Style* has comprehensive coverage of the bureaucracy but, by dedicating individual chapters to specific subjects without threading them together, he was not aiming to chart the bureaucracy's overall development.[19] Chua Mui Hoong's was an official commemorative volume rather than a scholarly piece and, for that reason, did not adopt an academic format.[20]

Also missing from this literature is a review of the development of Public Service capabilities, and training and executive development. Training refers to "the process of developing skills, habits, knowledge and

[16]Lee Boon Hiok, *Statutory boards in Singapore* (Singapore: University of Singapore, 1975). Also Lee Boon Hiok, "The Public Personnel System in Singapore," *Asian Civil Services: Developments and Trends*, eds. Amara Raksasataya and Heindrich Siedentopf (Kuala Lumpur: Asian and Pacific Development and Administrative Centre, 1980) 431–479; Jon S.T. Quah, "Statutory Boards," *Government and Politics of Singapore*, eds. Jon S.T. Quah, Chan Heng Chee and Seah Chee Meow (Singapore: OUP, 1987); Jon S.T. Quah, "Administrative Reform and Development Administration in Singapore: a comparative study of the Singapore Improvement Trust and the Housing and Development Board," PhD thesis, Florida State University, 1975.

[17]Gillian Koh, "Bureaucratic rationality in an evolving developmental state" *Asian Journal of Political Science*, 5.2 (1997): 114–141; David Seth Jones, "Recent reforms in Singapore's administrative *élite*," *Asian Journal of Political Science*, 10.2 (2002): 70–93; Jon S.T. Quah, "Improving the efficiency and productivity of the Singapore civil service," *Asian Civil Service Systems: Improving Efficiency and Productivity*, ed. John P. Burns (Singapore: Times Academic Press, 1994) 152–185; Jon S.T. Quah, "Transforming the Singapore civil service for national development," *Democratization and Bureaucratic Neutrality*, eds. Haile K. Asmerom and Elisa P. Reis (New York: St. Martin's Press, 1996) 294–312.

[18]Seah Chee Meow "Bureaucratic evolution and political change in an emerging nation: a case study of Singapore," PhD Thesis, Manchester: Victoria University of Manchester, 1971; Lee Boon Hiok,"The Singapore civil service and its perceptions of time," PhD Thesis, University of Hawaii, 1976.

[19]Jon S.T. Quah, *Public Administration Singapore Style* (Singapore: Talisman Publishing, 2010).

[20]Chua Mui Hoong, *Pioneers Once More: The Singapore Public Service, 1959–2009* (Singapore: Straits Times Press and Public Service Division, 2010).

attitudes in employees for the purpose of increasing the effectiveness of employees in their present government positions, as well as preparing employees for future government positions."[21] It is "the systematic modification of behavior through learning which occurs as a result of education, instruction, development and planned experience."[22] Such training in the context of the Singapore Public Service can take the form of equipping employees with specific skillsets to allow them to carry out their designated functions, such as finance, human resource, record-keeping or informational technology (IT). For employees at senior levels in the hierarchy, executive development programmes can enhance their management skills and provide them with the capacity to motivate and inspire teams and departments under their charge to contribute towards the Public Service's broader goals. Training can also acquaint employees with the context in which they have to operate, whether such contexts are the bureaucracy's distinctive culture and processes, or the sociopolitical environment of the particular vocation or profession.

All these different types of training, while equipping employees with attributes, knowledge and skills, build up the Public Service's capacity to perform its goals at the same time. As Herbert Simon pointed out, by preparing members of an organisation to reach decisions that are in the interest of the organisation on their own, training devolves the organisation from constant exercise of authority.[23] Internalising within officers the knowledge, skills, identifications, and loyalties of the organisation to act towards the organisation's interests in their discretion, training allows big organisations to function. This is especially so when organisations grow so large and dispersed over various physical locations, as in the case with any national bureaucracy, that direct command of the top leadership over subordinates is difficult, if not impossible. Hence,

---

[21]William G. Torpey, *Public Personnel Management* (Canada: D. Van Nostrand Company, 1953) 154.

[22]Michael Armstrong, *A Handbook of Personnel Management Practice* (London: Kogan Page Limited, 1996) 529.

[23]Herbert A. Simon, *Administrative Behaviour: A study of Decision-Making Processes in Administrative Organisation* (New York: The Free Press, 1976) 15. Also R. N. Spann, *Public Administration in Australia* (New South Wales: V.C.N. Blight, 1973) 84.

training, regardless of its specificity, allows a huge organisation like the Singapore Public Service to carry out daily routine functions effectively, essentially allowing the bureaucracy to perform competently.

The literature on the Singapore Public Service has not specifically examined executive development and training. Training has only been discussed as part of broader topics, such as personnel management.[24] The absence of a dedicated exploration on the subject of training and executive development in the Singapore Public Service is a distinct gap in the literature waiting to be filled.

This book offers a fresh perspective into modernisation by highlighting the critical role played by Public Service training. Existing studies of Singapore's development limited their analysis to the role played by the political elite, as recounted earlier. Without diminishing the contribution of Singapore's political leaders, this account points out that training and executive development allowed the Singapore Public Service to play an also instrumental role in the country's development. By professionalising and reforming the bureaucracy, training prepared and readied the Public Service to translate the grand vision of political leaders into policy details and then to implement these, directly transforming the country. This book postulates that training and executive development is an important ingredient in readying the bureaucracy to play a critical role in a country's modernisation.

---

[24] Several undergraduate-level essays did explore the subject but these were more than 20 years ago; Sim Sock Hoon, "Training in the Singapore Administrative Service," B.Soc.Sci. (Hons) academic exercise, National University of Singapore, 1985; Siow, Viola, "Training in the Singapore civil service: the way forward," B.Soc.Sci. (Hons) academic exercise, National University of Singapore, 1998; Lai, Tony, "Administrative training in the Singapore civil service: an evaluation of recent changes." B.Soc.Sci. (Hons) academic exercise, National University of Singapore, 1995. *Recent Theses Relating to Bureaucratic Training Concentrated on Organisational Change, Customer Service*, etc.; Saravanan s/o Sangiah, "Transformation of the Civil Service College into a Statutory Board: Causes and Implications," B.Soc.Sci. (Hons), Department of Political Science, National University of Singapore, 2003; Lim Peng Soon, "Organisational Change and the Impact on the Individual: A Phenomenological Study in the Transitory Experience of Employees in the Context of Transformational Change in Organisations," George Washington University, 2006; Rinkoo Ghosh, "An Empirical Study on a Customer-focused Strategy for a Singapore Government Training Organisation," Doctor of Business Administration, Graduate School of Business, Southern Cross University, 2008.

Examining the importance of training in the professionalisation of the Singapore bureaucracy also provides possible lessons and best practices that could be replicated or adapted in other jurisdictions seeking to reform their bureaucracies. Although any lessons will need to be contextualised within Singapore's unique circumstances, there could be practices sufficiently generic for replication in other bureaucracies. Some practices could also be de-contextualised and modified to suit local conditions. Minimally, Singapore's experiences can offer policymakers references on the use of training for bureaucratic reform.

Scope of Study

This book paints an administrative history of the various training initiatives guiding the Singapore Public Service, to present the argument that training and executive development served as a medium to reform the bureaucracy. Besides assessing executive training as a catalyst to promote bureaucratic change, tracing the evolution of these various initiatives fills the gap in the subject of training in the bureaucracy currently missing from the public administration literature.

To impose boundaries on the topic, the study focuses on centralised training. The terms 'training' and 'executive development' have been clarified in the earlier discussion rationalising this study. Training in the Public Service can be highly specialised and particular to the respective agencies, because the bureaucracy is made up of different agencies with wide-ranging portfolios. Induction training in uniformed agencies, for example, will immediately emphasise regimentation, while the organisational culture in agencies such as the finance ministry will be more analytically demanding. Training for civil defence personnel concentrates on the use of rescue equipment, while training for soldiers is dedicated towards the use of firearms. Without a common platform for comparison, hence, addressing the diverse range of specialised and particular modes of training can be inconclusive.

In contrast, centralised training brings together personnel of various vocations from all government agencies for common modes of instruction. Examining such universal training is thus more purposeful in assessing broad intents and effects pertaining to training across the bureaucracy. In particular, centralised leadership training typically receives inordinate amount of attention in bureaucracies. In theory, such training is dedicated towards the best and brightest of each bureaucracy and represents the best efforts towards developing the leadership which will steer the bureaucracy. Secondly, the impact of leadership training has the potential to shape and manage public agencies towards their respective organisational goals, maximising the greatest output from a single source of input. Through documenting an administrative history of centralised training initiatives, in particular leadership training, the scope of this study aims to draw out the thesis that training and executive development is a point through which change was introduced into the bureaucracy.

Articulating the definition of 'civil service' within the context of Singapore is important. Historian Edward Blunt traced the origins of 'civil service' to the East India Company (EIC), in the name of which Singapore was colonised in 1819. The EIC used the term to distinguish civilian employees from its military and ecclesiastical establishments.[25] The 1955 re-organisation of government structure saw the newly-created ministries — which succeeded departments — inheriting the 'civil service' nomenclature. However, the need to include statutory bodies structured outside of these ministries gave rise to the term "Public Service" to encompass the 'civil service' and these statutory boards.[26] Further, political scientist Lee Boon Hiok categorised the modern Singapore administrative machinery into three organisational types — traditional civil service, statutory boards, and government-owned companies.[27] Mobility in

---

[25] Edward Blunt, *The Indian Civil Service* (London: Faber and Faber Ltd., 1937) 1ff.

[26] *Colony of Singapore Annual Report 1955 (SAR 1955)* (Singapore, GPO, 1956) 252. While 'Public Service' and 'Civil Service', and 'public service officers' and 'civil servants', thus define different entities, they are used interchangeably in everyday discourse by Singaporeans, including public officers. In this book, references to 'Public Service' and 'public officers' include the 'civil service' and 'civil servants', but references by interviewees are left in their original to preserve the integrity of the artefacts.

[27] Lee Boon Hiok (1980) 441. The Constitution states that "the public services shall include (a) the Singapore Armed Forces; (b) the Singapore Civil Service; (c) the Singapore Legal Service; and (d) the Singapore Police Force". Republic of Singapore, *Reprint of the Constitution of the Republic of Singapore*, Singapore, 31 March 1980, Article 102.

appointments of personnel, especially the elite Administrative Service officers, across these organisational types is common, and personnel from these organisational-types do attend common centralised training. Naturally, the missions of different organisational-types impose specific training on their respective personnel at the agency level. This is another reason why it makes sense to limit the scope of this study to centralised training.

The period under study begins in 1959, when the Singapore Public Service was re-inaugurated from the colonial bureaucracy. The study finishes in 2001 when the main training institution, the Civil Service College (CSC), was reorganised into a statutory board. For the first time, the central institution responsible for training was detached from a government ministry to become a separate entity. This thus provides a fitting end-point for this study.

At the same time, the distance from the present timeframe, and a relatively uncontroversial topic, facilitates access to data underwriting the study. The time lag detaches the period under examination from the issues and concerns of the present context. It helps to neutralise any potential sensitivity of the information residing in government records and officials to be interviewed. This, and a seemingly innocuous topic such as administrative training, can enable relatively easier access to archival records and officials for oral history interviews.

As a study into the use of training and development to reform the Public Service, the book will touch upon reforms of the bureaucracy. However, it is not dedicated towards examing bureaucratic reforms. The specific subject of reforming the bureaucracy, such as anti-graft measures or tightening discipline, or factors such as the compact nature of Singapore's political system or strong political will of its ruling elite, will not be the focus. Nevertheless, these factors will be noted as they arise when examining the role of training schools and their impact on the professionalisation of the Singapore bureaucracy, which is the focus of the book.

To explore the proposition that training and executive development played a critical role in the reforms of the Singapore Public Service, allowing the bureaucracy to facilitate the Singapore's modernisation, this study addresses three sets of research questions:

1. What were the reasons and circumstances that gave rise to the various training initiatives and institutes throughout the history of the Singapore Public Service? This requires us to ask why did the Singapore bureaucracy invest so heavily in executive training and what did the government expect would be the outcome?
2. How did the Singapore bureaucracy undertake executive training in practice over these five decades? This will involve investigating:
   - What were the relationships between these training institutes and their stakeholders: the political masters, the larger bureaucracy, and the state?
   - What were the objectives and functions prescribed to these training endeavours? How did they carry out these objectives? What were the effects and impact of training upon the bureaucracy?
   - What types of executive training were delivered, and what programmes were mounted and for whom?
   - What were the changing roles played by these training initiatives as the bureaucracy and state evolved and modernised over time?
3. Stepping back and taking a long view after 50 years, what were the defining features and characteristics of Singapore's endeavours in institutionalising executive development and training?

Approach Taken

This study approaches the subject as an administrative history because the genre attends to the role of training in Singapore's public service reforms over time. It is a qualitative research, drawing on archival records and interviews with officials involved as the main approach. It does not dispute the importance of other methodologies but presents one approach to expand the field of public administration in Singapore, and adds to the diversity of the field of knowledge.[28]

Administrative history is best defined by Jos Raadschelders as "the study of the structure and functioning of government, the interaction between

---

[28] David McNabb, *Research Methods in Political Science: Quantitative and Qualitative Approaches* (New York: M.E. Sharpe Inc., 2010) 230.

society and government, and ideas about government-in-society."[29] This definition reiterates the importance of locating the study in the proper government-in-society context. The research questions of the 'whys', 'whats', and 'hows' of training in the Singapore bureaucracy cannot be explored in isolation; rather, these factors will be set against the dynamics of the broader society, government, and bureaucracy during a succession of distinct eras. Five periods characterised by key traininig initiatives can be identified within the time-scope of the study: (1) the colonial era (1819–1959), (2) the Political Study Centre (1959–1969), (3) the Staff Training Institute (1971–1975), (4) the Civil Service Staff Development Institute and the Civil Service Institute (1975–1996), and (5) the Civil Service College (1996–2001). Developments in each of these time periodisation will be interrogated at the levels of the bureaucracy, government, and society, to locate the study in the proper institutional and time contexts.

Methodology: Archival Research, Interviews, and Cross-Country Comparisons

Archival research is adopted in this study because government records are one of the most credible sources of information on government policymaking. Historian Kwa Chong Guan pointed out that government documents, as evidence, ground narratives reconstructing the past as objective and credible, because "they are records of transactions completed, responsibilities discharged and as such records of accountability."[30] Although the National Heritage Board Act stipulates that

---

[29] Jos Raadschelders, "Administrative History as a Core Dimension of Public Administration," 2008, Web, 6 July 2011, http://www.aspanet.org/scriptcontent/pdfs/FPA-AH-Article.pdf, 2. This is a refinement of earlier definitions, building upon the work of earlier scholars. See Lynton K. Caldwell, "The relevance of administrative history," *International Review of Administrative Sciences*, 21.3 (1955): 455; R. L. Wettenhall, "The challenge of administrative history: an Australian perspective," *Colony to Coloniser*, eds. J.J. Eddy and J.R. Nethercote (Sydney: Hale & Iremonger, 1987) 15; Jos Raadschelders, *Handbook of Administrative History* (New Brunswick, London: Transaction Publishers, 1998) 7.

[30] Kwa Chong Guan and Ho Chi Tim, "Archival Records in the Writing of Singapore History: A Perspective from the Archives," *The Makers & Keepers of Singapore History*, eds. Loh Kah Seng and Liew Kai Khiun (Singapore: Ethos Books and Singapore Heritage Society, 2010) 53.

government records more than 25 years old become "public archives", many records in the National Archives of Singapore (NAS) still have restricted access.[31]

Nevertheless, this project seeks to overcome this limitation by adopting several strategies, such as defining a comparatively uncontroversial topic as staff training as the subject of study, and adjourning the study in 2001, as dscussed earlier. This strategy has rewarded the author with access to some Civil Service College records, which were particularly useful in appreciating the high-level of thinking and planning leading to the inception of the Civil Service College. A mine of official information can also be found in the public domain. Both Singapore's National Library and the National University of Singapore Library retained large collections of government publications, including annual reports and periodicals published by the various training insitutes. As several Singapore researchers pointed out, limited access in NAS need not paralyse research: "By cross-checking and juxtaposing sources from multiple repositories, one could still piece together a relatively coherent picture of the historical episode."[32] Files from the Colonial Office (CO) in Britain's The National Archives (TNA) offered insights into the colonial bureaucracy, including its organisational character and issues such as localisation (also known as Malayanisation in Singapore and Malaya).

Oral history interviews may not be held in the same regard as official records but interviewees can be important witnesses to a stage of history.[33] Interviews with senior public officers involved with the bureaucracy's training schools were conducted to inform on this study. The purpose of these interviews was to draw upon as-yet untapped

---

[31] Republic of Singapore, "National Heritage Board Act, 1993," *Government Gazette, Acts Supplement*, 14 May 1993, Para 2.

[32] S. R. Joey Long, "Making and Keeping the History of the US Involvement in Singapore," *The Makers & Keepers of Singapore History*, eds. Loh and Liew (2010) 154. Also Ang Cheng Guan, "Writing Diplomatic History: A Personal Journey," *The Makers & Keepers of Singapore History*, eds. Loh and Liew (2010) 171–180.

[33] John Wanna, Christine Ryan and Chew Ng, *From Accounting to Accountability: A Centenarary History of the Australian National Audit Office* (Sydney: Allen & Unwin, 2001) x–xi; Lily Tan, "Archival Strategies for Oral Sources in Southeast Asia: Southeast Asia's Forgotten History," *Reflections and Interpretations* (Singapore: National Archives of Singapore, 2005) 35.

sources and, through integrating multiple perspectives, develop a holistic and detailed description of the events and dynamics pertaining to training and executive development in the Singapore Public Service.[34] In selecting interview subjects, a key criterion was identifying 'privileged witnesses' in order to extract information as sources for the study.[35] Most of these interview subjects were listed in various documentary sources, in many instances containing official designations, altogether making them desirable informants. A consideration was the positions they held and roles they played that had an impact on the developments of the various training schools. To temper against security and policy sensitivities, interview subjects were assured that the scope of interviews was restricted to the subject of training alone and until the period of 2001. The time lapse also allowed them the time to reflect and locate their recollections, though this may result in retrospective rationalisation which could limit objectivity.

Cross-country comparisons also help to situate the training initiatives of the Singapore Public Service and sharpen their features. For meaningful comparisons, jurisdictions should share characteristics similar to those of Singapore, such as British colonial tradition, Westminster parliamentary system of government, small jurisdictional size, efficient and incorruptible bureaucracy, and so on. Such specifications preclude comparison with some better-known institutions: the Australia New Zealand School of Government (ANZSOG),[36] Canada School of Public Service (CSPS), France's Ecole Nationale d' Administration (ENA),[37]

---

[34] Robert S. Weiss, *Learning from Strangers: The Art and Method of Qualitative Interview Studies* (New York and Toronto: Free Press, 1994) 9–10.

[35] *Ibid* 17 and 19.

[36] Rather than centralised training, Australian public officers have long received in-service training from external providers. ANZSOG is a consortium of universities and government partners across the country, and has to compete with other vendors in the market of bureaucratic training. See Spann (1973) 485; R. N. Spann, *Government Administration in Australia* (Sydney: George Allen and Unwin, 1979) 351. The Australia New Zealand School of Government, "Who We Are," Web, 5 October 2011, http://www.anzsog.edu.au/ content.asp?pageId=106.

[37] *Training in the Civil Service*, ed. R. A. W. Rhodes (London: Joint University Council for Social and Public Administration, 1977) 5; Geoffrey Fry, *Statesmen in disguise: The changing role of the administrative class of the British Home Civil Service, 1853–1966* (London: Macmillan, 1969) 148–151, 312, 324–325, 410–411; Lowe (2011) 314; Lai (1995) 33, 41–44.

Malaysia's National Institute of Public Administration (INTAN),[38] even UK's Civil Service College in view of Britain's much larger geographical size than Singapore. Nevertheless, as some of these were held as benchmarks of bureaucratic training, 'the holy grail of training' as Rhodes attested to the ENA,[39] references where appropriate will be made with these foreign civil service schools.

A more appropriate benchmark for comparison is Hong Kong, which shared with Singapore similar British colonial background, compact jurisdictional size, unitary-structure of government, and reputation of efficient and clean bureaucracy.[40] More direct comparison was hence made with Hong Kong's Civil Service Training and Development Institute (CSTDI).[41] There are other small former British colonies with Westminster styles of government and professional bureaucracies, such

---

[38] While INTAN is nominally a centralised school, it has seven regional campuses across West Malaysia and, Sabah and Sarawak. These regional campuses have to take into account distinctly different geographical and social contexts of their civil servant participants, even as similar courses are being conducted. See Malaysia, National Institute of Public Administration, "INTAN in Brief," Web, 5 October 2011, http://www.intanbk.intan.my/ i-portali/en/about-intan/intan-in-brief.html.

[39] *Training in the Civil Service*, ed. R. A. W. Rhodes (London: Joint University Council for Social and Public Administration, 1977) 5.

[40] Hong Kong's size of 1,104 square kilometres is the closest in terms of jurisdictional geography to Singapore's 791 square kilometres. Its seven million population size is proximate to Singapore's 5 million. Although it is not a Westminster parliamentary system, its bureaucracy inherited British practices and traditions. Hong Kong Government, "The Facts," Web, 4 August 2011, http://www.gov.hk/en/about/abouthk/facts.htm; Peter K.W. Fong, "Training as an Instrument of Organisational Change in Public Administration in Hong Kong," *Handbook of Comparative Public Administration in the Asia-Pacific Basin*, eds. Hoi-kwok Wong and Hon S. Chan (New York: Mercel Dekker, 1999) 255; Jane C.Y. Lee, "Transformation of Public Administration in Hong Kong: Managing an Expanding Economy in the Process of Political Transition," *Public Administration in the NICs: Challenges and Accomplishments*, eds. Ahmed Shafiqul Huque, Jermain T. M. Lam and Jane C.Y. Lee (London: Macmillan Press, 1996) 35–37. Transparency International's 2011 Corruption Perception Index ranked Hong Kong 12th globally, and fourth in Asia Pacific. Web, 7 December 2011, http://cpi.transparency.org/cpi2011/results/#CountryResults.

[41] Ahmed Shafiqul Huque, Grace O.M. Lee and Anthony B. L. Cheung, *The civil service in Hong Kong: continuity and change* (Hong Kong: Hong Kong University Press, 1998) 64–65; Ahmed Shafiqul Huque and Lina Vyas, *Public service in a globalized world: central training institutes in India and Hong Kong* (Aldershot: Ashgate Publishing, 2004) 64–67.

as Barbados, Botswana, Ireland, and New Zealand.[42] However, their locations, entire oceans and continents away from Singapore, together with the diverse cultural and contextual contrasts, complicate meaningful comparisons. In any case, the purpose of comparison was not an end in itself but to draw out the characteristics of Singapore Public Service's training institutes.

Outline

Following this introduction, Chapter 1 provides the colonial background to situate the context of the Singapore Public Service for subsequent discussion. As Singapore was claimed by the British as a base for her empire, the remit to the colonial bureaucracy on the island was to maintain stability at minimal cost. This chapter points out that in such institutional context, training for civil servants was not a priority for the colonial period.

The next five chapters will examine the five civil service training initiatives straddling across four decades. Chapter 2 introduces the Political Study Centre (1959–1969), set up by the new locally-elected PAP administration at self-government to socialise the bureaucracy to the new political milieu. Having served as executive of the colonial authorities for over a century, the bureaucracy at the threshold of decolonisation was steeped in colonial culture; its leadership disconnected from the local population, and frontline officers largely rent-seeking. Apart from being the vehicle through which the PAP government asserted control over the bureaucracy, the Political Study Centre was the platform through which the political leadership introduced — for the first time — the use of training for political socialisation to reform the Singapore Public Service.

---

[42] In Botswana, which topped Transparency International Corruption Perception Index in Africa, the civil service was described as competent, efficient, and free of personal corruption. Christopher Clague, "Bureaucracy and Economic Development," *Structural Change and Economic Dynamics* 5.2 (1994): 287–288; Ian Taylor, "The Developmental State in Africa: The Case of Botswana," *The Potentiality of 'Developmental States' in Africa: Botswana and Uganda Compared* eds. Pamela Mbabazi and Ian Taylor (Dakar: Codesria, 2005) 51, 44–56. New Zealand was ranked first internationally in Transparency International's 2011 Corruption Perception Index. Barbados was second in Americas and Ireland 19th worldwide. http://cpi.transparency.org/cpi2011/results/#CountryResults.

Chapter 3 discusses the Staff Training Institute (STI, 1971–1975) set up in the contours of the Singaporean developmental state. Rapid state-led development soon revealed the lack of requisite management training among civil servants responsible for planning, implementing, and managing these projects. This was a gap that the STI was set up to fill. After a decade of using training for political socialisation, the STI's role in equipping public officers for the developmental state returned the training-function to providing technical skills and knowledge for the bureaucracy.

The period 1975–1996 witnessed the Civil Service Staff Development Institute (CSSDI) and the Civil Service Institute (CSI), but both referred to the same agency and hence merit discussion together in Chapter 4. The CSI was the point through which reforms like computerisation were introduced across the Public Service. However, the CSI's maturity into an institution of training for the entire Public Service brought the dilemma between broad-based training and elite executive development to the fore. Given the importance accorded to the leadership corps of the bureaucracy, the CSI's inability to offer meaningful leadership programmes resulted in its supplanting by a dedicated leadership development unit.

Chapter 5 focuses on the first Civil Service College from 1993 when it was set up, until 1996 when it was renamed Institute of Policy Development. This embryonic Civil Service College brought to realisation a dedicated leadership development centre after decades of futile efforts to develop leadership training programmes. Its establishment amid various obstacles highlighted the critical importance of political support. As a platform dedicated towards fostering the *élan* of the Public Service, the Civil Service College manifested the use of executive development as a point of introducing reforms into the leadership elite.

Between 1996 and 2001, the two existing central training schools were consolidated under a new Civil Service College which devolved into a statutory board. Chapter 6 shows that these seeming myriad of re-labelling was actually a purposeful consolidation of various training functions. The ultimate aim of turning the CSC into a statutory board was to orientate the training functions into a focal point for reforming the bureaucracy. Thus, the transformation of the CSC was a remarkably purposeful alignment of training functions to introduce reforms into the Singapore Public Service.

The concluding chapter will finally sum up the key arguments in the preceding chapters. It provides the platform for the whole study — spanning the entire 40-year period under investigation — to be analysed. What were the factors facilitating the use of training and executive development in reforming the Singapore Public Service? Could a model of training-reform-modernisation be discerned from reflecting upon the 40 years of training and development in triggering bureaucratic reforms? Does the Singapore experience offer a template for replication in other bureaucracies seeking reforms?

Chapter 1

Neglect? The Origins of Singapore's Administration and Administrative Training Prior to Self-Government (1819–1959)

When the British laid claim to Singapore in 1819, the intention was not merely to seize the island as an end; the goal in appropriating Singapore was to exploit its strategic location as a base to stage colonial expeditions into the Far East. The brief to the bureaucracy set up to administer the island-base was singular, as will be seen in this background chapter — to maintain the island as a colonial base at minimal operating cost. This directive shaped the character of the bureaucracy, and ensured that training would never feature as a priority, during the periods of 1819–1867 when Singapore was ruled by the East India Company (EIC) and in 1867–1942, when it was transferred to the United Kingdom Colonial Office. After the Japanese Occupation (1942–1945), the late colonial period (1945–1959) saw various administrative reforms, including training. However, training in the local bureaucracy was subordinate to the broader British scheme to retain authority over the island. In 1959, Singapore was elevated to a complete self-governing state.

1.1 Administration by the East India Company and as Crown Colony: 1819–1942

In 1819, Stamford Raffles claimed Singapore for the British East India Company to exploit the island's strategic location as a base to stage colonial expeditions into China. As a commercial enterprise aimed at

maximising profit, administration was not a priority.[1] To keep costs
low, the EIC maintained "the minimum administrative infrastructure
necessary for the promotion of economic activities."[2] Whether Singapore
was reporting to Penang after the 1826 formation of the Straits Settlements
or to the EIC headquarters in Calcutta after 1832, the EIC kept the
bureaucracy small.[3] The India Office, taking over the Settlements after the
EIC's abolition in 1858, continued to curtail the size of administration.
Historian Lennox Mills summed up: "[T]he history of the Civil Service
in the Straits Settlements resolved itself largely into a struggle between
the local administration to increase and the Government of India still
further to decrease, the existing staff."[4]

The EIC used the phrase "civil service" to distinguish its civilian
employees from those in its military, maritime, and ecclesiastical
establishments.[5] There were two types of civil servants: covenanted and
uncovenanted officers. Covenanted civil servants were recruited from
England, after securing the nomination of a director of the EIC and
signing a 'covenant of faithful service.' In 1826, there were just 14
covenanted officers in the Straits Settlements, only three of whom served
in Singapore, reflecting the EIC's persistence in keeping administration
small.[6]

Although covenanted recruits were originally put through two years
of training at the EIC's school at Haileybury, the prevailing belief was that
formal training was unnecessary.[7] An English university education was
deemed sufficient in preparing EIC officers to administer the colonies.
Indeed, after Haileybury's closure in 1855, covenanted officers were drawn
from university graduates without any pre-service training. While officers

---

[1] Seah Chee Meow, "The Civil Service," *Government and Politics in Singapore*, eds.
Quah, Chan and Seah (1987) 96; Quah (2010) 26.
[2] Seah (1971) 4–5. See also Turnbull (2009) 34 and 54.
[3] C. M. Turnbull, *The Straits Settlements, 1826–1867: Indian Presidency to Crown Colony*
(London: University of London, 1972) Ch. 2.
[4] Lennox Mills, *British Malaya, 1824–1867* (Kuala Lumpur: OUP, 1961) 107.
[5] Blunt (1937) 1ff.
[6] Mills (1961) 104; Turnbull (1972) 74; Robert Heussler, *British Rule in Malaya: The
Malayan Civil Service and Its Predecessors, 1867–1942* (Oxford: Clio Press, 1981) 24.
[7] Blunt (1937) 35; Mills (1961) 111.

upon arrival in India did study local languages, this was not compulsory for those destined for the Straits Settlements. Training for civil servants in the Settlements, like counterparts in India, was on-the-job:

> On arrival... the young civilian [officer] is always put at first under a man who will look after him, and train him in the ways in which he should go. ... The young civilian must remember from that start that the training which he receives from others is of little importance compared with the training which is obtained by the simple process of keeping his eyes and ears open.[8]

For most civil servants in the Straits Settlements, "information regarding native laws and customs was gradually acquired in the course of duty."[9] Local studies were left "to individual initiative with no material inducement or reward."[10] This meant that most English civil servants were barely fluent in the Malay language and few learnt the Chinese vernacular tongues.

Morale was low as the Settlements was not an attractive posting.[11] The dearth of covenanted officers qualified to deal with local issues resulted in the need to recruit uncovenanted civil servants from among local European and Eurasian communities.[12] Uncovenanted officers were recruited for their local knowledge and administrative usefulness but were subordinate to covenanted officers, and had poorer salaries and service conditions than covenanted officers.

With both the EIC and the India Office focused on maintaining Singapore as a base at minimal costs, the island's infrastructure soon fell out of synchrony with its growth. As political scientist Seah Chee Meow pointed out: "Good administration could not be sustained by an incredibly small budget."[13] The local administration, under-staffed and demoralised, allowed municipal amenities to become

---

[8] Blunt (1937) 201 and 205.
[9] Mills (1961) 112.
[10] Turnbull (1972) 75.
[11] Robert Tilman, *Bureaucratic Transition in Malaya* (Durham: Duke University Press, 1964) 43. Morale was affected by poorer promotional prospects than officers in India, and lower socioeconomic status than local businessmen. Heussler (1981) 25.
[12] Mills (1961) 115.
[13] Seah (1987) 96.

poorly maintained even as commerce and the population expanded rapidly. These, in part, contributed towards the campaign by European merchants in Singapore to petition against the administration of the island from India. Historian Mary Turnbull observed that the petition to transfer the Straits Settlements from India "made no specific complaints about the Company's civil service, but many of the deficiencies of Indian administration stemmed from the shortcomings of the bureaucracy".[14] In 1867, Singapore and the Straits Settlements were transferred from the India Office to the direct rule of the Colonial Office in London.

As a Crown Colony ruled by the Colonial Office in London, Singapore's role remained as a base for Britain's Far Eastern empire and the character of the administration in Singapore unaltered.[15] The remit to the bureaucracy on the island continued to be maintaining a stable political and social environment, at the lowest possible operating cost, to serve the security of the Singapore base. In his study, Seah calculated that the British spent very little on the social development of Singapore during their colonial rule; their focus was on building up Singapore as a bastion of the metropole's broader empire.[16]

The highest administrative authority in Singapore was the Governor and the Executive Council he presided over. There was a Legislative Council but, without the assent or veto over bills introduced by the Governor, it was not a law-making body as commonly found in other jurisdictions. As the Governor and the Executive Council members were

---

[14]Turnbull (1972) 85.

[15]Lee Boon Hiok (1980) 437 suggested that the impetus for transfer among Singapore's mercantile community was really to press for British colonisation into Malaya to facilitate their commercial interests, more than complaints of administrative neglect. Also C. M. Turnbull, "Constitutional Development, 1819–1968," *Modern Singapore*, eds. Ooi Jin-Bee and Chiang Hai Ding (Singapore: University of Singapore, 1969) 183; Tilman (1964) 46.

[16]Seah (1971) 20, calculated that between 1867 and 1937 the British committed 36% of public expenditure on regime-maintenance roles, 45% on infrastructural expansion facilitating economic development, and only 13% on social services. Quah (1996) 290 added that the colonial bureaucracy was so focused on maintaining law and order and collecting taxes that it did not introduce any reforms throughout the colonial period.

officers of the Colonial Office, British civil servants effectively governed Singapore.

In 1869, the Colonial Office established a dedicated Straits Settlements Civil Service, separate from the Indian Civil Service, but difficulties in attracting officers to serve in the Settlements persisted.[17] Even after entrance examinations replaced the nomination-patronage system of recruitment dating back to the EIC days, cadets who excelled at the examinations preferred the Home and Indian civil services. In 1904, the Straits Settlements bureaucracy was renamed the Malayan Civil Service (MCS), acknowledging British consolidation of authority across the peninsula. The creation of a unified colonial civil service in 1934 finally allowed the posting of recruits to any parts of the British Empire, including less attractive posts like Malaya. The Malayan Establishment Office in turn was set up to deploy officers across the peninsula, including Singapore. The sum of these policies contributed to the emergence of a distinct MCS as precursor to the modern Singapore Civil Service.[18]

The Malayan Civil Service, ironically, was not opened to local Malayans. Cadets were required to be "natural-born British subjects of pure European descent on both sides".[19] Rather than harness the growing number of local inhabitants who attained tertiary education to the task of governance, separate schemes of service were created to stave off complaints of discrimination.[20] Local schemes of service were subordinate to the European-only MCS, with salary scales substantially lower than European officers because, according to the official justification, "Malaya is not a suitable country for the 'poor white'; unless a European can earn a wage on which he is able to live decently as a European

---

[17]Seah (1971) 9–11a; Turnbull (2009) 100.

[18]Seah (1971) 9; Lee Boon Hiok (1976) 94; Quah (2010) 28.

[19]Colonial Office (CO) Despatch 5819/12 in Eastern No. 67, Para 2, un-dated, cited in Seah (1971) 12 and Appendix A.

[20]Edwin Lee, "The Colonial Legacy," *Management of Success: The Moulding of Modern Singapore*, eds. in Kernial Singh Sandhu and Paul Wheatley (Singapore: ISEAS, 1990); James Chin, "History and Context of Public Administration in Malaysia," *Public Administration in Southeast Asia: Thailand, Philippines, Malaysia, Hong Kong and Macau*, ed. Evan Berman (London: Routledge, 2011) 143.

should, he merely brings discredit and contempt upon the European community."[21]

Such belief in the superiority of the European race, defined the qualities sought in the colonial civil servant — "strength of character, readiness to accept responsibility, care for the people whom the administrator was serving, albeit at times rather autocratically".[22] The assumption in the Colonial Service was that a liberal arts education would provide any Englishman with sufficient foundation to administer natives in the colonies.

The pattern of informal on-the-job training continued. Recruits learned from experienced officers the local customs and practices as they adjusted to their duties.[23] When the Colonial Office introduced formal training for recruits to the African Administrative Service in 1909, this did not extend to other colonial bureaucracies.[24]

All Colonial Service probationers were only provided with formal training in 1932, by means of a Colonial Administrative Service course. This was more academic than vocational. Veterans who had served in Malaya, and favoured maximum preparatory training prior to recruits taking up positions in country, did not find these training schemes beneficial. On the whole, learning on-the-job *in situ* continued to be regarded as more pertinent. "Even the C.O. [Colonial Office] itself took a somewhat patronising view of the lectures."[25]

In the 123 years of British rule prior to the Japanese invasion, Singapore was viewed by the metropole as a base for the extension of her Empire. The priority for the local administration was to maintain Singapore as a base at the lowest possible cost. The belief in the

---

[21] Seah (1971) 15, citing *Council Proceedings, 1920*, p. C7, calculated that a local officer needed to serve seven years to match the initial salary scale of the MCS European-cadet, and 22 years to reach the maximum $8,400 annual salary, which European officers could attain within 11 years.

[22] John Macpherson, "Foreword," Robert Heussler, *Yesterday's Rulers: The Making of the British Colonial Service* (London: OUP, 1963) x.

[23] Turnbull (2009) 100.

[24] Anthony Kirk-Greene, *On Crown Service: A History of HM Colonial and Overseas Civil Services, 1837–1997* (London: I.B. Taurius & Co., 1999) 17 and 27.

[25] Heussler (1981) 265.

superiority of English cultural background meant that the Englishmen needed no prior training to administer over the natives.

1.2 Administrative Developments under the Japanese Occupation: 1942–1945

The Japanese 70-day rout of the British through Malaya was such a piercing stab into the body politic that the colonial administration never recovered post-war. In the meantime, a Japanese-installed Municipal Administration staffed by Japanese civilian officials succeeded pre-war antecedent-departments in local governance.[26]

The Japanese intended to staff the Occupational civil service with their own, surmising that "many natives were incapable of administrative duties."[27] However, with the Japanese Empire stretching across Asia, few qualified Japanese were left to assume all the senior positions in Singapore. Many of these posts were staffed by lower-ranking Japanese officials, or even Taiwanese and Koreans from Japanese colonies.[28] Local rank-and-file civil servants were ordered back to resume their posts. One writer thought that the Japanese generals were "more familiar with the art of war than of public administration."[29] Turnbull recorded that a shortage of administrators resulted in positions being filled by "inexperienced men with inferior caliber".[30]

The inexperienced and weakened administration fuelled the deteriorating wartime socioeconomic dislocation. Shortage of staples coupled with non-existent economic planning led to spiraling inflation and black markets. The Japanese suppression of civil servants' pay to

---

[26]Turnbull (2009) 194; Lee Ah Chai, "Singapore under the Japanese, 1942–1945," B.A. (Hons) academic exercise, Department of History, University of Malaya, Singapore (1956) 5–8.

[27]Major-General Mauszo Fujimura, Military Administrative Inspector, "Japan Manuscript No. 103, Outline of Administration in Occupied Areas," 7–8, quoted in Paul Kratoska, *Japanese Occupation, The Japanese Occupation of Malaya: A Social and Economic History* (London: Hurst & Co., 1998) 51.

[28]Turnbull (2009) 202.

[29]Lee Geok Boi, *The Syonan Years: Singapore under Japanese rule, 1942–1945* (Singapore: NAS, 2005) 140

[30]Turnbull (2009) 210.

reduce expenditure resulted in many civil servants levying commission
for services and participating in black marketeering.[31]

Any evaluation of the Japanese Occupation *vis-à-vis* the bureaucracy
must take into account the endemic corruption among civil servants.
This was especially destructive upon the bureaucracy's institutional ethos.
At the same time, the British defeat eroded the pre-war deference among
local officers towards colonial authority, contributing to the rise of
post-war nationalism.[32]

1.3 Post-War Developments: 1945–1955

The British Military Administration (BMA) set up after their return
in 1945 further undermined British colonial authority in Singapore.
To be fair, the BMA faced immense challenges in restoring a civilian
government: chronic overcrowding, poor hygiene, and weak law and
order. A sampling of the administrative capacity to deal with these
problems can be gleaned from Turnbull's observations of the police force:
badly equipped, corrupt, and generally hated by the public. The Japanese
legacy of "corruption of public and private integrity" persisted during
BMA, evident in the "flourishing gambling dens and brothels… universal
profiteering, and bribery".[33] When its six-month mandate expired, the
acronym BMA had become Black Market Administration to the local
population. If Britain's defeat at the hands of the Japanese eroded her
colonial authority, BMA's incompetence and corruption emptied any
moral premise on which Britain could hope to resurrect her pre-war
empire.

With the return to civilian rule in 1946, Britain attempted to reassert
her colonial rule over Singapore to the *status quo antebellum*. The Malayan
Union proposal detached Singapore from the Malay peninsular, ostensibly
offering Singapore a more liberal constitution. However, concessions for
the election of local legislators were negated by the negligible powers
conferred them, and limiting voters to a small British-subject minority.
In reality, the constitutional 'liberalisation' was window dressing for

---

[31]Quah (2010) 32; Kratoska (1998) 66.
[32]Seah (1971) 26.
[33]Turnbull (2009) 229.

Singapore's separation from Malaya, which was destined for a more rapid march towards independence. Britain's oblique aim was to strengthen its control over Singapore as the hub of her post-war Far Eastern imperial defence.[34]

The constitutional separation from Malaya detached Singapore-specific departments from the pre-war Malaya-wide bureaucracy. This contributed towards a more distinct Singapore civil service (*see* Table 1.1). However, 11 pan-Malayan departments retained jurisdiction that included Singapore in the name of policy coherence across Singapore and Malaya. The Malayan Establishment Office continued to manage senior personnel appointments in Singapore.[35] While the Colonial Office directed that public services "must to the greatest extent be staffed by local people",[36] the Malayan Establishment returned to the pre-war practice of reserving senior positions for Europeans, denying local officers access to the higher echelons of the bureaucracy. The Administrative Service, which was the apex scheme of service, continued to be exclusively European. Discrimination in staffing the bureaucracy persisted on grounds that locals lacked "standards of conduct and moral values, which are productive of impartiality and integrity, a high sense of duty and service, sympathy and understanding".[37]

However, such a return to discriminatory staffing was no longer tolerated by local civil servants. In 1947, local officers petitioned the colonial government for wartime back-pay similar to those granted to British colleagues.[38] The government responded by setting up committees, ostensibly to review specific issues. However, the authorities selectively accepted recommendations favourable to them and rejected those sympathetic to local officers. Nevertheless, from among these, the

---

[34]Yeo Kim Wah and Albert Lau, "From colonialism to independence," *History of Singapore, 1991*, eds. Chew and Lee (1991) 117–118; Albert Lau, *The Malayan Union controversy, 1942–1948* (Singapore: OUP, 1991) 92.

[35]Seah (1971) 31.

[36]CO, *Organisation of the Colonial Service Command paper No. 197* (London, His Majesty's Stationery Office, 1946) A2.

[37]Malayan Union, *Report of the Asiatics in Senior Posts Committee* (Kuala Lumpur, Malayan Union Government Press, 1946) 11, NAS, Microfilm No. NA 1445/20397.

[38]Seah (1971) 32–37.

Table 1.1: Colony of Singapore Government, 1946–1955[39]

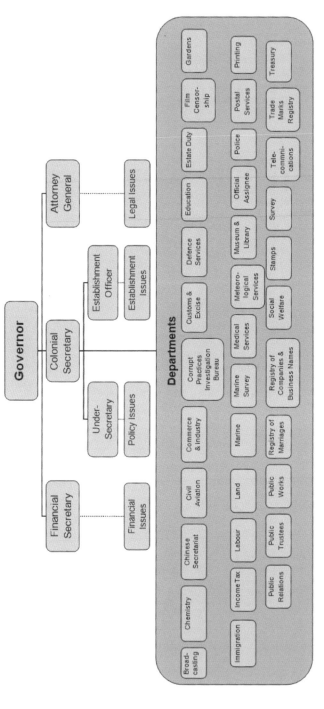

[39] Adapted from Seah (1971) 29.

Commission chaired by Harry Trusted, a British judge, standardised the erstwhile diverse schemes of services and grades into four divisions:

1. Division 1 were administrative and professional officers with high qualifications;
2. Division 2 were officers whose qualifications fell short of those in Division 1;
3. Division 3 comprised officers holding secondary school education; and
4. Division 4 contained the manual workers such as postmen, peons, etc.[40]

At Trusted's suggestion, local senior officers were also reorganised into the Higher Services Scheme, allowing them entry into Malayan Establishment positions.[41] For the first time, local officers broke the monopoly of European officers over senior positions. However, only 14 local officers were admitted into the elite Administrative Service, which topped the Division 1 hierarchy of the bureaucracy.[42]

The Trusted Commission also suggested creating a Public Service Commission (PSC) to handle personnel matters of civil servants in Malaya.[43] In 1951, a Singapore PSC independent of the Malayan Establishment Office was finally set up, taking control of the island's bureaucracy from the Malayan Establishment Office. This was a critical step towards subsequent localisation.

1.3.1 *Reforms in training*

The training of civil servants also benefitted from the wave of reforms though training reforms spun out of a drive to reimpose Britain's

---

[40] *Report of the Public Services Salaries Commission (Chairman: H. Trusted)* (Kuala Lumpur: Government Printing Office (GPO), 1947) 44, quoted in Seah (1971) 30.

[41] *Report of the Select Committee on the Public Services Commission* (Council Paper 180 of 1949), cited in Seah (1971) 39–40. The Higher Civil Service scheme was divided into Parts I and II. Entry to Part I was based on examinations and selection by the Public Service Commission. Part II officers were promoted from serving Division II officers. Lee Boon Hiok (1976) 110.

[42] George Bogaars, "Public Services," *Towards Tomorrow: Essays on Development and Social Transformation in Singapore* (Singapore: National Trade Unions Congress, 1973) 74.

[43] Quah (1987) 115–116.

colonial empire. British wartime soul-searching blamed the loss of its Far Eastern empire partly on the lack of proper training among her officials.[44] Ralph Furse, a senior Colonial Office official, argued that on-the-spot training was inadequate for the post-war setting: "Gone... are the days when the most obvious task of the administrator was to redress wrongs and to relieve suffering."[45] The problems of colonial development were increasingly sophisticated, expanding to include finance, economic planning, labour relations, social welfare, and land use. With American objections to Britain's plans to restore her colonial empire post-war, colonial civil servants would be operating "under the critical gaze of a much more vociferous and more sensitive international world".[46]

Furse recommended a three-stage training scheme spanning four years for all Administrative Officers of the Colonial Service. A Preliminary Course, providing cadets with a background of their work, would cover Colonial History, Colonial Systems of Government, native languages, and anthropology, "with special reference to the mentality of primitive peoples."[47] A two-year Apprenticeship followed, where the young officer would work under the mentorship of a senior officer in the field, to acquire an understanding of the local context he was serving in. The third stage would help officers understand the Colonial Office's policies across Britain's colonies.

Furse's recommendation was only partially taken up by a committee chaired by the Duke of Devonshire.[48] The Devonshire Committee agreed that pre-war training was "inadequate"[49] but striking the balance

---

[44]Memorandum by H.A.L. Luckham, a senior officer in the Malayan administration, to the CO., undated, quoted in Kirk-Greene (1999) 43.

[45]Major Sir Ralph Furse, Director of Recruitment, CO., "Memorandum on Post-War Training for the Colonial Service," submitted February 1943, CO, *Post-War Training for the Colonial Service: Report of a Committee appointed by the Secretary of State for the Colonies, Colonial No. 198* (London: His Majesty's Stationary Office, 1946) NAS Microfilm No. NA 1445/20450. Also, Kirk-Greene (1999) 46–47.

[46]Heussler (1963) 174.

[47]Furse (1946) 28.

[48]CO, *Post-War Training for the Colonial Service;* Kirk-Greene (1999) 44.

[49]Heussler (1963) 174.

between classroom-learning and learning *in situ* was not easy. Ultimately, limited funding and urgency to staff large numbers of vacant posts with the end of the war weighed against Furse's full training scheme. The resultant two Devonshire courses nevertheless introduced formal training into the Colonial Service. The First Devonshire Course in 1946 put recruits through a one-year programme in either Cambridge or Oxford universities, covering anthropology, economics, law, and colonial administration.[50] The Second Devonshire Course provided mid-career officers with seven months of seminars and research guided by faculties at Cambridge, London or Oxford universities.

However, debate raged on about the usefulness of formal training. Participants of the First Course actually argued "in favour of 'training on-the-job' followed by a course on the lines of a second course".[51] The Second Course also had less than satisfactory outcomes.[52] Still, the Devonshire Courses allowed the Colonial Service to keep pace with training policy in the British Home Civil Service. The Assheton Committee tasked with reforming the Home Civil Service acknowledged the need to graduate from on-the-job training to "a well thought out training scheme."[53] Accordingly, Administrative Class recruits underwent three-month-long courses covering subjects such as financial and parliamentary background of the administrator's work. However, the prevalent view in the British bureaucracy continued to hold learning from books a 'crime' "something that one just does."[54] Against that context, the Devonshire courses

---

[50]Heussler (1963) 197. Kirk-Greene (1999) 45 detailed the "Proposed Curriculum for the First Devonshire Course, 1946" across Oxford and Cambridge universities, with six months of language training to be taken at London University.
[51]J. B. Hooper, Supervisor, Colonial Service Courses, London, to O. H. Morris, CO, 8 January 1951, TNA CO 877/46/2.
[52]F. G. Carnell, "Colonial Service Second Course 1949/50," undated, TNA CO 877/46/6.
[53]"Report of the Committee on the Training of Civil Servants," Cmnd 6525 May 1943, para. 91, quoted in P. D. Lindley, *Civil Service College: A Short Account of the Administrative Processes which led to the Setting Up of the Civil Service College,* November 1978, p. 1, TNA JY 3/3. Also Geoffrey Fry, *Statesmen in Disguise* (London: Macmillan, 1969) 113; Dennis L. Bird, "Training Civil Servants: Some Reflections after 17 Years," *Public Policy and Administration* 7.2 (Summer 1992): 71.
[54]Lowe (2011) 313.

while "no more than exposure to scattered knowledge on a number of subjects... was an advance on training on the spot".[55]

More importantly, the Devonshire courses provided 'native officers' with training opportunities in England.[56] The inaugural First Devonshire Course saw a Malay officer among the 12 destined for the Malayan Civil Service.[57] Only in 1950 did such training opportunities in England cascaded down to Singapore. Four Singapore Administrative Service cadets attended the First Devonshire Course, but "[n]either the reports of their supervising tutors nor the standard of work performed since their return were entirely satisfactory, and as a result doubt has been expressed as to the advisability of sending future cadets to the First Devonshire Course."[58] The colonial authorities in Malaya and Singapore acknowledged that such training "broaden[ed the officer's] views by his travels outside Malaya",[59] but the actual value of such training was not thought to be anything more than that.

In sum, formal training despite the reforms continued *not* to be a priority. The motives behind reforms, in the face of post-war pressures for decolonisation, were really to perpetuate Britain's empire. Training reforms were "carried out in a defensive spirit given that colonies were under attack in the United Nations in the 1950's".[60] Even then, to colonial officials in Malaya and Singapore, reforms such as the Devonshire courses in the Colonial Office faraway, were not relevant or useful.

1.4 Limited Self-Government: 1955–1959

Meanwhile, the colonial authorities had to contend with the rising mixture of nationalism and frustrations among the local population

---

[55] Peter Harris, *Foundations of Public Administration* (Hong Kong: Hong Kong University Press, 1991) 194.

[56] Heussler (1963) 198.

[57] Wan Mansor Abdullah, *Service Par Excellence* (Kuala Lumpur: PNMB, 2004) 286.

[58] Urwick, Orr & Partners, Ltd, "Report No. 24, Higher Services (Part II), The Initial Training of Direct Entrants," undated, TNA CO 1017/6. Also W.C. Taylor, Acting Colonial Secretary, Singapore, to Chairman, Public Service Commission, Singapore, 28 April 1953, TNA CO 1017/6.

[59] *Ibid.*

[60] Harris (1991) 194.

in Singapore. The ethnic Chinese majority of the population had long been neglected by colonial policies. Limited job opportunities for graduates of Chinese-language schools and exploitative labour conditions were stoked by pro-Communist unionists to anti-colonial fervour. The 1954 Rendel Constitution, conceded by the British amid heightening demands for autonomy, allowed the election of a local government. However, Britain retained powers over legal, finance, and security subjects to preserve British interests, particularly the security of UK bases in Singapore.[61]

For the bureaucracy, the Rendel Constitution replaced Singapore's format of government with a ministerial system.[62] With the reorganisation of departments into ministries, the term 'Public Service' emerged as a reference to "The Government [i.e., the ministries], the City Council, the Harbour Board and the Improvement Trust",[63] the last three being statutory boards created by acts of legislation to carry out specific functions. A distinction was thus made that 'civil service' referred to the ministries that constituted the Government. 'Public Service' on the other hand referred to the broader organisation encompassing the 'civil service' and statutory boards.

The Labour Front emerged from the 1955 election to form a government under Chief Minister David Marshall. Marshall, a Jew and long-time resident of Singapore, had campaigned on the basis of decolonisation for the island. Locally-elected ministers, assuming responsibilities over six ministries, asserted the newly-introduced principles of ministerial responsibility and subordination of civil servants to political masters.[64] Reporting to these political heads were Permanent Secretaries, the most senior career-executives in each ministry, "responsible for the day-to-day administration of the Department, for formulating recommendations on policy for the Minister's consideration and for ensuring that policy decisions of the Minister and the

---

[61] Turnbull (2009) 244.
[62] Lee Boon Hiok (1980) 438–439.
[63] *SAR* 1955: 252.
[64] Seah (1987) 103–104.

Council of Ministers were put into effect."[65] This establishment of
the Permanent Secretary was important as a demarcation between the
elected and professional branches of government.[66] The British retained
the Attorney-General's Chambers, Chief Secretary's Ministry, and the
Financial Secretary's Office (*see* Table 1.2).

Among the Labour Front's first tasks was to accelerate
Malayanisation, i.e., replacing expatriate public officers with locals.
The resultant Malayanisation Commission recommended localisation
of four departments immediately, and the remaining 32 departments
within five years.[67] Accepting the recommendations, the Labour Front
Government localised six permanent secretaries but sought to retain
expatriates in key appointments for 10 years to prevent administrative
breakdown.

While the colonial authorities hoped for a pliant local government,
the Labour Front Government of Chief Minister Marshall manifested the
rising tide of nationalism among the population.[68] In May 1955, workers
on strike at the Hock Lee Bus Company and sympathising Chinese-school
students were so frenzied by the anti-colonial rhetoric from pro-
Communist unionists that fatal riots broke out. Marshall exploited the
British need to keep him in position — to prevent re-election of a
more extremist government — to press for constitutional concessions.
When the British agreed to discuss constitutional development, Marshall
sought for a fully-elected local government.[69] However, the British were
not assured by Marshall's ability to contain the Communist threat to
their bases. Failing to secure 'independence', Marshall resigned.

The crack-down on Communist-front groups by succeeding Chief
Minister Lim Yew Hock impressed the British sufficiently to grant a new

[65]Colony of Singapore. *Report of the Singapore Constitutional Commission* (Singapore:
GPO, 1953) Para 67.
[66]Lee Boon Hiok, "The Bureaucracy," *Management of Success*, eds. Sandhu and Wheatley
(1990) 92.
[67]Singapore, *Malayanisation, Statement of Policy* (Singapore, GPO, 1956) 1.
[68]James Low, "Kept in position: the Labour Front-Alliance Government of Chief
Minister David Marshall in Singapore, April 1955–June 1956," *Journal of Southeast Asia
Studies* 35.1 (2004): 41–64.
[69]*SAR 1956*: 271.

Table 1.2: Colony of Singapore Government (Limited Self-Government), 1955–1959[70]

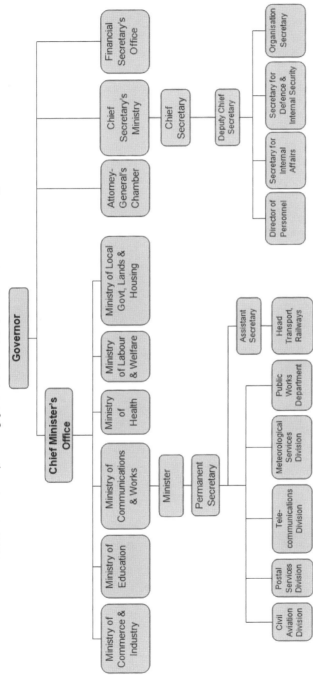

[70]Organisational structures of Ministry of Communications and Works and Chief Secretary's Ministry amplified for illustrative purposes. Organisational chart drawn up from information in Chan Heng Chee, *A sensation of independence: a political biography of David Marshall* (Singapore: OUP, 1984) 90; A. A.Williams, Deputy Chief Secretary, to multiple recipients, "Chief Secretary's Ministry — Organisation," 2 April 1955, File PRO 58/55, NAS Microfilm No. PRO 17/957; John Hingham to multiple recipients, "Constitutional changes — Organisation of Ministry of Communications and Works," 11 January 1955, File PRO 58/55, NAS Microfilm No. PRO 17/1003.

constitution in 1957.[71] Singapore would become a full self-governing state in 1959. A Council of Ministers, presided over by a Prime Minister, drawn from the fully-elected Legislative Assembly would exercise jurisdiction over domestic affairs, including the Public Service.[72]

Meanwhile, the pace of Malayanisation was exceeding the Labour Front Government's anticipation. By 1957, six of the eight permanent secretary posts were staffed by locals.[73] Stanley Stewart, a local Eurasian, even became Deputy Chief Secretary, subordinate only to the most senior appointment in the colonial bureaucracy. Many expatriates chose early retirement, apprehensive of career prospects with rising nationalism.[74] By 1957, 175 or 42% of the 416 expatriate officers had retired; another 36 had given notice to leave.[75] The Administrative Service witnessed 55% of the expatriate officers leaving within one year of Malayanisation, including nine of the 15 super-scale officers. The scramble to fill these appointments resulted in the downgrading of posts in order to relieve demand on the shrinking pool of Administrative Officers. Finally, 61 Administrative Officers — 22 of those with less than four years of service — were found to fill 65 posts.[76] The Chief Secretary reported to the Council of Ministers:

> ... Nothing can make up for the chronic lack of experience in the ranks of the Service. It is clear that the efficiency of the Administrative Service, which even now is not good, will deteriorate badly. If there was a wealth of experience and ability available in the ranks of the Clerical Service for senior Executive posts, the outlook would not be so grim. There is, however, a dearth of such talent... The prospect is an inexperienced Administrative Service, but also an inexperienced Executive Service 'supporting' it.[77]

---

[71]Turnbull (2009) 265–266 and 268.

[72]*SAR 1957*: 288; *SAR 1958*: 289.

[73]Colony of Singapore, "Singapore News Summary," 15 March 1957: 10.

[74]Compensation packages were more generous than those in other colonies. Seah (1971) 125.

[75]Governor of Singapore to Secretary of State for the Colonies, 11 March 1958, No. 43 Saving, TNA, CO1030/647.

[76]Director of Personnel to Chief Secretary, "Administrative Service — staffing position," File C.S.O. Conf. 15/56, in Seah (1971) 124.

[77]Chief Secretary to Council of Ministers, "Effects of Malayanisation on the Administrative Service," File C.S.O. Conf. 3/57, 4 February 1957, cited in Seah (1971) 124.

The Commissioner of Police admitted that the departure of expatriate officers was two-and-a-half years ahead of his estimate and prevented the Police from "maintaining present efficiency".[78]

The exodus of expatriate officers was hastened by growing signs of the People's Action Party (PAP) winning power at the impending 1959 elections. Having championed the plight of workers and Chinese school students, the PAP's popularity among the Chinese working class majority of the population helped it win the 1957 City Council elections. With the enfranchisement of 220,000 ethnic-Chinese residents under the new constitutional arrangements, the PAP's prospects at the 1959 polls were almost inevitable. However, British civil servants were "perturbed by the success and recent extravagances of the PAP".[79] In their eyes, the PAP had been associated with pro-Communist unions, most notably violence arising from the Hock Lee strikes and Chinese Middle Schools disturbances. Anti-colonial tirades from PAP leaders like Lim Chin Siong often broadened to attacks against English-educated professionals. Many expatriates chose to retire or requested to be posted to other British territories.

Nationalist sentiments and localisation also had ramifications within the bureaucracy. As Malayanisation resulted in local officers succeeding the top echelons, competing interpretations over the role of the civil service resulted in intra-bureaucratic tensions. One group sought to preserve the traditions of the colonial bureaucracy, including their entitlement to the perks and privileges of expatriate predecessors, the stratification between senior officers and rank-and-file staff, and the political neutrality of the bureaucracy. Another group led by Goh Keng Swee and Kenneth Byrne believed that local civil servants should seek independence rather than adhere to political neutrality, and prioritising perks and status.[80] Goh and

---

[78]"Appreciation of Situation in the Chief Secretary's Office following upon the retirements under the Compensation Ordinance," File C.S.O. Conf. 3/57, cited in Seah (1971) 24. Only 576 doctors were available when minimum standards required 1,600. "Doctors crisis worsens," *The Singapore Standard* 14 November 1957.

[79]Governor to Secretary of State for the Colonies, Personal No. 10, 22 January 1958. TNA CO 1030/651.

[80]Seah (1971) 70–71.

Byrne soon resigned to join the PAP to contest for the impending elections, but this intra-bureaucratic conflict would prove to have deeper ramifications.

On the eve of the 1959 elections, the Public Service was weakened by the rush to localise, especially among its senior leadership. Out of the 12,584 civil service positions, 2,634 posts or about 9% of the bureaucracy were vacant, and 187 of these vacancies were in the Division 1 grades, which consisted of the Administrative Service, Executive Service, and other professional schemes of service. Many local officers were quickly promoted to take over posts vacated by expatriates, including some not qualified for the responsibilities.[81] Efficiency suffered not just from the inexperience of the top echelons but also from the hollowing out of middle management to replace the higher hierarchical levels. The Chief Secretary assessed that "the Public Service has undoubtedly been seriously weakened, not so much in numbers as in experience."[82] Morale dipped with prospects of serving seemingly hostile political masters — the Chief Secretary found it necessary to address "reports that some civil servants were concerned about their future after the next elections", and directed:

> Permanent Secretaries, by their advice and example, should ensure that the Civil Service carried out the policy of the Government in office at the time, and that it would be their particular responsibility to establish feelings of mutual trust and confidence with the new Ministers, whatever their party.[83]

The Public Service at the threshold of decolonisation was pyramidal in personnel structure (*see* Table 1.3). The four personnel divisions organised according to job functions (following Trusted's reforms) was also dictated by officers' educational qualifications. Hence, officers in the Administrative Service leadership corps of the bureaucracy, and the executive and professional grades were organised into Division 1 by

---

[81] Seah (1987) 100.

[82] Governor to Secretary of State for the Colonies, No. 43 Saving, 11 March 1958, TNA CO 1030/647.

[83] H. Shaw, Governor's Secretary and Clerk to the Council of Ministers, to All Permanent Secretaries, and Secretary to the Chief Minister, "Informal Meeting of Permanent Secretaries," 5 March 1959, p. 2, Co.Min.15/55. Vol. 11, p. 2.

Table 1.3: Personnel Structure of the Singapore Public Service, 1959[84]

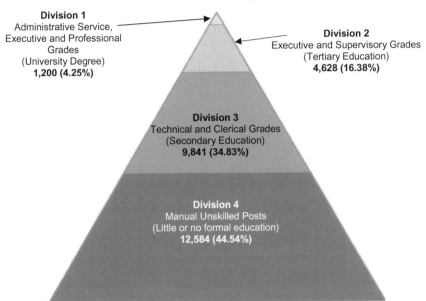

Division 1
Administrative Service, Executive and Professional Grades (University Degree)
1,200 (4.25%)

Division 2
Executive and Supervisory Grades (Tertiary Education)
4,628 (16.38%)

Division 3
Technical and Clerical Grades (Secondary Education)
9,841 (34.83%)

Division 4
Manual Unskilled Posts (Little or no formal education)
12,584 (44.54%)

virtue of their university-degree qualification. Conversely, officers with little formal education carrying out unskilled positions were categorised into Division 4. The colonial bureaucracy, on the eve of decolonisation, was very much in the same personnel structure as it was formed a century earlier: a small highly qualified elite presiding over a broader swathe of rank-and-file officers.

1.5 The Staff Training School, 1954–1959

A reform in this late colonial era was the introduction of the Staff Training School in 1954.[85] The dismal performance of Singapore's Administrative Service cadets at the Devonshire Course earlier led John Nicoll, the Governor of Singapore, to decide against sending local civil servants to

---

[84]Singapore, *Report of the Public Service Commission, 1959–1960 (PSC Report)* (Singapore: Government Printer, 1962) 4.
[85]*SAR* 1954: 213.

future courses:

> ... it is in my view, certainly for the Singapore cadet, important that greater emphasis should be laid, in any post-selection training course, on the more practical aspects of public administration. One of the main criticisms of the younger Singapore officers is that they are too academic in outlook and too little inclined to apply themselves to solid and detailed administrative tasks, and I do not consider the First Devonshire Course is best calculated to remedy this attitude.[86]

The need for formal training was not questioned. However, rather than classes at the University of Malaya, which his officers were exploring,[87] Governor Nicoll wanted:

> ... a Training Section in the [Colonial] Secretariat which would take charge of the newly entered cadet. It would be made clear that during this period, an officer's training was to be the first consideration; he would not be posted to any definite duties, but would be expected to devote a good proportion of his time to perfecting his writing and thinking in English and to case work and deviling on current files. ... the intention [is] to give the young officer by means of instruction and visits, a clear insight into the principles of public administration and the workings of Government departments, public authorities, such as the City Council, Singapore Harbour Board, etc.[88]

The Staff Training School was organised within the Establishment Branch in the Chief Secretary's Ministry (*see* Table 1.4) located at the Fullerton Building. Heading the School was the Staff Training Officer, reporting to the Director of Personnel. As a unit of the Chief Secretary's Ministry, the School drew from the budget of its parent ministry to run its activities; participants were not charged for the courses they attended at the School.

---

[86]Governor to Secretary of State for the Colonies, 10 July 1953, No. 1004 Saving, TNA, CO 1017/6. Also Urwick, Orr & Partners, Ltd, "Report No. 24, Higher Services (Part II), The Initial Training of Direct Entrants," undated, TNA CO 1017/6; Han Hoe Lim, Acting Chairman, Public Service Commission, to Colonial Secretary, 4 May 1953, TNA CO 1017/6.

[87]"Notes of a Meeting held at 2.30 p.m. on 8 May 1953 in the Vice-Chancellor's Room, University of Malaya," 9 May 1953, TNA CO 1017/6.

[88]Governor to Secretary of State for the Colonies, 10 July 1953, No. 1004 Saving, TNA, CO 1017/6.

Table 1.4: Organisational Structure of the Staff Training School, 1955[89]

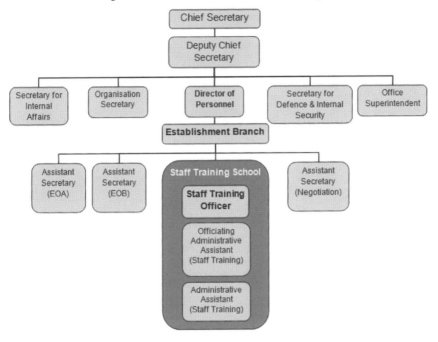

Two types of courses were held at the School.[90] Induction programmes ranged from those for Administrative Service cadets destined for senior echelons of the bureaucracy, to typists at the junior grades of the hierarchy. Vocational courses included those on supervisory skills, law, clerical work, and financial procedures.

The most significant training by the Staff Training School was the induction courses for Administrative Service cadets. A typical course spanned three weeks, covering topics like "Machinery of Government", "Social Welfare", and "Staff Relations and Negotiation".[91] Half of the

---

[89]Drawn up from A. A. Williams, Deputy Chief Secretary, to multiple recipients, "Chief Secretary's Ministry — Organisation," 2 April 1955, File PRO 58/55, NAS Microfilm No. PRO 17/957; Singapore, *Singapore Establishment Staff List, 1st April 1955 (SESL)* (Singapore: GPO, 1955) 1 and 16–18.

[90]*SAR* 1954: 214.

[91]J. Le Provost, Staff Training Officer, to The Public Relations Officer, "Staff Training: Part II Higher Services," 19 October 1955, CSO. 586/55/74, File PRO 561/55, NAS Microfilm No. PRO 24/1274–1276.

60- to 90-minute sessions in each class of 16 participants would be lectures, with the remaining time set aside for questions and discussions. Lecturers were senior officers from the departments responsible for the subjects, tasked "to give the officers attending the course a factual survey of the particular problem or Department, indicating the organisation required, the planning involved, and the main administrative problem to be found."[92]

Although its establishment suggested the authorities' interest in training public officers, the resources allocated to the Staff Training School were limited. Only a sub-unit of the Personnel Branch in the Chief Secretary's Office, without its own dedicated budgetary allocations, its staffing was reduced within three years.[93] The Staff Training Officer post was absorbed into the newly-created portfolio of Deputy Secretary (Training and Organisation), i.e., the officer had to split his attention between two subjects rather than concentrate on the training portfolio.[94] The School's facilities were also quickly found to be inadequate:

> The library is at present being used as the third lecture room and is therefore most of the time never available for its proper function. Besides, it is not possible to conduct a class of even eight people in the library (which has only one-and-three-quarters h.p. [horse power] air conditioning unit) for more than an hour without feeling the stuffiness of the room.[95]

This dilution of resources could have impacted the School's capacity to proffer higher quality programmes. Indeed, interest in the School's courses was not enthusiastic. While the 'ideal' class size of its Administrative Courses was 16, for example, classes in 1955 averaged 12 participants each.[96] Over time, the number of Division 1 officers attending courses at the School declined, with a corresponding increase in officers from Division 3 undergoing training at the School.[97]

---

[92] Le Provost to Public Relations Officer, 19 October 1955, File PRO 561/55, NAS Microfilm No. PRO 24/1273.

[93] *SESL* 1955: 17.

[94] *SESL* 1957: 17; *SESL* 1958: 16–18.

[95] Director of Public Works, "Application for Supplementary Vote, Singapore Estimates 1956," 28 May 1956, File Treasury 1955/56, NAS Microfilm No. MF 267.

[96] Tan to All Heads of Departments, 8 August 1956, File PRO 561/55, NAS Microfilm No. PRO 24/1231; *SAR* 1955: 254.

[97] *SAR* 1956: 278; *SAR* 1957: 295; *SAR* 1958: 308.

A source of 'competition' could be overseas training, which took up "the major part" of the 1955 training budget.[98] Within two years, the number of officers dispatched for foreign training more than doubled to 255.[99] Besides cannibalising into the School's budget, these overseas training opportunities inevitably posed more attractive options for public officers than local courses at the Staff Training School.

Even when the number of courses conducted by the School grew, the proportion of officers trained in relation to the whole Public Service was small. As a fraction of the total 48,000 officers, the 1,135 officers trained in 1955 constituted only 2.4% of the whole bureaucracy.[100] By 1958, only 3.4% of civil servants had been trained by the School.[101] Evidently, the mode of training for the larger majority of the bureaucracy was informal on-the-job training.

In a review years later, the Permanent Secretary of the Treasury admitted that the Staff Training School "has been looked upon primarily as a centre for elementary and introductory training... and not as an instrument for training in the higher levels of administration. It has been accepted rather than welcomed by Departments."[102] Although the colonial government decided to establish a school to train public officers, the resources committed towards this effort was limited. The shortage of instructional staff and inadequacy of facilities might have impinged on the quality of the School's training. Had courses been more useful to public officers, the demand for and attendance at these courses would naturally be much higher.

1.6 Conclusion

Records indicated that Governor John Nicoll and his staff did not make any comparable references to discussion on training in the British

---

[98] *SAR* 1955: 253.

[99] *SAR* 1960: 41.

[100] *SAR* 1955: 252.

[101] The size of the Public Service in 1958 remained at 48,000. *SAR* 1958: 308.

[102] Oon Khye Kiang, Permanent Secretary (Treasury), Ministry of Finance, 24 March 1962, "Training in the Singapore Civil Service," Try.Cf. 3711/56, File MC 218/62, NAS Microfilm No. AR 49/9/46.

Home Civil Service at that time. However, as a very senior officer in the Colonial Service, Nicoll would have been aware of the debates ongoing in Britain. While the prevailing wisdom in the Home Civil Service opposed a centralised training facility, Governor Nicoll chose to set up a Staff Training School for the Singapore bureaucracy in 1954. The Staff Training School in Singapore was significantly ahead of the British colonies in the region, and even the British Home Civil Service in its time; the Centre of Administrative Studies was only set up in 1963, and only in 1968 did the Fulton Committee recommended the Civil Service College.[103] Malaysia, which shared Singapore's colonial legacy, had a similarly-named Staff Training Centre, but this was only established after 1959.[104] Hong Kong, another British colony with similar jurisdictional features as Singapore, set up a Training and Examinations Unit in 1961.[105]

Governor John Nicoll should be credited for the instrumental role in setting up the Staff Training School. However, given his decisive role, would Nicoll's retirement in 1956 lead to a tempering of high-level attention towards the School? Did this, in turn, result in a reduction of resources to the School amid other compelling pulls on the limited budget? Did these developments undercut the School's capacity to expand the quantity and improve the quality of its training programmes?

The role of the Staff Training School should not be overplayed. The School was training more officers from the junior rungs of the hierarchy, which called into question whether it was meeting the original *raison*

---

[103]Lowe (2011) 313; Bird (1992) 71–72; Fry (1969) 132–133.

[104]Y. Mansoor Marican, *Public Personnel Administration in Malaysia*, Research Notes and Discussions Paper No. 12, 1979 (Singapore: ISEAS, 1979) 10–11, stated that INTAN was set up in 1963. National Institute of Public Administration (INTAN), "INTAN in Brief," Web, 16 November 2012, http://www.intanbk.intan.my/i-portal/en/about-intan/intan-in-brief.html indicated that INTAN was established in 1959.

[105]Government Printer, Hong Kong, *A Report on the Public Service 1965* (Hong Kong: Government Press, 1965) Para. 36, HKPRO, Accession No. A/55/81/2A; Hong Kong Government, *Report on Training of Government Servants 1952–1958* (Hong Kong: Establishment Branch, Colonial Secretariat, Hong Kong, 1958) 2, HKPRO; Ian Scott and John P. Burns, "Training," *The Hong Kong Civil Service: Personnel Policies and Practices*, eds. John P. Burns and Ian Scott (Hong Kong: OUP, 1988) 119.

d'etre of setting up the Staff Training School to train the Administrative Service and Division 1 officers. More attractive options, especially overseas training opportunities, contributed to the low number of officers — no more than 4% of the whole bureaucracy — who attended programmes at the School. The default mode of training across the bureaucracy was most certainly informal on-the-job training. The impact of the Staff Training School during this late colonial period can only be objectively assessed as negligible.

Summing up, the primary brief for the colonial bureaucracy between 1819 and 1959 was to maintain Singapore as a base for Britain's colonial empire, and to maintain the Singapore base at minimal operating cost. The metropole's goal of expanding and perpetuating its colonial interests, defined the nature of the bureaucracy — a small British elite presiding over a large swathe of locals occupying rank-and-file positions. Training in a bureaucracy bent on low-cost maintenance mode was not a priority, a development not uncommon across other British colonial possessions. Even when the Colonial Office began to initiate reforms in training — albeit to perpetuate colonial rule across its empire — these reforms were regarded by colonial officials in far-away Malaya and Singapore as of little usefulness. Instead, the establishment of the Staff Training School in Singapore customised training to take into consideration the local conditions for civil servants working in the island-colony. Still, the departure of the School's high-ranking patron (i.e., Governor John Nicoll), saw interest in structured training among colonial officials slipping, with the majority of civil servants undergoing informal on-the-job training. The token allocation of resources to the Staff Training School and more attractive overseas training options meant that the School had only a negligible impact on the training of civil servants during this period.

Chapter 2

Early Political Socialisation: The Political Study Centre and Staff Training (1959–1969)

At Singapore's decolonisation in 1959, the new locally-elected People's Action Party (PAP) government introduced the Political Study Centre to change the attitudes of public service officers. This chapter begins by setting the context of post-colonial Singapore. Public officers, having served only the colonial authorities, were nervous towards their new nationalist political masters. In turn, the PAP, anxious to pursue its nation-building agenda, was impatient with the Public Service.

Against this context, the PAP government imposed the Political Study Centre upon the Public Service to align public officers towards its worldview. As the emerging political elite still consolidating its authority at the threshold of 'state-formation', the PAP could not rely upon the bureaucracy — in its existing state of apprehension towards the recently-elected political masters — to carry out its governance priorities. The PAP government needed to realign public officers from the colonial mindset they were historically conditioned in towards an appreciation of their new operating milieu. Yet, this socialisation of the bureaucratic elite by the Political Study Centre was not an end-goal by itself. Seen against the larger political–bureaucratic relationship, the Political Study Centre was among various measures by the PAP government to assert its authority over the bureaucracy. At the same time, these measures sought to reform the Public Service for better delivery of its policies and programmes.

Public officers' translation of the PAP government's policy visions into actual programmes between 1959 and 1963, when Singapore acceded to Malaysia, attested to the success of the Political Study Centre. Public officers evidently moved away from the colonial era mindset as they hastened the pace of public housing construction, improved municipal amenities, lowered unemployment, and so on. These programmes certainly helped to persuade the electorate in rooting for the PAP's referendum for merger with Malaysia, which also saved the PAP government from collapse. More remarkably, that the Public Service stayed the course with the PAP government through the government's weakest point is a clear indication of the success of the Political Study Centre in socialising the Public Service.

The Political Study Centre, from that perspective, was an initiative by the PAP government to introduce change into and across the Public Service. For the first time, the function of civil service training was extended beyond the equipping of skills and knowledge to political socialisation. However, broadening the definition of training to include socialisation was at the expense of skills and vocational training as described in the previous chapter. The role of the Staff Training School set up by the colonial authorities was increasingly eclipsed by the Political Study Centre, as the latter rose in prominence. This prioritisation of political socialisation over vocational training in Singapore's state-formation continued even after Singapore separated from Malaysia to become an independent state, until 1969 when the Political Study Centre closed.

2.1 New Political–Bureaucratic Relations: Perception and Apprehension

On 3 June 1959, Singapore became a self-governing state, ending 140 years of British colonial rule. The newly-elected PAP government, headed by Lee Kuan Yew as Prime Minister, inherited the colonial government structure (*see* Table 2.1) and a $14 million budget deficit.[1] The Minister for Finance, Dr. Goh Keng Swee, set out to attract investment and create

---

[1] *SAR* 1959: 12; Singapore, *Towards a more just society* (Singapore: GPO, 1959) 1.

Table 2.1: Structure of the Singapore Government, circa 1959[2]

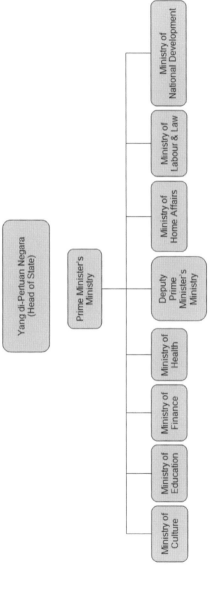

[2] Drawn up from information in Ministry of Culture, *What you should know about (Ministries and Departments)* (Singapore: GPO, 1959).

employment. To sweeten the investment atmosphere, the Minister for Labour and Law promised to protect workers' rights and urged them to forsake strikes. To build up manpower for the industrialising economy, the Education Ministry would emphasise mathematics and science. A Ministry of National Development would speed up housing construction to reduce slums and improve public hygiene. With Britain still controlling security and foreign relations, a Ministry of Culture sought to forge a sense of national identity among the population to prepare for full independence through merger with Malaya.

The PAP government was anxious to translate its pronouncements into actual policies, in light of the prevailing political context. While Prime Minister Lee Kuan Yew and fellow English-educated ministers like Toh Chin Chye, Dr. Goh Keng Swee, Kenneth Byrne and S. Rajaratnam controlled the government, they were wary of the threats posed by pro-Communists within the PAP ranks. From the PAP's formation in 1954, Lee and other English-educated leaders subscribed to a constitutional route to independence, through merger with Malaya. However, they needed the pro-Communists like Lim Chin Siong, whose eloquence in the Chinese-vernacular could mobilise the Chinese-speaking majority of the population. The pro-Communists in turn saw in Lee and the PAP the veneer of acceptability to the British who retained control over security. Although this *modus vivendi* allowed the English-educated moderates and pro-Communists to win the 1959 government, both camps knew an eventual split was inevitable. To stave off the risk of the Chinese-speaking being instigated into electing a Communist regime, the PAP ministers needed to quickly improve the lives of citizens. For the task of translating their political visions into policies and services to the citizenry, Lee and his ministers had to call on the Public Service.

The Singapore Public Service was re-inaugurated from the colonial bureaucracy at self-government. At 30,000 strong, it represented about 2% of the state's population of 1.5 million.[3] Too rapid a pace of Malayanisation had weakened the bureaucracy, especially in the higher

---

[3] *SAR* 1959: 42; *PSC Report*: 5; Governor to Colonial Secretary, No. 43 Saving, 11 March 1958, TNA, CO 1030/647.

services. By 1959, 405 expatriate officers had left; rather than retaining 267 expatriates in key positions as planned, only 104 remained. The Administrative Service that formed the leadership corps of the Public Service lost more than 55% of the expatriate officers, including nine of the 15 top-scale officers.

More importantly, the Public Service was nervous about its fate in the hands of new political masters. It had only served British colonial authority and some senior officers had earlier clashed with PAP leaders, particularly Dr. Goh Keng Swee and Kenneth Byrne, over whether the bureaucracy should remain politically neutral or help the nationalist movement.[4] The majority of the 1,200 Division 1 officers, including the Administrative Service leadership of the bureaucracy, were English-educated.[5] Unlike the Chinese-speaking majority of the population who voted in the PAP, most senior public officers were not ecstatic towards the new government. In the eyes of public officers like Goh Sin Tub, "when the PAP came in, the first fear was really the image which they [PAP leaders] had of being extreme, of being pro-Communist and of being anti-civil service."[6] PAP leaders had cultivated their nationalistic credentials by pitching against the colonial establishment, including Lee Kuan Yew and the English-educated moderates, though in more tempered tones than the pro-Communist elements. The general atmosphere among the English-educated upper echelon of the bureaucracy, hence, was one of apprehensive pessimism:

> There is a certain amount of question mark in my colleagues' minds and also in my own mind as to what pattern the Civil Service will take in future. With such a strong political party coming in, with a certain amount of antagonism to the old Civil Service which has stood for the colonial masters and implemented the will of the colonial masters, to put it in the language of the extreme left, the running dogs of the British, what future was there for these civil servants?[7]

---

[4]Governor to Secretary of State for the Colonies, Personal No. 10, 22 January 1958. TNA CO 1030/651.

[5]*PSC Report 1959–1960*: 4.

[6]Goh Sin Tub, Oral interview transcript, NAS, Accession no. 1422, Reel 4, p. 39. Also, Goh Koh Pui, Oral interview transcript, NAS, Accession no. 288, Reel 11, p. 5.

[7]Goh Sin Tub, Oral interview transcript, Reel 5, p. 43.

The fears of public officers appeared to be realised when the new government's first measures seemingly targeted the Public Service. The English-language criterion for entry into the executive ranks was lifted, ostensibly to draw in more talents.[8] Salary-cuts followed quickly, to mitigate the budget deficit, according to the PAP. Although only the top 35% were affected, public officers protested.[9] S. R. Nathan, a welfare officer in the Ministry of Labour then, related his shock "as the pay cut took away a third of their monthly income."[10] Postal clerk Lee Gek Seng had to borrow for hire purchase payments. Nathan "wondered if the Chinese-educated left had taken over."[11]

Lee Kuan Yew and his ministers, for their part, were "exasperated" by what they perceived as their public officers' lack of "appreciation of the grave challenges before us, and the fact that we had to prevent the Communists from exploiting the grievances of the Chinese-speaking whose voting strength was now decisive."[12]

Senior public officers, it seemed to Lee and his ministers, had become conditioned to ruling by *fiat* of colonial authority. Sequestered in the comfort of their offices, they became far removed and disconnected from the local population. To be sure, there were obviously exceptions, but such was the population's impression of the bureaucracy, including rampant corruption among frontline public officers. Police constables were accepting $10 bribes to turn a blind eye to traffic offences; a driver's licence could be guaranteed for $100, while back-room-rates for priority allocation of new government flats was $90.[13] Even office-boys expected 10 to 20 cents for handing out forms at government departments. The extent of street-level corruption according to one Singaporean then: "people had to pay [police] officers to get them to investigate crimes. The rich and powerful could bribe the police to get people out of jail."[14]

---

[8] *Singapore Legislative Assembly Debates (SLAD)* 21 July 1959, Section 368.
[9] *SAR* 1959: 13.
[10] Quoted in Yap, Lim and Leong (2009) 173.
[11] S.R. Nathan, *An Unexpected Journey: Path to the Presidency* (Singapore: S. R. Nathan, 2011) 205.
[12] Lee Kuan Yew (1998) 319.
[13] Yap, Lim and Leong (2009) 175; Cheong (2013) 296.
[14] Tee Kim Leng, quoted in Yap, Lim and Leong (2009) 175.

Hence, Lee recalled that, while public officers objected, the Chinese-speaking majority of the population supported measures *vis-à-vis* the bureaucracy — "Some of the senior officers had to give up their maids — too bad, but the country was facing greater hardships and perils, and we had to convince people that this government would govern in the interests of all."[15]

2.2 The Political Study Centre

Against this backdrop of terse relationship between the new political masters and the Public Service, the Political Study Centre was established on 15 August 1959. Dr. Goh Keng Swee, the Minister for Finance whose portfolio oversaw the Public Service, outlined the need for the Political Study Centre — civil servants "because of past training and background... in the traditions of the British system, particularly the Colonial system... have not been made aware of the importance of keeping in touch with the masses."[16] Worst, they were not "able to see how they have been separated from the masses, why that is a bad thing and why it is necessary for them to know what the masses think about political affairs, their hopes and aspirations, so that the execution of government policy can be made more effective."[17] Dr. Goh clarified the PAP government's notion of political neutrality expected of the bureaucracy:

> It is not sufficient just to say that the civil servants are there to carry out the policies and instructions of Ministers. When they carry out policies, they necessarily must have a wide sphere of discretion. It is not possible for Ministers to give directives in detail to enable the civil servant to meet any possible eventuality. If the role of the civil service were just to carry out instructions in a mechanical way,... you can be sure that the Government would not be able to make any impact upon the people.[18]

The Political Study Centre was thus necessary to educate public officers on the dynamics of the political milieu in which policies would

---

[15]Lee Kuan Yew (1998) 319.
[16]Quoted in *Straits Times (ST)* 29 July 1959: 14.
[17]*SLAD*, 12 December 1960, section 386.
[18]*Ibid.*

be formulated and implemented:

> The Civil Servant participates in the democratic state by contributing his skill and experience in running the administrative machinery. He can hardly hope to be an effective administrator if he is unaware of the political milieu in which he must operate or if he is unsympathetic to the long-term objectives which the government sets out to achieve.[19]

Not surprisingly, the Political Study Centre immediately fell under a cloud with many feeling it was set up to indoctrinate or brainwash public officers towards siding with the PAP. Quizzed by the Opposition, the Finance Minister had to assure the Legislative Assembly that the Centre's training was "completely impartial... we are not attempting to brainwash the civil service and ask them to subscribe to our ideology, because we rate the intelligence of the civil service high enough to know that such a course of action would be foolish and futile."[20] Nevertheless, questions persisted over the role of the Political Study Centre, and Dr. Goh had to repeatedly clarify that the Centre was not intended to indoctrinate public officers: "Surely the civil servants could have seen through it."[21] The Centre's name was not helpful. Available sources cannot address the intriguing question, given that Dr. Goh, Lee Kuan Yew, and other PAP ministers were English-educated professionals, why a more innocuous name was not chosen over the semantically-loaded Political Study Centre.

2.2.1 *Organisational structure and staffing*

The Political Study Centre — located at No. 4 Goodwood Hill, the former residence of the colonial Financial Secretary — was set up within the Establishment Division of the Ministry of Finance.[22] Selected to head the Centre was George Thomson, a former Colonial Service officer who "understood what we wanted and soon grasped the part

---

[19]Dr. Goh Keng Swee, "Message from the Minister," *Bakti: Journal of the Political Study Centre* 1 (July 1960): 3.

[20]*SLAD*, 11 December 1959, Section 990.

[21]*SLAD* 12 December 1960, Section 389.

[22]Ministry of Culture, *What you should know about the Ministry of Finance* (Singapore: GPO, 1959) 6; *ST* 29 July 1959: 14.

he had to play."[23] Aspersions were soon cast on Thomson being a British spy, and the Communist background of the Centre's other instructor.[24] Gerald de Cruz, a Eurasian, was indeed an ex-Communist who embraced the "opportunity I'd long awaited to expose — and explode — the Communist ideology and Party tactics from the inside. As a practitioner of Malayan Communism for many years, I knew the Communist philosophy, practice, and 'dirty tricks' techniques inside out."[25] With Malaya and Singapore embroiled in a state of Emergency against communist guerrillas for the past decade, teaching senior public officers Communism is intriguing. To the PAP government, the leadership of the bureaucracy must have been direly disconnected with political realities to warrant such a course.

2.2.2 *Training activities and participants*

The Political Study Centre's curriculum were drawn up by a committee led by S. Rajaratnam, the Minister for Culture, and comprised several PAP leaders.[26] Courses spanning over two-and-a-half weeks would put classes of 20 permanent secretaries and directors through seminars to "make civil servants understand the new dynamic forces that face Asia and, by such understanding, transform a colonial civil service into a civil service that will be adequate to meet new needs arising from revolutionary changes".[27] A participant of the inaugural course described that:

> ...there were stimulating lectures, lively Q&A [question and answer], and uninhibited discussions covering the general history of East–West relationship,

---

[23] Lee Kuan Yew (1998) 321. Also Richard Clutterbuck, *Conflict and Violence in Singapore and Malaysia, 1945–1983* (Colorado: Westview, 1985) 383; *SLAD*, 11 December 1959, Section 990.

[24] *SLAD*, 11 December 1961, Sections 1865–1881.

[25] Gerald de Cruz, *Rojak Rebel: Memoirs of a Singapore Maverick* (Singapore: Times, 1993) 185–186.

[26] Lee Kuan Yew, *SLAD*, 11 August 1960, Section 572.

[27] Cheong Hock Hai, "The first course at the Political Study Centre," *Bakti* 1 (July 1960): 28. Also Khoo Seang Hoe, for Permanent Secretary (Establishment), to Permanent Secretary, Ministry of Culture, "Courses at the Political Study Centre," 22 September 1959, File MC 146 Pt 1, NAS Microfilm AR 8/16/219.

population changes in Singapore, our economic problems, our problems in nation building, communist tactics both here and in the Federation with their threats to Malayan nationalism. Theory and practice were equally studied and political institutions were studies against the background of political thought.[28]

These courses received attention from the political leadership. Dr. Goh Keng Swee was one of the ministers who lectured at the classes, while the Prime Minister visited in the evenings "to have informal but very informative sessions with the civil servants, at which questions were freely asked and answers honesty given."[29]

By 1960, the Political Study Centre was organising 16 similar courses a year; a total of 297 civil servants ranging from Permanent Secretaries and school principals to Division 2 officers and teacher-trainees underwent training at the Centre.[30]

In addition, "General Lectures" were held on Saturday evenings, well outside the official working hours, on issues impacting on the government and the Public Service.[31] Between September and December 1959, for example, Prime Minister Lee Kuan Yew lectured on "The Parliamentary System in a Plural Society", and Dr. Goh Keng Swee spoke on "The Ideal Civil Servant in a Revolutionary Situation". Two academics lectured on "Muslim Political Thought" and "Economic Development in Malaya".

Records indicated that neither participants nor their parent-ministries needed to pay any fees for the courses at the Political Study Centre. As a sub-unit of the Ministry of Finance, the Political Study Centre drew on the ministry's budget to fund its activities.

[28]Cheong (1960): 28. Also Permanent Secretary (Establishment), to Permanent Secretary, Ministry of Culture, "Courses at the Political Study Centre," 22 September 1959, File MC 146 Pt 1, NAS Microfilm AR 8/16/219.

[29]De Cruz (1993) 185. Also Vernon Palmer, Oral interview transcript, NAS, Accession no. 1423, Reel 9, pp. 72–73; *SLAD*, 11 December 1961, Section 1876.

[30]*SAR 1960* 43; *SLAD*, 12 December 1960, Section 388.

[31]"Programme of General Lectures at the Political Study Centre," 11 September 1959, File MC 146 Pt 1, NAS Microfilm AR 8/16/223. Also, Oon Khye Kiang, Permanent Secretary (Treasury), to All Permanent Secretaries and Heads of Departments, "General Lectures at the Political Study Centre," 2 January 1960, File MC 146 Pt 1, NAS Microfilm No. AR 8 /16/194.

2.2.3 *Bakti: Journal of the Political Study Centre*

In July 1960, the Political Study Centre published the inaugural issue of its journal. The title *Bakti*, was explained to mean "service in the highest form... [including] devotion to God, love for parents, service to king and country and doing good to one's community but also any kind of service in the highest order."[32]

Envisioned as a quarterly priced at 50 cents, *Bakti*'s "articles will aim to be, not the authoritative type which forecloses discussions but the intelligent type which stimulate discussion."[33] The head of the Political Service Centre, George Thomson, urged heads of ministries to write and encourage contributions from their staff. The intended audience were evidently officers who had a grasp of the English language in the Executive, professional, and clerical schemes of services rather than street-level or lower-educated frontline civil servants.

The bulk of *Bakti*'s repertoire were articles from newspapers, essays by academics, and transcripts of speeches by ministers and senior public officers. The inaugural edition, for example, carried an article by the Minister for Culture.[34] Issue 3 included the English translation of an editorial in the local Chinese-language daily.[35] Several issues featured topical interests like "The Emergence of South-East Asia", "Education and National Independence", etc.[36] Public officers contributed reports on courses and suggestions on policies.[37] However, the most prolific writer was Thomson, whose articles featured in almost every edition of the journal.[38]

---

[32]Sheh bin Alwi, "Bakti," *Bakti* 1 (July 1960): 2.

[33]Thomson to All Permanent Secretaries and Heads of Departments, "Political Study Centre Magazine," 19 May 1960, File MC 131, NAS Microfilm No. AR 8/3/107. Also Goh, "Message from Minister," *Bakti* 1 (July 1960): 3.

[34]S. Rajaratnam, "Culture: Fact and Fiction" *Bakti* 1 (July 1960): 8–14; Prof. K.G. Mydral, "Economic Planning in Asia," *Bakti* 1(July 1960): 4–5.

[35]"Good government creates goodwill; bad government engenders resentment," *Bakti* 3 (April 1961): 29–30.

[36]"The Emergence of South-East Asia," *Bakti* 3 (Apr 1961): 9–11; T.L. Green, "Education and National Independence," *Bakti* 4 (March 1962): 17–18.

[37]Cheong (2013) 27–28.

[38]For example, G. G. Thomson, "A New Self for Singapore," *Bakti* 1 (July 1960): 23–26; G. G. Thomson, "Can Democracy Survive?" *Bakti* 2 (November 1960): 15–19; G.G. Thomson, "Politics and the Civil Servant," *Bakti* 4 (March 1962): 14–16.

A fair assessment of *Bakti* is difficult without the availability of its circulation data. It was not conceived as a commercial undertaking and, without a proper publishing infrastructure, Thomson had to solicit for "volunteers [i.e., free-of-charge] in each Department who will distribute and sell the copies for us."[39] Notably, *Bakti*'s publication fell behind schedule, with the fourth edition late by a year.[40]

2.2.4 *Responses of officials to the Political Study Centre*

No evaluations of the Political Study Centre are available but impressions can be drawn from the recollections of some public officers. Tan Chok Kian, who was at the Ministry of Finance at that time, remembered, "most civil servants, I think, took it well. Of course, they said, 'Well, we're all going back to school. We're going to be brainwashed, what have you,' but I would say generally it was an eye-opener."[41] Ngiam Tong Dow, at the Ministry of Commerce and Industry then, said: "I would not use the word 'brainwash'. It was changing the mindset of the old Singapore civil servants."[42]

Most officers acknowledged a better appreciation of the political milieu and roles they had to play in that context. Teo Kah Leong, then-Permanent Secretary in the Ministry of National Development, recalled leaving the Political Study Centre initiated into "the background and principles of the communist regimes [and] communism.... *Many of us in those days were very vague about communism.*"[43] Vernon Palmer remembered his stint at the Centre helped him "to understand the Communist's mind".[44] Such candid acknowledgement of their 'vague'

---

[39]Thomson to All Permanent Secretaries and Heads of Departments, "Political Study Centre Magazine," 19 May 1960, File MC 131, NAS Microfilm No. AR 8/3/107.

[40]The second and third issues were published in November 1960 and April 1961, months behind Thomson's original timeline of 1 October 1960 and 1 January 1961 respectively. *Ibid*; *Bakti* 2 (November 1960); *Bakti* 3 (April 1961).

[41]Tan Chok Kian Oral interview transcript, NAS, Accession No. 1400, Reel 1, p. 4 and Reel 3, p. 20.

[42]Ngiam Tong Dow, Interview with Author, 10 January 2013. Also Goh Sin Tub, Oral interview transcript, Reel 4, pp. 39–40.

[43]Teo Kah Leong, Oral interview transcript, NAS, Accession No. 1431, Reel 4, p. 38.

[44]Palmer, Oral interview transcript, pp. 72–73.

conceptions of communism among top-level public officers thus justified the rationale for the Political Study Centre.

Ngiam Tong Dow thought that the Political Study Centre was the game changer: "Because it changed the mindset: you are no longer the masters, now you are the servants of the people."[45] Tan Chok Kian said:

> It really gave the civil servants a new outlook, a new dimension of what life was, what the new environment was. Whilst you [as a civil servant] are apolitical, you had to know more about politics that henceforth the government is...governed by politicians with ideologies...party philosophies and ideas and so on. ...it was just not the case of sitting in your offices and handing out decisions, that you had to get to know what's going on down at the grassroots levels.[46]

Teo Kah Leong remembered that:

> We began to realise that while we are taking decisions, we had to consider not only the technical aspects of the problem, we had to consider the political aspect as well....We had to work very closely with the politicians and whenever we made recommendations, we also had to weigh the purely, shall we say, the technical aspects of the matter against the political side, to weigh the two together.[47]

Public officers' conceptualisation of the bureaucracy's political neutrality, in the light of their stints at the Political Study Centre, was best reflected by Ngiam Tong Dow:

> In the tradition of the British civil service, I am political but not partisan. There is separation between the state and the executive. The executive, however, has to remember that our duty is to implement the will of the people manifested through the elected prime minister.[48]

This was in line with the tenets of Westminster political neutrality summed up by Kernaghan and Langford — politicians make policy decisions and public servants execute those decisions; meritocracy rather than political affiliation as the basis of public servants' appointment and

[45]Ngiam Tong Dow, Interview with Author, 10 January 2013.

[46]Tan Chok Kian, Oral interview transcript, pp. 20–21.

[47]Teo Kah Leong, Oral interview transcript, p. 39.

[48]Ngiam, quoted in *Dynamics of the Singapore Success Story: Insights by Ngiam Tong Dow*, ed. Zhang Zhibin (Singapore: Cengage Learning Asia Pte Ltd, 2011) 103.

promotion; public servants advise ministers in private while ministers accept responsibility for departmental actions.[49] Ridley elucidated the tradition of the civil servant's identification with successive political masters in Westminster systems: "the British civil servant is expected to be a chameleon changing colour as government change."[50] Rhodes, Wanna, and Weller elaborated on the non-partisan and professional traditions of Westminster bureaucracies as eschewing "direct involvement in political life", that is, "Civil servants did not run for office, give political speeches, or campaign for one side or the other."[51] Hence, while the socialisation efforts at the Political Study Centre were criticised, they did not appear to deviate from the principles expected of the bureaucracy in Westminster systems of government.

One year on, the Minister for Finance was satisfied with the results:

> The senior officers who went through these courses — many of them for the first time — understand now why Government policy is what it is, and they are therefore able to exercise their own initiative in promoting our policies instead of being jogged along by their Ministers.[52]

2.3 State Formation: Reining in and Reforming the Public Service

The establishment of the Political Study Centre together with the range of seemingly harsh measures by the PAP government upon the bureaucracy can be better appreciated in the context of a nascent state in the throes of 'state-formation'. 'State-formation' theorists led by Stein Rokkan and Charles Tilly observed that as states in Europe were formed, they underwent phases of 'penetration' and 'standardisation'. 'Penetration' is defined by these scholars as the actions of the emerging élite to establish their presence, impose their authority, and assert

---

[49]Kenneth Kernaghan and John W. Langford, *The Responsible Public Servant* (Nova Scotia: Institute for Research on Public Policy, 1991) 56–57.

[50]F. F. Ridley, quoted in Quah (1996) 294–295.

[51]R.A.W. Rhodes, John Wanna and Patrick Weller, *Comparing Westminster* (Oxford: OUP, 2009) 65–66.

[52]*SLAD*, 12 December 1960, Section 388.

their control over a territory.[53] 'Standardisation' refers to the forging of a common culture across the territory. The cultivation of a shared identity among the population towards the state gives rise to the 'nation'. While 'state' refers to a defined territory where ruling elite exercises its authority at will upon the population, 'nation' is a progression of the 'state' where the population actively identifies with and participates in the state. 'Standardisation' measures, hence also known as 'nation-building', could include the imposition, use and presence of similar administrative procedures, identification documents, curricula for schools, uniforms for public officers, etc.

In all these processes, the bureaucracy played a defining role as agent of the state. By erecting and maintaining government offices and infrastructure such as post offices and utilities, and by enforcement actions especially through the use or threat of force, civil servants serve as instruments for 'penetrating' the state's authority across the territory. Similarly, state officers in insisting that the population adhere to prescribed administrative procedures and identification documents, by propagating common educational curricula in schools, through wearing of uniforms, etc., homogenise a population into a 'standardised' culture.[54]

Examined against this 'state-formation' theory, socialisation and other measures by the PAP government *vis-à-vis* the Public Service were manifestation of the 'penetration' process. As the emerging elite, the PAP

---

[53]Stein Rokkan, "The Basic Model", *State formation, nation-building and mass politics in Europe: the theory of Stein Rokkan,* ed. Peter Flora (Oxford: Oxford University Press, 1999) 131–134; Charles Tilly, "Reflections on the history of European state-making," *The Formation of National States in Western Europe,* ed. Charles Tilly (Princeton: Princeton University Press, 1975) 65; David Waldner, *State-building and late development* (Ithaca: Cornell University Press, 1999) 21; Steven Van de Walle and Zoe Scott, "The Role of Public Services in State- And Nation-Building: Exploring Lessons from European History for Fragile States," Governance and Social Development Resource Centre Research Paper, 2009, pp. 9–14.

[54]State-formation theorists expanded other aspects of state- and nation-building, such as 'accommodation', 'participation', 'redistribution', etc. However, the current context of analysis focuses this discussion on the initial 'penetration' and 'standardisation' phases of state-building.

was still insecure politically. The seemingly punitive measures were, in Goh Sin Tub's words:

> ...to tell the Civil Service: 'This shows you who is boss. We are the piper and we call the tune.'...a punishment if you like, a stroke of the cane if you like, which the PAP had to administer, and to administer in fulfilment of its promise to their text that it had made against the Civil Service. And it was salutary. Once and for all. One stroke of the cane and it's all over. Then immediately after that, the whole programme to win over the Civil Service, setting up the Political Study Centre, training, brainwashing, if you like, the senior civil servants and the down the line.[55]

However, these measures also manifested a 'standardisation' effect: by bridging public officers' disconnect with the citizenry, these measures sought to forge a common identity among the population. Similarly, while the Political Study Centre's socialisation of public officers was evidently 'penetrative', to stamp the PAP government's authority over the bureaucracy, it also sought to 'standardise' the public officers, drawing them closer to the citizenry they were supposed to serve.

Seen in this light, the Political Study Centre and other government measures taken toward the Public Service served the simultaneous aims of 'showing who is boss' and introducing genuine reforms. Indeed, Prime Minister Lee Kuan Yew located the Political Study Centre within a larger 'effort to bring the administration to the people':

> A most significant change in the past year is the conscious effort to bring the administration to the people. A Political Study Centre was started to educate and explain our political and ideological problems to the administrative officers of the state. Senior officers were asked to rethink our political problems. Counter clerks and other officials who deal with the public now understand that they are servants and not masters of the people. And the police have been brought down to the people to be their friend and protector, not their guardian and punisher. ...This is a constant and continuing process, and the work must go on. But after one year, there are clear signs that the position has changed for the better.[56]

---

[55]Goh Sin Tub, Oral interview transcript, Reel 5, p. 45.
[56]Lee Kuan Yew, "People, Administration and the Economy: Broadcast over Radio Singapore (2 June 1960)," NAS, *Papers of Lee Kuan Yew* (Singapore: NAS, 2012) 184.

In October 1959, the PAP government mounted Operation Pantai Chantek to clean up public parks. The idea hailed from Ong Eng Guan, the Minister for National Development, "a copycat exercise borrowed from the Communists — ostentatious mobilisation of everyone including ministers to toil with their hands and soil their clothes in order to serve the people."[57] Public officers, for their part, were expected "to contribute in a small way to help in beautifying the new State of Singapore and would add a positive contribution for the welfare of the common people."[58] Making public officers leave the comfort of their offices to undertake physical labour in front of the public was undoubtedly another assertion of authority by the PAP government over the bureaucracy. Having public officers worked among citizens also drove home the message that public servants were meant to serve the public.

By 1960, the PAP government tightened its control over public officers. The Prevention of Corruption Ordinance increased penalties for graft.[59] The Public Service Commission was empowered to initiate disciplinary proceedings against errant staff.[60] In 1962, a Central Complaints Bureau allowed citizens to lodge complaints against public officers who were rude or misbehaved towards them.[61]

Summing up the PAP government's intentions, Finance Minister Dr. Goh Keng Swee pointed out that public officers needed to move away from the colonial mindset:

> The people are now the real masters of the Government, whose responsibility is to serve the people. The people are the real employers of the public servants and the payers of their salaries. Therefore, it is only right that public servants should be courteous to the public in the performance of their duties. But in order to adapt themselves to these changed relationship Government

---

[57] Lee Kuan Yew (1998) 322.

[58] Chairman, Organising Committee, Operation Pantai Chantek, to Permanent Secretary (PS), Ministry of Culture, "Operation 'Pantai Chantek'" 19 October 1959, File MC 132, NAS Microfilm AR 8/16/194; Memo from Chairman, Organising committee, Operation Pantai Chantek to Chairmen to Singapore Telephone Board, Singapore Harbour Board, Singapore Polytechnic, Ministries and other organisations, 12 October 1959, File MC 132, NAS Microfilm AR 8/16/194.

[59] *SLAD*, 13 February 1960, Sections 379–382.

[60] *PSC Report 1961*: 2 and 10; *PSC Report 1962*: 3 and 11.

[61] *SAR* 1962: 77–78,

employees will have to undergo a new process of training. This is a kind of brainwashing and time is required for re-adjustment and adaptation.[62]

Whether genuine reforms or 'showing who is boss', these measures affected the Public Service severely. In fact, a PAP leader wrote an open letter to Prime Minister Lee Kuan Yew about "the deliberate hostility being stirred up in certain sections of the Party towards the English educated... [causing] a growing sense of suffocation felt by teachers, lawyers, doctors and engineers"[63]. Public officers might not complain publicly but those most aggrieved chose to leave altogether. Civil servant Goh Koh Pui remembered, there was "quite a big [number of] resignations from the Administrative Service."[64] His colleague, George Bogaars, recorded "the resignations of some half a dozen or more top civil servants who found their positions untenable."[65] A PAP politician added 300 others from the professional services.[66] Bogaars later wrote:

> The damage this did to the civil service was serious since it deprived the administration, at a time when it could least afford it, of very experienced officers who could, not only carry forward the administration but help in training and guidance of the large batches of new entrants who had to be recruited to fill up vacancies created by expatriate retirements and Malayanisation. These officers who had resigned had been recruited before the Second World War into the Straits Settlements Civil Service and had seen their service in many parts of the Malay Peninsula. Their withdrawal compounded the difficulties that were to face the civil service in the new chapter of political history that had begun.[67]

The departure of unhappy senior public officers, nevertheless, removed the resistance within the bureaucracy to the PAP government. At the same time, these departures opened up the upper echelons to rising high-calibre young officers.[68] Altogether, this change in Public Service's leadership facilitated the PAP government's efforts to align the

---

[62]Dr. Goh Keng Swee, "Courtesy is democratic citizenship," *Bakti* 3 (April 1961): 30.
[63]*ST* 20 December 1959: 7.
[64]Goh Poh Kui, Oral interview transcript, p. 5.
[65]Bogaars (1973) 78.
[66]Yap, Lim and Leong (2009) 174.
[67]Bogaars (1973) 78.
[68]There included Sim Kee Boon, J.Y. Pillay, Howe Yoon Chong, G.E. Bogaars, Pang Tee Pow and K.P.R. Chandra. Yap, Lim and Leong (2009) 174.

Public Service. With the benefit of hindsight, Quah pointed to these measures as a concerted socialisation effort by the PAP government.[69]

2.4 The PAP Split, Merger into Malaysia, and the Role of the Public Service

The political context was meanwhile evolving dramatically and the effects of the socialisation and reform of the bureaucracy would play their parts. In April 1961, Ong Eng Guan, having been sacked from his ministerial post for challenging the PAP leadership, resigned his Legislative Assembly seat to trigger a by-election. Despite its efforts, the PAP's candidate was routed by Ong. More significantly, the PAP's defeat alarmed the Malayan government to the risk of Singapore — under a weak PAP government — falling to the communists and threatening Malaya's security.[70]

In May 1961, Malayan Prime Minster Tunku Abdul Rahman, erstwhile cool about Singapore's reunion with Malaya, reignited the possibility of merger. A Singapore under its jurisdiction would allow the Malayan government to arrest communists within the PAP, which Lee Kuan Yew and the English-educated leaders could not do without backlash from the Chinese masses. Lim Chin Siong and the pro-Communists naturally resisted Singapore coming under the Malayan government.

As merger became a battle for survival between PAP leaders and pro-Communists, Lim Chin Siong led supporters to defect *en masse.*[71] The party organisation collapsed: 35 of the 51 branch committees, and 19 of the 23 organising secretaries deserted the PAP to join Lim's newly set-up Barisan Socialis.[72]

As the PAP clung onto government with a four-vote legislative margin, negotiations with the Federation government produced results. Malaya, Singapore, and the Borneo territories would merge to form

---

[69]Jon S. T. Quah, "Culture change in the Singapore Civil Service," *Civil service reform in Latin America and the Caribbean,* eds. Shahid Chaidhry, Gary Reid and Waleed Malik (Washington, D.C.: The World Bank, 1994).

[70]*SAR* 1961: 2–3; Tan Siok Sun (2007) 92–99; Turnbull (2009) 277–278; Lee Kuan Yew (1998) 344, 362–372.

[71]*SAR* 1961: 7–8; Tan Siok Sun (1998) 99–102.

[72]Turnbull (2009) 279, Yap, Lim and Leong (2009) 211–212.

Malaysia.[73] The Barisan Socialis, with its survival at stake, demanded a referendum on merger. The PAP government agreed to a referendum, but rather than 'for or against' merger, over the terms of merger.[74]

Against this background, the PAP government drew on the Public Service in its campaign for merger. As the incumbent government, the PAP saw as its right to mobilise all resources of the state, because merger — in its view — was a state-wide cause. Union with Malaya would allow Singapore to become independent, provide for economic growth, thereby generating revenue to fund programs to improve the population's standards of living.

In its campaign, the PAP government highlighted its public service achievements to ingratiate itself with the population. On the government's behalf, the Ministry of Culture published pamphlets drawing attention to the government's accomplishments.[75] Prominence was accorded to the 44,251 public housing units completed since self-government, housing 20% of the population, complete with utilities and amenities.[76] Electricity supply was extended to 15 villages, improving living conditions of about 35,000 people.[77] Twenty-one primary schools and eight secondary schools were constructed, increasing school enrolments by 76,028 to 397,005.[78] The Economic Development Board, these publications proclaimed, would "induce investments totalling something like $1,740 million and to create economic and social opportunities that would meet the needs of our vast growing population".[79]

Results of the September 1962 referendum was an overwhelming 71% support for PAP's Alternative 'A'.[80] PAP's win halted the tide of its

---

[73] *SAR* 1961: 9–10; Lee Kuan Yew (1998) 400–401; Yap, Lim and Leong (2009) 232–233.
[74] *SAR* 1962: 22.
[75] Ministry of Culture, *One year of peaceful revolution, June 3, 1959 to June 3, 1960* (Singapore: Ministry of Culture, 1960); Ministry of Culture, *Year of progress, June 1960–June 1961* (Singapore: Ministry of Culture, 1960); Singapore Ministry of Culture, *Year of fulfilment, June 1961–June 1962* (Singapore: Ministry of Culture, 1962).
[76] *SAR* 1960: 256; Ministry of Culture, *Year of fulfilment,* (no page nos.).
[77] Ministry of Culture, *Year of progress.*
[78] *SAR* 1959: 208; *SAR* 1962: 296: Ministry of Culture, *Year of fulfilment,* (no page nos).
[79] Ministry of Culture, *Year of progress.*
[80] *SAR* 1962: 24.

fall, from the by-election defeats to the mass defections to the destruction of its branch organisations. Its majority in the Legislative Assembly continued to be tenuous, with the razor-thin majority negated after more defections to Barisan Socialis. It also took the Anglo-Malayan-Singapore Internal Security Council's 1963 arrest of Barisan leaders, for consorting with plotters of the Brunei revolt, to ease the pressure off the PAP. However, the 1962 referendum, stemming PAP's plummet and ensuring Singapore's merger with Malaysia, saved the PAP government from certain political collapse.

The Public Service evidently played a role in PAP's success at the referendum. Behind the statistics, cited to lend credence to the PAP government's having improved the population's standard of living, was the handiwork of public officers. Permanent secretaries, directors, and heads in ministries and state agencies translated the PAP's political visions into specific policies, and then cascaded these into detailed actionable plans. Public officers across the rank-and-file, actualised these plans by building thousands of public housing units and implementing other essential public services. Prime Minister Lee Kuan Yew would later credit the construction of the first few blocks of public housing apartments in his Tanjong Pagar constituency for helping him hold on to his ward.[81] Hence, the work of the Public Service gave the PAP government the evidence of its public service for the citizens, and converted these into votes for the government at the referendum.

In this regard, the Political Study Centre, as part of the measures by the PAP government to rein in and reform the Public Service, delivered its objectives. Public officers professed a better understanding of the intentions of the PAP government, and a deeper appreciation of the political milieu in which government policies and programmes needed to be formulated and delivered. For those whom Dr. Goh Keng Swee labelled as 'die-hards' in his evaluation to the Legislative Assembly,[82] the courses at the Political Study Centre probably sealed their decisions to leave the Public Service. The resignations of these senior officers removed the high-level resistance within the bureaucracy towards the PAP

---

[81]Yap, Lim and Leong (2009) 259.
[82]*SLAD*, 12 December 1960, Section 387.

government. Also, by facilitating the rise of younger officers who were more receptive towards the government, these departures consolidated the PAP government's control over the bureaucracy and allowed the PAP government to have a cooperative agent to implement its policies and programmes.

2.5 The Staff Training Centre

The Political Study Centre's success in socialising public officers was, however, at the expense of staff training. The Staff Training School set up by the colonial authorities continued after self-government to conduct induction and functional skills training. In late 1959, its name changed to the Staff Training Centre.[83]

As the Political Study Centre was set up, the resources of the Staff Training Centre were gradually hollowed out to support the former. The Director of Training who headed the Staff Training Centre, namely George Thomson, was concurrently appointed head of the Political Study Centre and progressively spending more time at the latter (*see* Table 2.2).[84] Although the Staff Training Centre was allocated three officers and the Political Study Centre one instructor, both Centres were sharing two officers by 1961.[85] The Political Study and the Staff Training Centres were in all purposes one entity, the latter subsumed under the banner of the Political Study Centre.

While the Political Study Centre had its own building, complete with lecture hall, seminar rooms, and canteen, the Staff Training Centre occupied half a level in the Fullerton Building which housed other departments. The Staff Training Centre's sole lecture hall could be

---

[83]*SAR* 1959: 45; Lee Kuan Yew, "On Improving the Apparatus of the State: Speech at the End of the First Course for Assemblymen on the Work of Government Ministries and Departments at the Staff Training School (29 October 1959)," NAS, *Papers of Lee Kuan Yew* 134–136; Ministry of Culture, "Address by the Prime Minister, Mr. Lee Kuan Yew, to Assemblymen and Civil Servants on the conclusion of the Second Course for Legislative Assemblymen at the Staff Training School on November 16, 1959," NAS Document lky19591116; *ST* 29 October 1959: 7, *ST* 15 November 1959: 5.

[84]"Staff Training in Singapore Government Service," 8 June 1962, File MC 218/62, NAS Microfilm No. AR 819/32.

[85]State of Singapore, *Directory* (Singapore: Ministry of Culture, 1961) 45.

Table 2.2:   The Political Study Centre and Staff Training Centre, 1962[86]

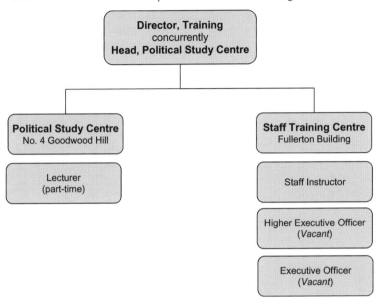

partitioned into two discussion rooms but "the partition is not sound proof, and it is not possible to hold two lectures simultaneously."[87] By 1963, the Staff Training Centre had lost most of the important training. Induction for the élite Administrative Service and Executive Service were transferred to the Political Study Centre. Apart from induction for in Division 3, the majority of the courses it held were for interpreters and translators.[88] The Staff Training Centre had effectively become a school for training the lower rank-and-file hierarchy of the bureaucracy.

Apart from an analysis in Seah's 1971 study, no formal evaluation of the Staff Training Centre can be found. Seah attributed the Staff Training Centre's difficulties to resourcing, coordination among relevant agencies, and attitudes towards training. To illustrate, Seah pointed

---

[86]Drawn up from information in "Staff Training in Singapore Government Service," 8 June 1962, File MC 218/62, NAS Microfilm No. AR 819/32.
[87]"Staff Training in Singapore Government Service," 8 June 1962, File MC 218/62, NAS Microfilm No. AR 819/32; *SAR* 1960: 42.
[88]*SAR* 1963: 449.

to the Centre's 1962 budget being only 4% of that of the Teachers'
Training College.[89] Poor liaison among the Public Service Commission,
Establishment Division and Staff Training Centre led to the Centre not
receiving updated lists of recruits, resulting in laggard induction of new
officers across the bureaucracy. With poor resources affecting capacity,
the Centre's courses were superficial, providing only basic knowledge
rather than actual 'real' training; participants apparently preferred on-
the-job training. The government was not unaware and a Commission
of Inquiry recommended tighter coordination among the agencies to
improve the training of civil servants.[90] However, the attitudes among
senior civil servants towards training also contributed to the Staff Training
Centre's difficulties. The 17 heads of departments, responding to a survey
initiated by the Permanent Secretary of the Treasury, indicated that only
6% of their staff, in their opinion, needed training. More importantly,
most department-heads did not see the Staff Training Centre as useful,
preferring staff to attend courses elsewhere.[91] In contrast, the Political
Study Centre did not suffer the limitations of its poorer sibling.

Their enthusiasm was also due to the more interesting and relevant
curriculum at the Political Study Centre.

Ngiam Tong Dow, in retrospect, explained that the political leadership
was more interested in cultivating the Administrative Service than the
Staff Training Centre. The Administrative Service was an elite scheme
of service originating from the colonial bureaucracy. It was modeled
after the British administrative class to provide the leadership corps
for the bureaucracy. Ngiam, who joined the Administrative Service
after self-government, pointed out that the Prime Minister and his
Finance Minister in particular were focused on developing a small
Administrative Service leadership cadre to lead and manage the broader
public service:

> The whole concept was that we must have a core of men. What Dr. Goh
> called the Praetorian Guards...So we must develop a core of Praetorian

---

[89]Seah (1971) 155.

[90]*Ibid* citing *Commission of Inquiry into Government Annually Recurrent Expenditure:
Horizontal Report No. 3*, Paras 39–65.

[91]Seah (1971) 156–158.

Guards to safeguard the sovereignty of the country. And this whole idea of developing a civil service is to develop the Praetorian Guards. So I think Lee Kuan Yew and Dr. Goh Keng Swee, they were not really interested, if I may say so, [in the] Staff Training Centre.[92]

2.6 Priority of Socialisation: State Formation through Merger and Independence

Hence, while the Political Study Centre was successful in re-orienting public officers, this broadening of the definition of training to include socialisation was at the expense of vocational training and the Staff Training Centre. With state-formation as the overarching context, the importance accorded to socialisation is understandable, even necessary.

2.6.1 *Merger into the federation of Malaysia*

The organisation of the Public Services was one of the key questions leading up to Singapore's Merger into the Federation of Malaysia, and among "the inevitable disputes between the two Governments."[93] In the course of Merger discussions, Federal Deputy Premier Tun Abdul Razak and Singapore Prime Minister Lee Kuan Yew agreed there were five areas which needed close examination by senior civil servants from both sides. "Establishment and Organisation" was one of the sub-committees under the ambit of an "Inter-Governmental Committee on Merger of Singapore with the Federation of Malaya".[94]

Eventually, the Merger with Malaysia saw Singapore transferring to the Central Government the administrative portfolios of "civil aviation, meteorological services, transport, telecommunications, post,

---

[92]Ngiam Tong Dow, Interview with Author, 10 January 2013.

[93]The Earl of Selkirk [UK High Commissioner to Singapore and UK Commissioner-General for Southeast Asia], to Secretary of State for the Colonies, Inward Telegram Secret No. 559, 4 December 1962, TNA, CO 1030/1067.

[94]Copy of Letter from Permanent Secretary, Ministry of External Affairs, Federation of Malaya, Kuala Lumpur to the Prime Minister, Singapore, 26 November 1962, TNA, CO 1030/1067. Also Tun Haji Abdul Razak bin Dato Hussien [Deputy Prime Minister, Malaya], to Lee Kuan Yew, Prime Minister, Singapore, 17 November 1962, TNA, CO 1030/1067, and Lee Kuan Yew, to Tun Haji Abdul Razak bin Dato Hussien, Deputy Prime Minister, Federation of Malaya, 20 November 1962, TNA, CO 1030/1067.

judicial services, audit, immigration and passports, defence, police and prisons."[95] Among these, the most significant was the Police Force along with the Special Branch responsible for internal security.[96] The Singapore State Government retained the Ministries of Culture, Education, Finance, Health, Home Affairs, Labour and Law and National Development. The change into a state-level Public Service, as part of a federal bureaucracy, appeared more nominal than substantial. Apart from the security agencies, the Singapore Public Service post-Merger continued *status quo ante.*

Following Singapore's accession into Malaysia, the Political Study Centre continued to feature prominently while the Staff Training Centre languished in its shadows. The "scope of work of this [Political Study] centre was expanded to include the Federation of Malaya, Sabah and Sarawak at the request of the governments of these territories."[97] Within three months of Merger, the Political Study Centre conducted eight courses for the Sarawak Civil Service and Sabah government.

> During each course, the political, economic and social problems of the region were discussed in the light of the new national pattern of responsibilities and the new attitude and methods of working required of a Civil Service in a community with full adult suffrage and a full parliamentary system of Government.[98]

Civil servants from the Federation government were sent to attend the courses organised in Singapore. In contrast, there were no mention of the Staff Training Centre in any public records between 1964 and 1966.[99]

2.6.2 *Full independence for Singapore*

On 9 August 1965, Prime Minister Lee Kuan Yew suddenly proclaimed the independence of Singapore. While Singapore's separation was

---

[95]Yang di-Pertuan Negara's Speech, *SLAD*, 29 November 1963, Section 119.
[96]*SAR* 1963: 444; Bogaars (1973) 81; Lee Kuan Yew (1998) 512–513.
[97]Seah (1971) 448.
[98]*SAR* 1964: 448.
[99]*SAR* 1964–1966.

unexpected, relations between the Federal government and the Singapore State government were already "far from happy."[100] The deteriorating Malaysia–Singapore relations leading to the latter's separation is the subject of several dedicated books[101] and not the focus of this study. To briefly provide context for discussion, the conflict between the United Malays National Organisation (UMNO), which led the Barisan Nasional coalition government in Malaysia, and the People's Action Party in Singapore was fundamentally racial: PAP's meritocratic approach to governance challenged UMNO's affirmative action policies aimed at preserving Malay political dominance. Other issues expanded the contestation while rhetoric from both sides of the Causeway fanned hostilities. However, bloody riots in 1964 underscored the racial undertones of the Malaysian–Singapore conflict, which complicated the search for an acceptable solution to abate the spiralling tension. Eventually, to avoid further acrimony and violence, key UMNO and PAP leaders agreed to separate Singapore from the Federation to its own independence.

The suddenness of Singapore's independence surprised even its own Public Service; except for a handful of very senior officers, the rest of the bureaucracy was completely kept in the dark.[102] The bureaucracy scrambled to set up the functions of a sovereign state. Chan surmised that, "When Singapore separated from Malaysia, the island fortuitously was managed by a politicised and relatively skilled bureaucracy."[103] The delicacy of the situation required a keen appreciation of the political context: while the Malaysian government formally separated Singapore from the Federation, some radical elements in Malaysia were threatening

---

[100]Turnbull (2009) 287.

[101]Two books focusing on Singapore's Merger with and Separation from Malaysia are Albert Lau, *A Moment of Anguish: Singapore in Malaysia and the Politics of Disengagement* (Singapore: Times, 1998) and Tan Tai Yong, *Creating 'Greater Malaysia': Decolonization and the Politics of Merger* (Singapore: ISEAS, 2008).

[102]Only three civil servants knew of Singapore's impending Separation: Stanley Stewart, Head of the Civil Service, Wong Chooi Sen, the Cabinet Secretary, and George Bogaars, Director of Special Branch. Lee Kuan Yew (1998) 631.

[103]Chan Heng Chee, "Political Developments, 1965–1979," *History of Singapore,* eds. Chew and Lee (1991) 161.

to abrogate Singapore's independence.[104] A state of war remained with Indonesia in view of Jakarta's Confrontation. Securing Singapore's borders while rallying the international community to recognise and guarantee its sovereignty, and expanding trade to bolster its economic viability all became Singapore's paramount priorities. George Bogaars, a senior civil servant at that time, wrote later:

> Up to then the main focus of attention of the civil service had been domestic and internal matters. The paramount concern had been on political stability and security and the development of social and economic services to sustain this stability. The civil service has been conditioned over the previous decade to think largely in terms of Singapore's internal problems.[105]

Thus, the rush to set up the Ministry of Foreign Affairs and Ministry of Interior and Defence and change functions of other ministries to meet the demands of a sovereign state (*see* Table 2.3). More challenging than structures was staffing new ministries and adjusted portfolios with the right people. The shortage of staff with the competencies and stature compelled the Civil Service to search the private sector for people to hold high-level appointments in the nascent Foreign Service.[106] Even as officers were pulled away to staff newly-created portfolios, deputies and subordinates might not be qualified to take over vacated leadership positions. "Fortuitously," as Chan put it, Singapore's public officers had by this time "shared the same ideology as the ruling leadership and was sensitive to its political tasks."[107] An outcome she attributed to the "reorientation and retraining of the Civil Service" through the Political Study Centre.

Unsurprisingly, with the state at the threshold of state-formation following independence, political socialisation was given greater priority, much more than skills training. The retiring Head of the Civil Service highlighted the continued importance of political socialisation in the

---

[104]Lee Kuan Yew, *From Third World to First: The Singapore Story, 1965–2000, Memoirs of Lee Kuan Yew* (Singapore: Singapore Press Holdings and Times Editions, 2000) 22.
[105]Bogaars (1973) 81.
[106]Chan (1991) 162; Bogaars (1973) 82.
[107]Chan (1991) 162.

Table 2.3: Structure of the Singapore Government, Circa 1965[108]

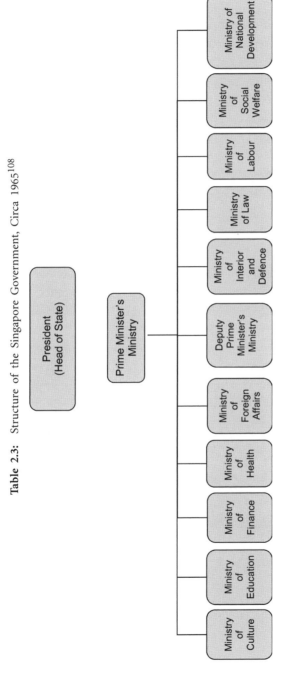

[108]Drawn up from Parliament of Singapore, *Parliamentary Debates Republic of Singapore, Official Report*, First Session of the First Parliament, 8 December 1965–31 December 1965, 24: 1.

context of state-formation:

> ...we must understand that the position of the Administrative Service in newly emerging and independent developing countries is different from that of Colonial and pre-self-governing days. Whilst we still should not take part in politics, we cannot disregard politics in that there must be a keen sense of political awareness and a better standard of political assessment of conditions, problems and situations on our part, if we are going to advise our Ministers better in the formulation of policy, and understand and loyally carry out policies laid out by the Government.[109]

2.6.3 *Closure of the Political Study Centre and Staff Training Centre*

In 1969, the government closed the Political Study Centre. After 10 years of operation, the Centre was deemed to have achieved its purpose remarkably: "All senior members of the Civil Service have undergone courses at the centre."[110] The government press statement announcing the closure added that newly-recruited civil servants, having gone through National Service and been brought up in an environment of nation-building, would have a better appreciation of national objectives. Another possible reason might be the confidence of the PAP government in its political power, including its control over the bureaucracy. The strongest indicator of the PAP's power was the overwhelming 84% popular vote through which the PAP was returned to power at the 1968 elections.[111]

While the Staff Training Centre remained in operation, it continued to provide only vocational training to rank-and-file public officers.[112] Induction courses for the élite Administrative Service and other Division 1 officers were not returned to the Staff Training Centre even with the closure of the Political Study Centre. After 1969, the official *Singapore Year Book*, which had devoted sections of varying lengths to key

---

[109] S. T. Stewart, "The New Civil Servant," *Bakti* 4.1 (November 1966): 1.

[110] Among the Political Study Centre's three senior officers, Thomson was posted to the Ministry of Foreign Affairs, Deputy Director Lee Ting Hui to Ministry of Education and Staff Tutor Gerald de Cruz to Ministry of Culture. *ST* 3 August 1969: 13.

[111] *SAR* 1968: 6.

[112] *SAR* 1969: 227.

developments at the Staff Training Centre since its 1954 inception, no longer mention the Centre.[113]

With the closure of the Political Study Centre, a gap in the training of senior officers thus arose. Given that these public officers occupied key positions in the bureaucracy, this training gap is a significant and glaring one.

2.7 Summing Up: Reforming the Bureaucracy

This chapter has described the use of the Political Study Centre as a point to change the attitudes of the bureaucracy. At self-government in 1959, the Singapore Public Service re-inaugurated from the colonial bureaucracy was apprehensive towards its new political masters: the People's Action Party had since its formation accentuated its nationalistic credentials by pitting itself against the colonial establishment. The PAP leaders on their part were exasperated that the bureaucracy, after 140 years as agents of the colonial authorities, was insensitive to the emerging political context: the Chinese-educated majority of the population, who now held electoral sway, was so aggrieved by colonial rule that they could be easily fanned into voting in a communist regime. While senior civil servants were largely disconnected with the public they were supposed to serve, street-level bureaucrats indulged in corruption, and the bureaucracy — still steeped in colonial-era organisational culture — was seen as ineffectual by the local population.

Consequently, the PAP government set up the Political Study Centre to reform the bureaucracy. By socialising senior civil servants to a deeper appreciation of the political context against which policies would be made, the Political Study Centre was not simply introducing change into the bureaucracy. Rather, in re-orienting these officers away from the colonial-era organisational culture towards an alignment with the newly-elected PAP government, the Political Study Centre cultivated a loyalty towards the emerging state among them. As they returned to their leadership positions of various ministries and departments, these

---

[113] *SAR* 1971ff. From 1971, the *SAR* series changed its format to report on developments in the year preceding the title. Hence, *SAR 1971* recorded events in 1970.

senior civil servants carried with them that new alignment with the new government across the Public Service. Through socialising the bureaucratic elite, the Political Study Centre in effect was spreading reforms across the bureaucracy. The Political Study Centre was thus a catalytic point of change in the Singapore Public Service.

In seeking to break the bureaucracy away from its colonial-era traditions, the Political Study Centre was not modelled after any British institution. In fact, the prevailing attitude in the UK Home Civil Service continued to be learning on-the-job, "sitting by Nellie".[114] Several more years would to pass before the Centre for Administrative Studies was set up in 1963 as Britain's first dedicated civil service training institution.[115]

The Political Study Centre's socialisation aim draws comparison with training institutions in communist states. As Lee Kuan Yew and his fellow ministers were at that time co-habiting with pro-Communist cadres within the PAP, they might be aware of China's Central (Communist) Party School.[116] No records, however, suggest any reference to foreign training institutions in the setting up of the Political Study Centre.

This use of training for socialisation, though, was at the expense of skills and vocational training. Lee Boon Hiok surmised that the PAP "believed that the new recruit to the Civil Service would require only a brief and therefore not a very thorough course to familiarize himself with the workings of the Civil Service. The civil servant would thus, for the rest of his career, have to gain expertise while 'on-the-job'."[117] Resources from the Staff Training Centre were thus diverted for political socialisation. The Staff Training Centre, in contrast to its role in training senior officers before 1959, became relegated to training the rank-and-file of the bureaucracy.

---

[114]Lowe (2011) 313. Also Robert Pyper, *The British Civil Service* (Hertfordshire: Prentice Hall/Harvester Wheatsheaf, 1995) 42.

[115]Desmond Keeling, "The Development of Central Training in the Civil Service, 1963–1970," *Public Administration* 49(1971): 53–54.

[116]Zheng Yongnian and Lye Liang Fook, "China's Central Party School: Adapting to Changes (II)," EAI Background Brief No. 182 (2004): 1; Zheng Yongnian, *The Chinese Communist Party and Organisational Emperor* (London: Routledge, 2010) 168.

[117]Lee Boon Hiok (1980) 450.

Through the lens of state-formation theory, such emphasis on political socialisation represented the efforts of the emerging political elite to 'penetrate' its authority across the new state. The bureaucracy, in particular, having served colonial authorities for an extended period, was in all purposes a colonial institution. Together with other measures *vis-à-vis* the bureaucracy, the Political Study Centre was meant to show 'who is the boss'. Asserting control over the bureaucracy would allow the new political elite — in particular Lee Kuan Yew and his inner core of English-educated ministers — to harness the Public Service as its agents of policy implementation. At the same time, these measures brought public officers closer to the citizenry, which served to forge a common identity among the people of Singapore, an aspect of 'standardisation' in state-formation theory. The role of the Public Service in state-formation, and the effects of socialisation at the Political Study Centre, became all the more evident when the PAP experienced its worst crisis in 1961.

The success of the Political Study Centre's socialisation was best demonstrated when public officers stuck with the PAP government in 1961. Following the Hong Lim electoral debacle and the massive defection of pro-Communist elements within its ranks, the PAP was hanging on by a wafer-thin legislative majority. At this point, when the PAP leadership was at its most weakened, had public officers remained disgruntled, they could have taken the opportunity to not comply with instructions from their political masters.

A logical explanation would be public officers' adherence to constitutional requirements, conditioned by British tradition, to abide by political masters regardless of their attitudes towards the government. Another explanation could be public officers' fears of Singapore — and the bureaucracy — falling under the control of pro-Communists. If the PAP had appeared harsh, an even more leftist pro-Communist regime could escalate to outright persecution of public officers. Indeed, George Bogaars reflected years later, when he went on to become the Head of the Civil Service, that Singapore's civil servants at that point of decolonisation could have it worse:

> It would have been one of the easiest things for the Government to have gone along with the general mood and fashion of the day — a mood and fashion which had started in the newly independent countries of Asia after

the Second World War — to denigrate and abuse the civil service until by gradual exhaustion it loses all confidence in itself as well as the respect of the public for which it is paid to serve. The results of such attrition are a collapse of the Administration and its floundering in inefficiency, corruption, and graft. These were already apparent in certain parts of Asia, though the cause was attributed to everything else except the political pandering to popular sentiment to get even with civil servants and the bureaucracy who apparently represented the past colonial masters.[118]

The most compelling explanation for the bureaucracy's support for the PAP government at its most vulnerable was the successful socialisation of public officers to align with the PAP. Indeed, despite the initial apprehension towards the PAP and the weakened state of the ruling party, public officers continued to extend their support to the political masters. Much of the policies that helped the PAP win electoral votes, such as public housing, better municipal amenities, larger student enrolment, and other socioeconomic improvements, were translated from the political visions of the PAP into actual realities by public officers. Given that popular support for the PAP at the Merger Referendum saved the PAP from collapse, public officers through their policies played a not uncritical role. The socialisation of the Public Service through the Political Study Centre was thus largely successful. To quote a civil servant at that time:

> I think the whole thing went through in a very satisfactory way in a sense because it corrected the situation within so short a period. If you look at it in retrospect, it was a correction of an image of the Civil Service within a very short time. And after that, the PAP could use the civil servants.[119]

Bogaars, taking a long view of the evolution of the bureaucracy years later as Head of the Civil Service, was sure that socialisation of civil servants through the Political Study Centre played an instrumental role in aligning the bureaucracy, leading the civil service to support the Government when it was at its weakest and under attack:

> The politicisation of the civil service ... by the Political Study Centre ... [was], by and large, successful. There was a gradual understanding and perception of the civil service of political matters and the issues which concerned the

[118]Bogaars (1973) 78–79.
[119]Goh Sin Tub, Oral interview transcript, Reel 5, p. 45.

electorate and influenced Government policy. This was tested during the next half decade when the extreme left in the People's Action Party under Communist control broke away from the party in a bid to seize political power for themselves.... The civil service had to be mobilised across the full range of its functions and activities to meet the attack at all points.[120]

Political scientist, Chan Heng Chee, went so far as to suggest that the PAP leadership, in view of the internal party struggle, "forged an alliance with the civil servants through re-socialisation and politicisation of the Civil Service" through the Political Study Centre.[121] Although the timeline of events did not fit her argument, the Political Study Centre was set up in 1959 earlier than the rise of intra-PAP fissures in 1960, Chan was perceptive in pointing out that PAP leadership essentially formed an alliance with the bureaucracy, and the Political Study Centre was a critical element in that alliance. In fact, so profound was the Centre's impact on the ruling party that when the PAP suffered electoral slippage 30 years later, PAP leaders invoked references to the Political Study Centre to remind civil servants of the importance of political sensitivity in policy-making.[122]

In retrospect, therefore, through various socialisation efforts, the PAP government aligned the Public Service to share its goal of independence through peaceful and constitutional merger with Malaya. With the bureaucracy thus persuaded, the PAP government could rely on public officers supporting its merger campaign even when the party was weakened by internal strife. A Public Service that was aligned to PAP government could be counted upon to pursue the interests of Singapore, as it became a state of Malaysia with the success of merger.

The inception point of change, however, began with the Political Study Centre.

---

[120]Bogaars (1973) 80.

[121]Chan Heng Chee, "The PAP and the Structuring of the Political System," *Management of Success*, eds. Sandhu and Wheatley 5.

[122]Ong Teng Cheong, "Bridging the perception gap," *Petir* (August 1992): 18.

Chapter 3

Towards Managing the 'Developmental State': The Staff Training Institute (1971–1975)

In 1971, the Staff Training Institute (STI) was established to build up the capacity of the Singapore Public Service to keep pace with the needs of the emerging developmental state. As Singapore embarked upon rapid state-led economic development after independence with the aim of ensuring the survival of the new nation-state, the bureaucracy was expected to play the role of an 'economic general staff'. Yet, without the requisite management training, this was a role public service officers were not prepared for. Attracting and retaining qualified and talented officers to lead and manage this developmental state was further complicated by more attractive career prospects in the booming private sector.

The STI was a response to level up the management skills of public officers to help drive and oversee state-led development. This equipping of managerial skillsets was particularly critical with the appearance of a gap in executive training, following the closure of the Political Study Centre and the end of centralised training of the elite Administrative Service and Division 1 officers. At the same time, the introduction of management training at the STI would boost the career development of public officers and help sweeten the attractiveness of the Public Service in recruiting and retaining qualified and talented personnel.

The chapter, in describing the organisational structure and personnel staffing of the STI, accounts for the considerations driving these developments and draws out the STI's relationships with its supervising agency and the broader bureaucracy. The manner in which the STI structured and deployed its resources illustrates how the Institute sought to carry out its mission and objectives through its training activities. While the period covered was a mere four years, it warrants a specific chapter because the STI laid the foundation upon which subsequent training initiatives arose.

3.1 The Changing Context

On 15 March 1971, Minister for Finance Hon Sui Sen opened the Staff Training Institute (STI).[1] This was two years after the closure of the Political Study Centre, which, having taken over the training of the elite Administrative Service as mentioned in the preceding chapter, resulted in a gap in the training of senior bureaucrats. The Staff Training Centre, which provided vocational training for the lower hierarchy of the Public Service, also diminished further in importance.

No publicly available records can account for the training of public officers between 1969 and 1971, but training did continue. Herman Hochstadt, then-Deputy Secretary in the Ministry of Finance (MOF) whose portfolio covered personnel matters, explained that the management training for officers in the Administrative and Executive Services was largely on-the-job during this period. However, this was:

> ... supplemented, when perceived to be needed and feasible, by *ad hoc* participation on sponsorship from individual ministries and departments with support of MOF, which had central control over finance and personnel, at part-time programmes and courses by various organizations such [as] SAMTAS and later SIM.[2]

Hochstadt was referring to the Supervisory and Management Training Association of Singapore, a professional body, and the Singapore Institute of Management, an educational institution. Both were outside of the government and Public Service.

---

[1]*ST* 16 March 1971: 17.
[2]Herman Hochstadt, Deputy Secretary, Ministry of Finance, 1969–1972, email correspondence with Author, 22 August 2012 and 2 January 2013.

Hence, the training of senior public officers between 1969 and 1971 was outsourced. This out-placing of senior officers' training was not driven by innovative thinking in public administration. Rather, it was an abandonment of formal structured training, returning to pre-1954 colonial practice of *ad hoc* on-the-job coaching by more experienced officers. By 1971, even within the top Administrative Service, for instance, 86 of the total 176 officers had not undergone any induction training. By the government's own admission, "more than 50% of the officers are relatively new and untrained".[3] As the PAP government obviously recognised the value of training, having harnessed training to socialise civil servants upon forming government, a deliberate policy to marginalise training was unlikely. Perhaps the lowering of training as a priority resulted from the flurry of activities with the sudden thrust of independence upon the country. Even when the importance of their training was recognised, senior officers were probably preoccupied with urgent tasks at hand and could ill afford time for training. The need to finance new priorities of nation-building, as mentioned in the previous chapter, added pressure on the limited budget. In the face of such urgent tasks and competing pulls on resources, an unconscious diversion of the Public Service's attention away from training — rather than a deliberate neglect — was understandable, if not inevitable.

3.1.1 *Matching pace with the developmental state*

The setting up of the STI pointed to the government's dissatisfaction with such unstructured arrangements. According to the then Minister for Finance:

> At present, on-the-job training is provided on an *ad hoc* basis, if at all, within prevailing constraints and resources in the ministries and departments. This is obviously unsatisfactory, and a conscious effort will have to be made to provide adequate on-the-job training to supplement on-course training.[4]

---

[3] Hon Sui Sen, Minister for Finance, quoted in *ST* 16 March 1971: 17.
[4] Hon Sui Sen, Minister for Finance, Singapore Parliament, *Parliamentary Debates: Official Report* (Singapore: Government Printer, 1971) 24 March 1971, columns 1172–1173.

Minister Hon Sui Sen elaborated that "the need was recognized for developing a core of well trained and efficient civil servants with *imaginative concepts of management,* if we are to maintain and even surpass the level of economic and social growth that Singapore has achieved over the last 10 years."[5] Implicit therein was the recognition that public officers were unable to match the pace of Singapore's development or changing domestic needs. Indeed, political scientist Quah commented that:

> While Singapore's bureaucracy was not deficient in skilled manpower required for developmental programmes — the problem was not one of quantity as the size of the bureaucracy was quite large for a small country — the problem involved upgrading the quality of bureaucrats.[6]

The unconscious neglect of training exposed a need "to produce well trained and efficient civil servants equipped with knowledge of modern management".[7]

Part of the reason public officers could not keep pace was Singapore's remarkable speed of development. Chalmers Johnson included Singapore among the East Asian capitalist developmental states.[8] That is, a government "hegemonic in a commanding height . . . mobilize[s] economic and political resources" to actively drive the economy.[9] The policy

---

[5]Ministry of Culture, "Speech by the Minister for Finance at the opening of the Course 'Techniques of Project Development and Analysis' conducted jointly by Staff Training Institute and the United Nations' Asian Institute of Economic Development and Planning — 9.00 a.m. on 24 July 1972 at Regional English Language Centre, Orange Grove Road," 24 July 1972, NAS Document PressR19720724a, Microfilm NA1254.

[6]Quah (1975) 574.

[7]Jon S. T. Quah, "Public Administration in a City-State: The Singapore Case," *Comparative Study on the Local Public Administration in Asian and Pacific Countries,* ed. Keiso Hanaoka (Tokyo: EROPA Local Government Centre, 1984) 208–209.

[8]Johnson started off with explaining Japan's rapid economic recovery, before extending his developmental state model to cover the East Asian newly-industrialising economies including Singapore. Chalmers Johnson, *MITI and the Japan Miracle* (California: Stanford University Press, 1982); Chalmers Johnson, "The nonsocialist NICs: East Asia," *International Organisation,* 40.2 (March 1986): 559; Chalmers Johnson, "The Developmental State: Odyssey of a Concept," *The developmental state,* ed. Meredith Woo-Cummings (New York: Cornell University Press, 1999) 40.

[9]Linda Low, "Introduction and Overview" *Developmental States: Relevancy, Redundancy or Reconfiguration?* ed. Linda Low (New York: Nova Science Publishers, 2004) 5.

instruments 'guiding the market' were "formulated by an elite economic bureaucracy, led by a pilot agency of 'economic general staff'."[10] Developmental states relied on "a highly elaborate, resourceful, and centralized administrative apparatus for effectively implementing national planning priorities and administering direct and indirect control over the industrialization process."[11]

The genesis of Singapore's developmental state was traced to 1959, when the PAP embarked upon state-led industrialisation upon winning self-government.[12] Economic development would soak up unemployment and fund social expenditure to uplift the well-being of citizens. Post-independence, the PAP government's survival focus led to rapid economic development. The structure of government, besides the security and social ministries, was geared entirely towards economic development and infrastructural expansion in support of that economic development (*see* Table 3.1). GDP grew from an already respectable 8.9% in 1965 to 15.2% in 1968. These figures were all the more impressive when set against the uncertainties post-Separation, especially when Britain announced its early withdrawal. With the UK bases accounting for 20% of Singapore's economy and 25,000 local jobs, British withdrawal was threatening to halt Singapore's economic engine.[13] Despite such gloomy outlooks, the Singapore economy powered on to score 17.5% in 1971.

The massive scale of development across Singapore exacerbated the government's need for the requisite capacity to manage the developmental

---

[10]Robert Wade, *Governing the Market: Economic Theory and the Role of Government in East Asian Industrialisation* (Princeton: Princeton University Press, 1990) 25–27.

[11]Yun-han Chu, "State structure and economic adjustment of the East Asian newly industrialising countries," *International Organisation*, 43.4 (Autumn 1989): 656. Also, Peter Evans, "Transferable lessons? Re-examining the institutional prerequisites of East Asian economic policies," *Journal of Development Studies*, 34.6 (August 1998): 70–74.

[12]Linda Low, "The Singapore developmental state in the new economy and polity," *The Pacific Review* 14.3 (2001): 416; Linda Low, "Singapore's Developmental State between a Rock and a Hard Place," *Developmental States*, ed. Low, 163–164; Gillian Koh, "Bureaucratic rationality in an evolving developmental state," *Asian Journal of Political Science*, 5.2 (December 1997): 116–117. Also, Cheng Siok Hwa, "Economic change and industrialization," *History of Singapore*, eds. Chew and Lee (1991) 190–193; Bogaars (1973) 82.

[13]Turnbull (2009) 309.

Table 3.1: Structure of the Republic of Singapore Government, 1968[14]

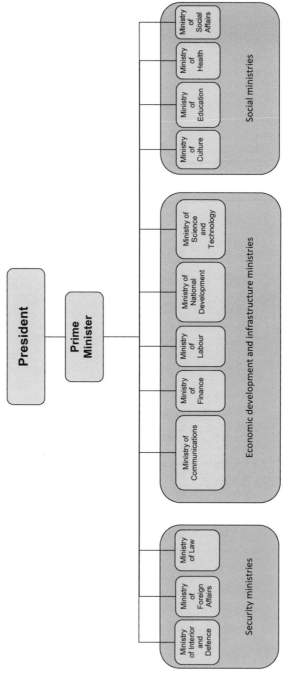

[14]Drawn up from information in *SAR 1968*: 6–7; Hochstadt, email correspondence with Author, 3 January 2013.

state. The use of public enterprises to lead Singapore's development strategy sharpened the need for managerial skills among public officers. Chan pointed out that Singapore had established statutory authorities to address particular development issues, such as the Housing and Development Board (HDB) to construct public housing, the Development Bank of Singapore (DBS) to finance industrial start-ups, and so on. This "choice of the statutory authority as an organizational form released bureaucrats from the conventional rules and regulations of the Civil Service to permit flexibility and experimentation in new areas, with the minimum of control from the legislature."[15] However, this "economic and administrative innovation" also compelled public officers to quickly acquire the managerial skills to preside over large state-led enterprises. George Bogaars, then Head of the Civil Service, wrote that:

> ...the rapid economic and social developments of the past few years had considerably expanded the scope of activities and responsibilities of Government and accelerated the pace of administration. The Government had become increasingly involved in businesses and industrial enterprises. All this had created a demand for properly trained civil servants with experience and knowledge of modern management techniques and with imaginative concepts of management.[16]

The proliferation of multinational corporations (MNCs) into the economy brought public officers face-to-face with some of the top executives from around the world, many of whom were highly qualified. For Singapore's bureaucrats to be effective planners, regulators, and policymakers, dealing with overseas MNCs and local companies while keeping an eye on the country's overall development, the need for Singapore's public officers to be equipped with management training became real and urgent.

Hence, the STI was set-up to provide the bureaucracy, particularly top public officers, with the requisite management training to match the country's pace of development. The STI's establishment in effect was an acknowledgement and rectification of the inadequacy of on-the-job

---

[15]Chan Heng Chee (1991) 164.
[16]Bogaars (1973) 83.

training.[17] The STI also brought the training functions back in-house within the Public Service.

3.1.2 *Retaining talents*

At the same time, the STI also aimed to strengthen the Public Service's human resource management amid the changing economic context. The booming economy and influx of MNCs in the 1970s resulted in a keen competition for qualified manpower; in particular, "managerial skills were at a premium".[18]

However, the Public Service was losing its lustre as a career choice, due to poorer remuneration and training, compared to the private sector. Officers in the Singapore Public Service were organised into four divisions. Division 1 consisted of staff in administrative and professional grades with honours-class university-degrees.[19] Division 2 included executive and supervisory grades with general degrees or pre-university education. Division 3 contained technical and clerical grades with secondary school education, and Division 4 were officers carrying out manual duties.

Graduates with university-degrees typically began their careers as Executive Officers (EOs), a scheme of service in Division 2 (*see* Table 3.2). EOs could be promoted to Higher Executive Officer (HEO) grade and Senior Executive Officer (SEO), a Division 1 grade. Graduates with Honours-class degrees could jump-start their careers as SEOs in Division 1.

The SEO-grade was equivalent to the Administrative Assistant (AA), the entry-point of the elite Administrative Service.[20]Originating from the colonial bureaucracy and modeled after the British Administrative Class, the Administrative Service was the leadership corps of the bureaucracy;

---

[17]Quah (1984) 209.

[18]Turnbull (2009) 328.

[19]John Ewing-Chow and Teo Hee Lian, "Management Training in the Singapore Civil Service," unpublished paper, 1 September 1982, John Ewing-Chow, Papers, 13.

[20]By the late 1970s, the grade structure adjusted slightly with the introduction of a Senior Administrative Assistant (SAA) and removal of the Secretary grades. Lee Boon Hiok (1980) 447, 462, and 478.

Table 3.2:   Grade Structure of University-Graduates in the Public Service, 1971[21]

	Executive Service	Administrative Service
Division 1		Permanent Secretary (PS)
		Deputy Secretary (DS)
		Secretary
		Principal Assistant Secretary (PAS)
		Assistant Secretary (AS)
	Senior Executive Officer (SEO)	Administrative Assistant (AA)
Division 2	Higher Executive Officer (HEO)	
	Executive Officer (EO)	

its role was secondary only to that of the political leadership.[22] It is no wonder that the Administrative Service was cultivated by the PAP government as its 'Praetorian Guards' after it assumed power at self-government.[23] Administrative Service officers (AO) could be promoted from EO-grades but many AAs entered as 'returned scholars'. These referred to graduates, some from local universities but most were from prestigious overseas institutions, where they studied on government scholarships. Scholarships were awarded to students who excelled at their pre-university examinations, to identify and nurture talented personnel

---

[21] The EO scheme also admitted applicants with Higher School Certificate (equivalent to the UK-based General Certificate of Education Advanced Level) or polytechnic-diplomas, but with lower salary points than university graduates. No single document among currently available records captures the Public Service's grade structures. This section is drawn up from Singapore, *Directory* (Singapore: GPO, 1970) 18–25, updated 31 October 1971; Singapore, *Establishment List for the Financial Year 1st April 1974 to 31st March 1975 (Estab List)* (Singapore: GPO, 1974) 185–202; John Ewing-Chow, Management Training Officer, STI, circa 1974, Interview with Author, 28 December 2011; Teo Hee Lian, Language Education Officer, CSSDI, circa 1976, Interview with Author, 3 January 2012 and email correspondence with Author, 2 January 2013; Hochstadt, email correspondence with Author, 2 January 2013.

[22] Anthony Tan Kang Uei, "Meritocracy in the Singapore Civil Service: recruitment and promotion of Administrative Service officers," B.Soc.Sci. (Hons) academic exercise, National University of Singapore, (1997) 24.

[23] Ngiam, Interview with Author, 10 January 2013.

early. Upon completion of their studies, 'scholars' would serve in the Public Service for a number of years. Progression rungs up the AO career ladder, after the AA-grade, were Assistant Secretary (AS), Principal Assistant Secretary (PAS), Secretary, Deputy Secretary (DS) and finally Permanent Secretary (PS), the highest appointment in the Public Service.

The impact of private sector competition for manpower was best illustrated by a newspaper report at that time. *The Straits Times*' survey of 50 senior officers found that 32 senior officers, all graduates with Honours-class degrees, would leave for better pay and only 13 would serve long-term in the bureaucracy. The newspaper opined that "the gap between wages in Government and the private sector has steadily widened during the past five or six years."[24] Fresh graduates with Honours-class degrees could start their careers earning $250 more per month in the private sector; Superscale-A officers could earn more than their $3,000 monthly salary in the private sector. This lure of monetary incentives, surmised political scientist Seah Chee Meow, was due to a weak sense of identification with the Public Service:

> ... the bureaucratic ethos (such as pride in serving in the bureaucracy) is not effectively instilled among the bureaucrats who tend to be more susceptible to purely monetary considerations ... due to the fact that many of the bureaucrats (especially those in the senior or division one grade) have not been in the bureaucracy for a long time. They have yet to internalise many of the norms of the bureaucracy.[25]

Remuneration for civil servants would be raised progressively to match the pay-scales in the private sector, but only several years later rather than immediately.

In the meantime, the government would improve the career development of public officers. Closer supervision was introduced to tighten on-the-job training. A senior officer, with the rank of Deputy Secretary, was appointed at the Ministry of Finance to oversee the enhanced scheme. The career advancement of officers was also to be more

---

[24]*ST* 25 April 1971: 8. Also, *ST* 21 March 1971: 10.
[25]Seah Chee Meow, *The Singapore Bureaucracy and Issues of Transition* (Singapore: University of Singapore, 1975) 21.

purposefully charted out through a programme of planned postings. The abilities, potential, and even inclinations of officers would be considered for the postings of officers. Minister Hon Sui Sen reiterated that "Postings of young officers will be made with the career development of the officers in mind and not merely because the postings are administratively convenient or expedient."[26]

The centerpiece of the government's plan to attract and retain talented manpower was the Staff Training Institute. The STI in the first instance was to provide formal training to make up for the unconscious neglect of training in the years after independence. Specifically, the STI's primary role was to equip senior public officers, particularly the pinnacle Administrative Service officers, with the requisite management skillsets to manage the emerging Singapore developmental state. While ramping up the capacity of the public service, the training of the individual officer would grow his capacity to better perform on his next job. By thus preparing an officer for advancement in his career, training in the STI aimed to attract and retain talented officers amid the competition for manpower from the private sector.

3.2 The Staff Training Institute

Planning for the STI benefitted from the advice of two British management consultants.[27] No indication, however, suggested any reference to the Fulton Report in Britain, recommending the setting up of a Civil Service College in the Home Civil Service, or the École Nationale d' Administration (ENA). By all accounts, there were no attempts to model the STI on any civil service schools in other jurisdictions. To site the STI, the former residence of a colonial official at Lorong Langsir, off Stevens Road, was identified and renovated into an instructional facility by March 1971.[28]

---

[26]*ST* 25 April 1971: 8. Also *ST* 21 March 1971: 10.
[27]*ST* 16 March 1971: 17; Bogaars (1973) 83.
[28]Ewing-Chow, Interview with Author, 28 December 2011.

3.2.1 *Organisational structure*

The STI was set up within the Treasury Division in the Ministry of Finance (*see* Table 3.3).[29] The Permanent Secretary (Treasury) was assisted by three Deputy Secretaries. During this period, Herman Hochstadt was the Deputy Secretary who — as part of his broader portfolio — oversaw the STI through the Personnel Administration Branch (PAB).[30] Locating the STI under the bureaucracy's central personnel agency indicated that training was seen as a human resource subject. Heading the PAB was a Secretary-grade officer, Miss Lim Hsiu Mei.

In 1973, Miss Evelyn Chew, Principal Assistant Secretary in the MOF's Personnel Administration Branch, was posted to the STI as Acting Director (*see* Table 3.4).[31] Chew would be familiar with the STI, having been assisting Lim Hsiu Mei at the PAB, making her lateral transfer optimal. The Language Training and Management Training sections undertook the STI's training functions, supported by the Administration Section.

In October 1973, a high-level Steering Committee on Training was set up to 'advise' the Director STI.[32] However, one senior member of this Committee remembered that "the Committee did not meet very often."[33]

---

[29] *Directory 1970* 18–25 updated 31 October 1971 and 31 July 1972; *Estab List 1974* 185–202. Also, Hochstadt, and Lim Hsiu Mei, Secretary, Personnel Administration Branch, Ministry of Finance, circa 1971, Interview with Author, 21 August 2012; Hochstadt, email correspondence with Author, 2 January 2013.

[30] STI, *Report of Activities, July–December 1972*; *Directory 1970* 25 updated 31 October 1971. John Tan would have been able detail the developments in this early period of STI but he could not be located.

[31] STI, *Report of Activities, July–December 1972* 3; *Estab List 1974–1975* 186–187; *Directory 1970* 21. As late as June 1974, Evelyn Chew was signing off as Acting Director. See Evelyn Chew, Acting Director, Staff Training Institute, "Letters to the Editor, Govt replies: Civil servants and that cloak of anonymity," *ST* 17 June 1974: 14.

[32] Beside Head of Civil Service, Bogaars, members were Tan Chok Kian, Permanent Secretary (Finance) (Budget); Ngiam Tong Dow, Permanent Secretary (Finance) (Development); Peter Tan, Secretary, Public Service Commission; Miss Lim Hsiu Mei, Deputy Secretary (Personnel Administration). STI, MOF, *Training Programme 1975*, January 1975, 1.2.

[33] Ngiam Tong Dow, Interview with Author, 10 January 2013. Tan Chok Kian, Lim Hsiu Mei and Evelyn Chew also could not recall much about this Committee. Lim Hsiu Mei, email correspondence with Author, 17 January 2013; Evelyn Chew, Director, STI, 1973–1975, email correspondence with Author, 12 April 2013.

Table 3.3: The Staff Training Institute in the Ministry of Finance, 1971[34]

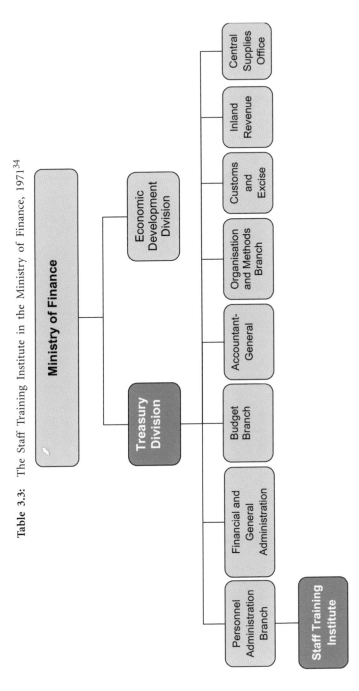

[34]Drawn up from information in *Directory 1970* 18–25 updated 31 October 1971 and 31 July 1972. Organisational units arranged left to right according to the sequence they were presented in the original documents.

Table 3.4: Internal Structure of the Staff Training Institute, circa 1974[35]

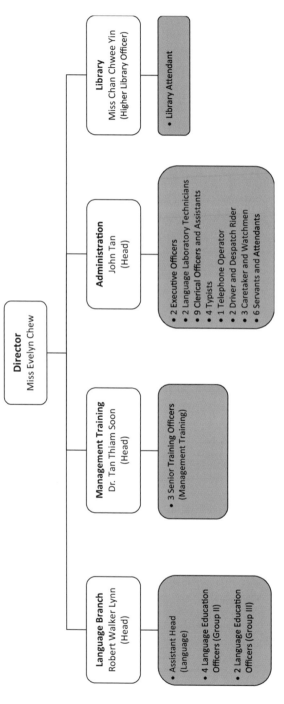

[35]Developed from information gathered from *Estab List 1974–1975* 186–187; STI, MOF, *Training Programme 1975*, January 1975 1.2; *Directory 1970* 21 updated 31 October 1971; Lim Ang Yong, Interview with Author, 21 June 2012; Ewing-Chow, Interview with Author, 28 December 2011.

3.2.2 *Personnel staffing*

Personnel for the STI were drawn from within the Public Service. The STI did not contemplate whether instructors should be recruited from among academics or civil servants, a question debated over when staffing Britain's Centre of Administrative Studies and later the UK Civil Service College.[36] By 1974, the STI had a total of about 45 staff, 12 of whom were engaged in direct training duties.[37]

The post of Director of STI was a civil servant, exercising the bureaucracy's authority over the Institute and linking the STI with the larger bureaucracy. The decision could also stem from administrative convenience by deploying a senior officer from the Finance Ministry who had the competency and was available to start the new school. Recruiting from outside the Public Service would have required time, apart from the new entrant's unfamiliarity with the workings of the bureaucracy.

Similarly, the teaching staff was drawn from among civil servants with the number kept small. The Finance Minister explained that "in view of the very wide field that we are going to cover, it will not be possible for us to have full-time staff lecturers in all the various courses that we want."[38] From the perspective of the MOF, maintaining a small staff of instructors could also keep expenditure low. However, the small instructional cadre would not affect classes, as the Institute planned on calling upon senior civil servants and officers from statutory boards to lead lectures for intermediate, advanced, and induction courses.[39]

Even so, the gap in management training expertise within the bureaucracy compelled the STI to look elsewhere for the relevant staff. As late as 1973, management trainers were still not recruited.[40] Only in 1974 were six Management Training Officers appointed in the STI. A Management Training Officer recruited around that time pointed out

---

[36]Lowe (2011) 314.

[37]*Estab List 1974–1975.* 8.

[38]Hon Sui Sen, Minister for Finance, *Parliamentary Debates*, 24 March 1971, column 1172.

[39]Public officers conducting lectures at the STI were paid allowances at the rate of $25 an hour for intermediate and advanced courses, and $4 to $10 for language courses. STI staff were not paid. *Ibid.*

[40]*Estab List 1974–1975* 186–187.

that "the economy was taking off and lots of people were joining the MNCs — National Semi-Conductor, Texas Instruments, hundreds of companies were coming in. There was shortage of manpower."[41]

Eventually, a University of Singapore academic was seconded to the STI as Head of Management Training.[42] Tan Thiam Soon quickly realised that the existing civil servant-trainers were not equipped to teach management courses beyond the induction and supervisory courses. As a result, Tan had to bring in colleagues from the university to lecture in the STI's management courses.[43] The Head of Language Training, Robert Walker Lynn credited as "instrumental in developing the Language section of the Institute,"[44] was also from outside the civil service.

Finding the appropriate instructional staff with management expertise continued to be challenging against the background of a booming private sector. "For [Financial Year 1974], $143,370 was not spent because suitable staff including Training and Senior Training Officers and Language Education Officers were not recruited despite several attempts to do so through circulars and advertisements."[45]

Remarkably, while much preparation had gone into planning the STI, such as identifying and renovating facilities, little advanced planning had focused on staffing it with the appropriate instructors. Tan Thiam Soon recalled that while his secondment from the University of Singapore was for a one-year term, there was no succession plan for the STI's management training officers to take over his position.[46] Eventually, when Tan returned to the university, the position of Head of Management Training was left vacant for some time.[47]

---

[41] Ewing-Chow, Interview with Author, 28 December 2011.
[42] Tan Thiam Soon, Interview with Author, 21 November 2012.
[43] These included Dr. Gan Huat Tatt and Kek Soon Eng from the University of Singapore, and Lawrence Wong from the Singapore Institute of Management. Tan Thiam Soon, Interview with Author, 21 November 2012.
[44] Chew, email correspondence with Author, 13 April 2013. Also, Ewing-Chow, Interview with Author, 28 December 2011; Teo Hee Lian, STI, Interview with Author, 3 January 2012.
[45] Hon Sui Sen, Minister for Finance, *Parliamentary Debates*, 17 March 1975, column 462. Also *ST* 2 October 1974: 19 Advertisements Column 3.
[46] Tan Thiam Soon, Interview with Author, 21 November 2012.
[47] Ewing-Chow, Interview with Author, 28 December 2011.

3.2.3 *Resources and Support*

As a sub-unit of the Finance Ministry, the STI drew from the MOF's budget to run its activities; participants and their parent-ministries did not have to pay fees for the courses attended. A good working relationship with MOF headquarters facilitated the resourcing of the Institute, but the STI still faced logistical difficulties. Despite customised renovations, John Tan, the Head of Administration who had supervised these upgrading works, wrote two years after the STI's opening that "the existing premises have proved inadequate as more courses are mounted."[48] Inadequate equipment also prompted an obviously informed Member of Parliament to notice, during debates on the STI's 1971 budget, the absence of "votes for audio-visual equipment."[49] To which, the Finance Minister replied: "It is always possible, of course, to get it on loan from the various organizations."[50]

3.2.4 *Organisational objectives and training activities*

Although established in 1971, the STI's objectives were only publicly articulated in its *Training Programme 1975*, its inaugural course prospectus:

> The objective of the Staff Training Institute is to enhance the efficiency of the public sector by providing in-service training courses in the following areas:
>
> - Induction
> - Management and Supervision
> - Specialised and Vocational
> - Language[51]

These courses aimed at "[m]aking officers aware of modern management concepts and tools" and "[s]howing officers how these

---

[48]STI, *Report of Activities, July–December 1972*, 7 March 1973, 3.

[49]J. Conceicao, Member of Parliament for Katong, *Parliamentary Debates*, 24 March 1971, column 1171.

[50]Hon Sui Sen, Minister for Finance, *Parliamentary Debates*, 24 March 1971, column 1172.

[51]STI, *Training Programme 1975*, January 1975, 1.1.

Table 3.5:   Courses conducted by Staff Training Institute, 1971

Courses	Division	No. Held	No. of Participants
Induction Courses		3	80
Administrative Officers	1	1	39
General Executive Officers	2	1	25
Defence Executive Officers	2	1	16
Management Courses		7	164
Intermediate Administrative Officers Course	1	3	70
Executive Officers Course (Intermediate)	2	4	94
Specialised & Vocational Courses		31	880
Management Services Training Course	1/2	1	20
Faster Reading	1/2	2	40
Preparation of Confidential Reports	1/2	4	97
Courtesy and Telephone	3/4	24	723
Leadership Training		15	256
Outward Bound School	1	4	15
National Youth Leadership Training Institute	2/3	11	241
Language Training		8	309
Adult Education Board	1/2/3	8	309
Total		64	1,689

concepts and tools can be applied in the Public Service." In addition, they were meant to equip officers with "basic administrative skills."

In the first nine months of its operations, the STI had organised an impressive 64 courses and trained a total of 1,689 participants (*see* Table 3.5).[52] Closer scrutiny revealed that some courses were conducted on behalf of the STI by external institutions. All 15 Leadership Training courses were undertaken by the Outward Bound School and National Youth Leadership Training Institute.[53] After paring away courses by external agencies, the STI conducted only 41 courses involving 1,124 participants.

[52] John Tan, "Review of Activities of Staff Training Institute," *Management Development (MD)* 1 (September 1973): 8–10.

[53] Language classes were also conducted by an external Adult Education Board initially. Leadership Training eventually disappeared from the STI's collateral material. STI, *Training Programme 1975*, January 1975, 1.1.

After a full year of operation, the STI had built up its capacity to provide a wider range of programmes.[54] Personnel with the requisite knowledge and competency were brought on board, such as the secondment of Tan Thiam Soon from the University of Singapore to start up the Management Training Section or the recruitment of Robert W. Lynn to head the Language Branch. Beyond the number of courses held or participants trained was the broader variety of class offerings. For instance, management type courses grew from just two classes in 1971 to five courses in 1972. Tan, who drew up the management training curriculum, pointed out that the subject of 'management' in those days was not overly business oriented; "The emphasis was not on finance, accounting, not on that, it is mainly on management and administration [of personnel]."[55] Vocational courses also increased from four to nine, attesting to the STI's growing capacity. Still, in proportion to the overall strength of the civil service that was around 63,000 at that time, the 1,287 civil servants trained by the STI represented only 2% of the whole bureaucracy.[56]

An examination of the training activities indicated that the STI essentially embraced the roles played by the former Political Study Centre and Staff Training Centre. A dual emphasis was apparent — dedicated training for the top echelon of the bureaucracy and training opportunities to the lower strata of the Public Service.

Courses for the leadership corps of the bureaucracy were receiving distinctly greater amount of attention. In its first year of operation, the STI had substantially more courses for officers in Divisions 1 and 2; while those in Divisions 3 and 4 only had three courses, those in the higher echelon had 10 courses. Divisions 1 and 2 officers also had more differentiated development opportunities, with intermediate level management courses already on offer. These attested to the greater amount of attention by the STI staff to focus on the training of officers in Divisions 1 and 2. Induction courses for the Administrative Service officers also saw the mustering of Permanent Secretaries and senior

---

[54]Consolidated from John Tan (1973) 8–10.
[55]Tan Thiam Soon, Interview with Author, 21 November 2012.
[56]*Estab List 1974–1975* 8 indicated the total number of civil servants then was 63,050.

officers from various ministries and statutory boards as lecturers; these courses for cadets in the premier scheme of service spanned 10 days. In comparison, induction courses for the Division 2 General Executive scheme of service were only a week long; lecturers were scheduled to be "senior departmental officers and Institute staff".[57] Induction for clerical assistants in Division 3 was only three days and completely led by SIT staff.[58] By 1975, the Induction Course for the Administrative Service had stretched to two whole weeks. However, the Induction Course for the Executive Service had been reduced to three days. By then, the STI had also rolled out an "Intermediate Administrative Officers' Course" and courses on management principles and practices for senior officers, attesting to the inordinate amount of attention at planning and designing courses specifically for the elite scheme of service and higher echelons of the bureaucracy.

3.2.5 *Emphasis on the entire public service*

Efforts were made to emphasise the STI's role in offering training to the entire bureaucracy, which meant including the lower-grade rank-and-file officers: "We will have courses for Personal Assistants, Receptionists, Telephone Operators, and Counter Clerks. We have courses in the Outward Bound School and in the National Youth Leadership Training Institute for officers in supervisory positions."[59] Minister Hon Sui Sen reiterated that "STI has been running a wide range of courses for officers in *different grades* and *different Services.*"[60] The intent was to point out the government's commitment to also offer training opportunities to *junior*-grade officers.

The STI essentially succeeded the roles played by the Political Study Centre and the Staff Training Centre, albeit consolidating the training of elite and rank-and-file into one agency. The focus on training the elite

---

[57]STI, *Report of Activities, July–December 1972*, 7 March 1973, Appendix B3.

[58]STI, *Training Programme 1975*, January 1975, 111.1–111.2.

[59]Hon Sui Sen, Minister for Finance, *Parliamentary Debates*, 24 March 1971, column 1171; *ST* 25 March 1971: 2.

[60]Ministry of Culture, "Speech by the Minister for Finance," 24 July 1972.

was a legacy of the Political Study Centre. Indeed, the induction courses for officers of the Administrative Service and the Executive Service were previously conducted by the Political Study Centre before it closed. Most of the courses for the junior grade officers, such as induction for the Clerical Service, vocational training, and language training, used to be held at the Staff Training Centre.

Besides such core structured courses, the STI was also involved in other occasional training activities. For instance, the Institute collaborated with the union of public service employees to conduct courses on the Government Instruction Manual.[61] These courses were essential, even critical, as they helped new executive officers pass their probationary examinations to be emplaced and receive salary-increments. In conjunction with its parent Finance Ministry, the STI organised a seminar on "Enhancing Productivity in Government Operations" for 100 senior public officers in 1974.[62] With the Singapore government subsequently launching a nation-wide Productivity Campaign, this could be a preparatory workshop for changes that would be introduced across the bureaucracy, and indeed, across the country.

3.2.6 The 'Management Development' bulletin: The 'gospel of good management'

In September 1973, the STI and the Finance Ministry's Management Services Unit jointly published a bulletin titled *Management Development*. On the front page of the inaugural issue, Minister for Finance Hon Sui Sen, likened *Management Development* to an evangelist serving "to spread as widely as possible the gospel of good management, which we want to infuse the whole Civil Service."[63]

The periodical had an editorial board, chaired by Lim Hsiu Mei, the Deputy Secretary at the Finance Ministry overseeing personnel matters

---

[61] *ST* 2 September 1971: 4; Lim Ang Yong, Interview with Author, 21 June 2012.

[62] *ST* 12 August 1974: 23; Cedric Pugh, "Budget Innovation in Singapore," *Government Budgeting in Developing Countries*, ed. Peter Dean (London and New York: Routledge, 1989) 100.

[63] "Message from Minister for Finance," *Management Development (MD)* (September 1973): 1. *Management Development* was to run continuously until 1984.

and the STI. Members of the Board included Evelyn Chew, Director of STI, and Robert W. Lynn, STI's Head of Language Training.

The similarity between *Management Development* and the earlier *Bakti* cannot be missed. *Bakti* complemented the Political Study Centre's courses by disseminating articles on the political context of Singapore's state-formation process and the role expected of the bureaucracy, to a wider audience across the Public Service. Likewise, *Management Development* sought to spread information on various aspects on management across the Public Service. The inaugural edition introduced "What is 'management services'", and subsequent issues explained "Management by Objectives".[64] Most of these were contributions from officers across the Public Service, contrasting with *Bakti*'s offerings of speeches by political leaders or articles reproduced from other publications. The articles in *Management Development* were also relatively well-written and replete with bibliographic references.

3.2.7 *Evaluation of STI's Programmes*

Whether formal evaluations were undertaken on the STI's training programmes cannot be ascertained.[65] Among academics, only Quah reviewed that "STI was merely a training institution and did not have a research programme."[66]

One internal report on a single course can shed some light on the conduct of training in the STI. The report was written up by John Ewing-Chow, in his third week as a Training Officer, after attending and administering a course on Management Principles and Practice for Division 1 public officers. Ewing-Chow wrote that course participants were unfamiliar with the Institute's role and course offerings, despite

---

[64]Lau Kim Boo, "Management Services Concept," *MD* 1 (September 1973): 4 and 11; Wong Tuen Seng, "Management by Objectives — An Expository Note" *MD* 5 (September 1974): 2–5.

[65]Official records pertaining to STI cannot be found in the public domain; the catalogue of the National Archives of Singapore did not list any such records. Without consulting official records evaluating the STI's training programmes or the Institute's performance, a fair assessment of the STI at this juncture is not fair.

[66]Jon S. T. Quah, "The Study of Public Administration in the ASEAN Countries," *International Review of Administrative Sciences*, 46 (1980): 358.

the publicity given to the STI over the years. On the course itself, he thought that interesting sessions, such as a Management Game, were let down by vague objectives and unclear instructions. Topics on Organisation, Planning, and Control would be more useful for officers with top management exposure rather than young participants. Case studies should be civil service-oriented to enhance identification with the scenarios. Between the two trainers, the civil servant rather than the academic came across to be more emphatic when acknowledging obstacles in practice. Ewing-Chow reflected that "[i]t is therefore a good selection principle... to bring together participants of similar ages and educational backgrounds, not only for status reasons but also for a better learning environment."[67] While this sampling cannot be taken as representative of all courses, it is nevertheless illuminating.

Another perspective on the STI was found in an interview with J. F. Conceicao in *Management Development*. The Chairman of the Parliamentary Public Accounts Committee lamented that many civil servants were focused on the mechanics of their jobs. Beyond vocational development, civil servants should appreciate their roles in relation to the community and the country:

> ... the kind of orientation provided by the Political Study Centre was [thought] no longer necessary. Now surely if you take away that institution, you must devise some means of orientating people constantly to the fact that they are serving the public.... Training, seems to be its just like industrial training without sending the guy to the factory. It's a waste of time. Same thing with the training in the Civil Service, it has to be tied to career development. If you are thinking in terms of the [Executive Officer] and the chap down the line, you're training them not only to function, but for a fulfilment of a function which if well fulfilled could entitle the chap to [promotion].[68]

3.3 Some Comparisons

The STI's establishment was particularly timely, considering developments in civil service training across other Westminster jurisdictions. In Britain,

---

[67] Ewing-Chow, "Report on Management Course A, 16 to 21 December 74," JEC Papers.
[68] "Interview with Mr. J. F. Conceicao," *MD* 11 (March 1976): 6. Although the article was published after the STI was renamed, the conduct of the interview in 1975 meant his views pertained to the period of the STI.

after years of debate, the UK Civil Service College was finally set up in 1971. Proponents for a central training school for the UK Home Civil Service, with the Assheton Committee in 1944 among the earliest advocates, had long been tempered by institutional inclination towards on-the-job training.[69] The Centre for Administrative Studies set up in 1963 was a major step towards a central institution, but "only a very small proportion of the civil service had access to what might be described as proper training, and this was of an exclusively introductory type."[70] The 1968 Fulton Committee finally provided the strongest impetus for reforming the subject of training in the bureaucracy and the Civil Service College was established in 1971.[71]

The UK Civil Service College's realisation brought to the fore other dilemmas in civil service training. These ranged from whether academics or civil servants make the most appropriate instructors, should the curriculum be academically-rooted or oriented to the work and life of the bureaucracy, to whether the College should be headed by an academic or career-civil servant.[72] The eventual decision was an eminent Professor Eugene Grebenik as principal and an under-secretary William Graham Bell as deputy, and the faculty was a mix between career civil servants and academics.[73] Even so, these arrangements were, by no means, the final word on the long-standing debates between civil servants or academics as instructors, or even between advocates of a central training institution and those for 'sitting next to Nellie.' Nevertheless, the creation of a dedicated school in Britain underscored the recognition of the need for bureaucratic training in that jurisdiction.

Similarly, training in the Hong Kong bureaucracy was gradually taking off after a late start; a Training and Examinations Unit was created under the Appointments, Training, and Discipline Division within the

---

[69] Lowe (2011) 313; Pyper (1995) 42.

[70] Pyper (1995) 42. Also Bird (1992) 71.

[71] Lowe (2011) 313–314; Pyper (1995) 43.

[72] E. Grebenik, "The Civil Service College: The First Year" *Public Administration* 50 (1972): 135.

[73] Bird (1992) 72.

Colonial Secretariat's Establishment Branch in 1961.[74] Its mandate was to upgrade the skillsets of local officers in order to speed up the localisation of the Hong Kong Public Service. Considering the similar jurisdictional sizes and common colonial traditions, Hong Kong's Training Unit was several years later than Singapore's Staff Training School. Nevertheless, while the post-colonial Staff Training Centre languished as Singapore concentrated on political socialisation, bureaucratic training grew steadily in Hong Kong.

By 1971, a dedicated Government Training Division separated from other shared portfolios.[75] It continued to coordinate internal training within various government departments, and training for civil servants in local and overseas universities.[76] Its Staff Training Centre, on the other hand, was similar to Singapore's STI, comprising language training sections and a section on General and Administrative Training. A huge number of its officers taught languages, particularly the English language, but the Hong Kong context also required civil servants to be equipped with various Chinese dialects. The General and Administrative Training section carried out courses on supervisory skills, communications, administrative skills, and the like, for executive officers, clerks, secretaries, and other officers of rank-and-file grades. In this regard, the types of training carried out by the Hong Kong Staff Training Centre and its main targeted audience were similar with those of Singapore's STI. The exception was the management training for the leadership corps, which was the impetus for the birth of the STI against the context of a developmental state. In Hong Kong then, there were no similar management type courses for its leadership of the bureaucracy.

In Malaysia, with which Singapore shared a common colonial and bureaucratic tradition, the Staff Training Centre set up between 1959 and 1963 had graduated into a National Institute of Public

---

[74]Hong Kong, *Report on the Public Service 1965*, Para 36, HKPRO, Accession No. A/55/81/2A; Scott and Burns (1998) 119.

[75]Hong Kong, *Report on the Public Service 1971/72*, 41, HKPRO, Accession No. A/55/81/9B.

[76]*Ibid*, 32–33 and 41, HKPRO, no. A/55/81/9B. Also Hong Kong, *Report on the Public Service 1967/68*, 39, HKPRO, A/55/81/5A; Hong Kong, *Report on the Public Service 1969*, 25, HKPRO, A/55/81/7A.

Administration (Institut Tadbiran Awam Negara, INTAN) by 1972.[77]
While the British neglected training during their "leisurely pace" of
colonial "maintenance role", independence and development highlighted
the need for administrative training.[78] Interestingly, apart from remedying
"deficiencies in the existing training systems", INTAN's creation was
catalysed by two 'stimuli':

> First, there was growing awareness within the civil service of its role as an
> agent of change and the consequent need to equip itself for this role. Second,
> there was pressure from the ADS [Administrative and Diplomatic Service],
> the elite bureaucratic cadre, whose members felt "threatened by a gradual
> but steady diminution of power" brought about in part by their relative
> inability to cope with the new demands made on them, systematic training
> and career development was seen as an immediate need in the process of
> 'rejuvenating' the elite cadres.[79]

INTAN's mission was similar to Singapore's STI, providing induction,
basic training, and refresher training. However, its aim of "training for
career development" was more ambitious, which INTAN appeared capable
of delivering.[80] From 1970, INTAN was partnering with local universities
to conduct courses on management science and public administration
leading to the conferment of diplomas.

Currently available records and those officials interviewed for this
study indicated that there were no references to Malaysia's experience
when the STI was being set up. The striking similarities in the respective
circumstances leading up to the setting up of Singapore's STI and
Malaysia's INTAN could be due to the near identical geographical–
jurisdictional context and colonial bureaucratic tradition. Quah certainly

---

[77]Marican 10–11; INTAN, "INTAN in Brief," Web, 16 November 2012, http://www.
intanbk.intan.my/i-portal/en/about-intan/intan-in-brief.html
[78]Elyas bin Omar, "The Civil Service Systems in Malaysia," *Asian Civil Services*, eds.
Raksasataya and Siedentopf (1980) 272; Noor Hazilah Abd Manaf, "Civil service system
in Malaysia," *Public Administration in Southeast Asia: Thailand, Philippines, Hong Kong
and Macao*, ed. Evan Berman (London: Routledge, 2011) 216.
[79]Marican (1979) 11, quoting extracts from Staff Training Centre, Malaysia, and
Development Administration Unit, Malaysia, *Training and Development in West Malaysia*
(Kuala Lumpur: Prime Minister's Department, 1969).
[80]Omar (1980) 272–273.

attributed British negligence of structured training and favouring on-the-job training as reasons for the late development of civil service training in both former UK colonies, compared to the rest of Southeast Asian states.[81] In any case, compared with developments in other Westminster jurisdictions, the STI was a timely catching-up in civil service training for Singapore.

3.4 Conclusion

Against the context of the Singapore developmental state, the STI was set up for the purpose of building up the capacity of the Administrative Service corps to *manage* the country's rapid economic development. The developmental state loomed large from the prism of the state; the political leadership's grand strategic goal was rapid, large-scale, state-led economic development. In turn, this developmental state goal highlighted the perspective from which senior ranks of the bureaucracy contemplated the situation: a lack of management skills among civil servants to lead, plan, regulate, and manage the developmental state.

The STI was meant to be the point through which public officers were introduced to and be equipped with management skills. In the face of competition for limited qualified manpower, the STI was part of an overall effort to boost public sector HR management, to attract and retain good public officers. All things considered, the STI was thus set up as a point to reform the Public Service.

In the evolution of training in Singapore's bureaucracy, the STI represented a return to the traditional functions of competency training, after a momentary neglect due to the priority accorded to using training for political socialisation. Quah observed that "STI reflects a shift in emphasis from the political training courses of the PSC [Political Study Centre] to more practical and comprehensive training programmes for civil servants."[82] After 10 years of continued rule, the

---

[81] Jon S.T. Quah, "Study of Public Administration in the ASEAN Countries" *International Review of Administrative Sciences*, 46 (1980): 358. Quah identified STI as Singapore's first training school, discounting the Political Study Centre or the Staff Training Centre as bureaucratic training schools.

[82] Quah (1980): 358.

hold of the PAP government over the state was sufficiently secured and
political socialisation was no longer as compelling as at the onset of
self-government.

However, at the same time, focusing on technical competencies
was also a natural progression from the Political Study Centre. The
Political Study Centre succeeded in aligning civil servants into sharing the
worldview of the PAP government. Assured of a dependable bureaucracy
and their civil servants' loyalty to the new state, the focus could shift
towards building up the technical competencies of the Public Service, and
hence that of the STI. As the successor to the Political Study Centre, the
purpose of the STI was to build up basic competencies and management
skills.

Furthermore, the shift in training policy towards technical skills was
recognition that basic training in the Public Service had largely been
neglected in the period following independence. For a government that
ostensibly recognised the value of training and having harnessed training
to socialise the bureaucracy, how did the PAP allow such a lapse in
the priority of bureaucratic training? The answer is likely that the PAP
had competing priorities in the wake of independence, and civil service
training had become a casualty of the country's primary goal of rapid
development.

The preoccupation with the urgent tasks of state-building and the
competing pull on limited resources in the aftermath of independence
might have led to an unconscious distraction from training in the Public
Service. This risk was articulated by the civil servants responsible for
leading training. John Ewing-Chow and Teo Hee Lian, two trainers who
started out their careers with the STI and eventually rose to become
directors of the Public Service school, wrote years later that "[t]he 1970s
was . . . a time when [with] the priority going to pressing issues related to
economic restructuring, housing, health, education, and defence, further
development of training in the public sector had to take a back seat."[83]
In this regard, establishing the STI was more than a shift from political
socialisation to practical training; it represented renewed emphasis on
training in the Singapore Public Service.

---

[83] Ewing-Chow and Teo (1982) 3.

The STI was not modelled after any foreign civil service training organisations in other jurisdictions. In setting up the STI, records available and officials interviewed attested to no references to the British Civil Service College, the French École Nationale d'Administration, the Malaysian INTAN, or any other foreign bureaucratic schools. The STI was Singapore's exploration of its own approach towards training, an experiment to fill the gap of management training among civil servants amid the needs of the developmental state. This streak to go its own way could reflect distrust or an eschewing of foreign models; at the same time, it also reflected a sense of growing confidence within the bureaucracy, or the government, of its own budding competencies and capabilities. Without the boundaries of foreign models, the STI was certainly able to customise its structure, goals, and activities to local necessities, and took into consideration local constraints. For example, it was able to work around the lack of management expertise within the bureaucracy by seeking for the secondment of academics to build up capacity in this domain. In all purposes, the STI represented an experiment on the part of the Singapore Public Service in training.

All its efforts notwithstanding, the STI and its work should not be exaggerated. It was always a small organisation, with 45 officers by 1974, of which 12 were in direct training positions. Especially stark was the lack of expertise to conduct management training, with only four trainers even when supplemented by seconded academics. Of the 56 courses the STI conducted in 1972, only five — or less than 10% — were management courses. All 15 leadership courses were undertaken on its behalf by external agencies. The bulk of the STI courses were functional and vocational courses. This concentration on training the rank-and-file of the bureaucracy appeared to have reversed, even subverted, the original intent of setting up the STI to equip the Administrative Service officer with management skills.[84]

Unsurprisingly, while the STI might have publicised its mission and training activities formally, it was apparently not well-recognised even among public officers. The STI's organisational goals were set out by the Minister for Finance, and courses were offered across the Public

---

[84]Sim (1985) 22.

Service through regular circulars. In 1975, the STI even published a *Training Prospectus*, setting out in detail its objectives and its offerings of training courses. Yet, in reality, the STI was not very well-recognised among public officers, as evidenced by Ewing-Chow's report on a course. Several course participants had queried STI staff on what was the STI, what were its roles, who were the staff of the STI, and what were the courses available at the STI. Hence, for all the STI's professed mission and goals, in reality, it was not really well-known among public officers, who were its intended clientele.

The Staff Training Institute appeared from the start to be a temporary milestone towards a larger and longer-term scheme of training. Even as its Lorong Langsir premise was being renovated into the STI in 1971, the plan was already laid to eventually locate the Institute with a Civil Service Centre to be set up in the former Tanglin Barracks.[85] Within two years, the STI's Lorong Langsir premises had become inadequate for the expanding needs of the STI. However, rather than the scheduled relocation to Tanglin, plans were unveiled in 1973 to move the STI to Kent Ridge, where "the present extent and scope of activities will be intensified."[86] In 1975, following the move to the brand-new complex, the Public Service's training school was renamed the Civil Service Staff Development Institute, thus ending the tenure of the Staff Training Institute from 1971 to 1975.

---

[85]*ST* 16 March 1971: 17; *ST* 12 February 1972: 14.
[86]John Tan (1973) 8.

Chapter 4

Symbolism and Tinkering: The Civil Service Staff Development Institute and the Civil Service Institute (1975–1996)

This chapter examines the central training school of the Singapore Public Service between 1975 and 1996. Although the school was known as the Civil Service Staff Development Institute (CSSDI) and then the Civil Service Institute (CSI), the two names referred to the same organisation and hence, merit discussion under the same banner. The 20-year period is addressed in three parts to draw out the various stages in the school's evolution.

In 1975, the Staff Training Institute changed its name to the Civil Service Staff Development Institute when it moved to new premises, and tried to extend 'training' into more comprehensive staff 'development'. The first part of this chapter examines the context leading up to this new phase of training in the Singapore bureaucracy.

The second part of this chapter deals with the Civil Service Institute. While the name change from the CSSDI was no more substantial than nominal, the Institute did begin to grow in capacity and training offerings in the 1980s. Through its expanding range of courses, especially those on language, productivity, and computerisation, the was introducing reforms into and across the Public Service.

The third part of this chapter addresses the challenges facing the CSI. In particular, the tension between broad-based training and developing the elite was brought to the fore with the gradual evolution of the CSI into a training institution for the entire Public Service. This aspiration contrasted with the CSI's inability to provide leadership development programmes for the elite Administrative Service officers, at least in the eyes of the Public Service leadership. By the early 1990s, the establishment of a separate training centre for the AOs ended the CSI's monopoly of training in the bureaucracy. In 1996, the CSI was reorganised into a department within a new Civil Service College. Thus, the CSI's 20-year tenure as a separate and sole central training school of the Public Service came to an end.

4.1 From CSSDI to CSI: A Quiet Graduation and an Overnight Name Change

In June 1975, *Management Development* announced that "[t]he Civil Service Staff Development Institute (CSSDI), formerly known as Staff Training Institute, moved to its permanent premises in Heng Mui Keng Terrace, off Pasir Panjang Road."[1]

This allocation of a brand-new building to the CSSDI was significant; until then, the Public Service's schools were set up in existing government quarters. In contrast, facilities in the new building were state-of-the-art; a 185-seat lecture theatre, with the latest sound systems and cinema projector, was complemented by syndicate rooms, language laboratories, a library, and a 52-room hostel.[2] One staff recalled that "CSSDI had the most modern building and office in the whole Civil Service."[3]

The context against which the new facilities were allocated to the CSSDI was interesting. Apparently, the building was originally planned as Singapore's contribution to the United Nations.[4] One former Permanent Secretary recounted:

> The CSSDI building at Heng Mui Kheng Terrace — this was originally designed and built to accommodate a UN-sponsored regional training and development institute under the auspices of ESCAP [Economic and Social Commission for the Asia and the Pacific] but, owing to differences between ESCAP officials and Singapore authorities on immunities, privileges, and

[1] "Civil Service Staff Development Institute — New Premises," *MD* 8 (June 1975): 9.
[2] CSSDI, *Training Programme 1976* (Singapore: CSSDI, 1975) I.3; *Training Programme 1979*, 3.
[3] Ewing-Chow, Interview with Author, 28 December 2011.
[4] Ewing-Chow, Interview with Author, 28 December 2011; *ST* 4 May 1970: 7; *ST* 7 November 1970: 12.

benefits to be extended to UN personnel to be attached to and engaged for the UN-sponsored institute, the offer to ESCAP to host the institute in Singapore was rescinded by the Singapore government; the building and facilities were, on completion, handed over to a newly formed CSSDI for use for its programmes and courses.[5]

More importantly, the name change to 'Civil Service Staff Development Institute' reflected the institute's direction towards 'staff development', according to Miss Evelyn Chew, the Director overseeing the transition.[6] Chew's supervisor, Miss Lim Hsiu Mei, Deputy Secretary (Personnel Administration Branch), concurred that the name change represented a progression from "mere training to a higher level of developing staff across the entire civil service."[7] Hence, the name-change with the move to new facilities in Heng Mui Keng reflected an elevation in training.

4.1.1 *Organisational structure and personnel staffing*

The CSSDI reported to the Personnel Administration Branch of the Ministry of Finance's Budget Division.[8] This reporting line was a continuation from that of STI although the MOF had undergone some changes following a reorganisation. The earlier Treasury Division was renamed Budget Division, which continued to oversee the PAB. Hence, human resources remained a subject of resourcing and training remained a part of personnel management to the bureaucracy.

The CSSDI also received policy direction on the training of Division 1 officers from the Establishment Unit in the Prime Minister's Office, signalling the government's attention to "an urgent situation ... to spot

---

[5] Hochstadt, email correspondence with Author, 22 August 2012. ESCAP was the name, from 1974, of the Economic Commission for Asia and the Far East (ECAFE). ESCAP, "History," http://www.unescap.org/about/history, accessed on 27 December 2012.

[6] Evelyn Chew, Director, STI/CSSDI, 1971–1979, email correspondence with Author, 30 January 2013.

[7] Lim Hsiu Mei, Deputy Secretary (Personnel Administration Branch), MOF, 1975, email correspondence with Author, 17 January 2013. In *Directory 1975*: 123, the subjects under Lim's oversight included "Career Development, Training."

[8] *Training Programme 1976*: I.1; Ministry of Culture, Singapore, *Singapore Government Directory 1977 (Govt Directory 1977)* (Singapore: Ministry of Culture, 1977) 139; *Estab List 1976*: 2; *ST* 17 March 1976: 6.

talent at the top",[9] "because of the void in numbers of able officers in the 30- to 45-year-old age group caused by many promising officers leaving to join the private sector in the years of rapid economic growth."[10] Internally, the CSSDI's structure remained the same as that of the STI.

The CSSDI retained the same staff establishment as the STI.[11] Tan Thiam Soon and Robert W. Lynn remained Heads of Management Training and Language respectively, but both left soon after, and the positions became vacant.[12]

Lynn had identified a successor before his departure. Miss Teo Hee Lian, a young Administrative Service officer, had impressed the CSSDI faculty while attending induction. Transferring her to the CSSDI was not easy as the AOs were typically posted to policymaking positions in ministries, but Teo eventually became a CSSDI Language Education Officer.[13]

Competition from the private sector was another issue. When the CSSDI sent a Management Training Officer, John Ewing-Chow, for post-graduate studies, he was instructed to avoid business-related fields, such as Masters in Business Administration, to avoid exposing him to private sector poaching.[14] Difficulties in recruiting staff with administrative experience and training expertise continued to hinder the CSSDI's capacity build-up.[15]

---

[9]Lee Kuan Yew, Prime Minister, *Parliamentary Debates*, 16 March 1976, columns 333–334. Other officers continued to be managed by the MOF Establishment Branch and Public Service Commission.

[10]Circular by Head of the Civil Service, quoted by Lee Kuan Yew, *Parliamentary Debates*, 16 March 1976, column 334.

[11]Of the total complement of 41 officers, 10 were directly involved in training duties. *Estab List 1974–1975*: 8.

[12]Tan Thiam Soon, Interview with Author, 21 November 2012; Teo Hee Lian, Interview with Author, 3 January 2012.

[13]Posted to the CSSDI in 1976, Teo went to the University of Lancaster for a Master's degree in linguistics in 1977, and returned to the CSSDI in 1978. *MD* 30 (January 1981): 16; Teo Hee Lian, Interview with Author, 3 January 2012.

[14]Ewing-Chow did a Masters in Administration. Ewing-Chow, Interview with Author, 28 December 2011.

[15]*ST* 17 February 1984: 13.

Table 4.1: Structure of the Civil Service Staff Development Institute, 1975[16]

Director
Miss Evelyn Chew

Language Section
Robert Walker Lynn
(Head)

- 3 Language Education Officers
- 2 Language Laboratory Technicians

Management Training Section
Tan Thiam Soon
(Head)

- 2 Senior Training Officers (Management Training)
- 3 Training Officers (Management Training)

Administration Section
John Tan
(Head)

- 3 Executive Officers
- 9 Clerical Officers and Assistants
- 3 Typists
- 1 Telephone Operator
- 2 Driver and Despatch Rider
- 5 Caretaker and Watchmen
- 3 Office Attendants

Library

- 1 Library Officer
- 1 Library Attendant

[16]Developed from information gathered from *Estab List 1976*: 188–189; *Training Programme 1976*: I.1.

4.1.2 *Objectives and training activities*

The CSSDI was officially opened by the Minister for Finance on 10 March 1976. Its aims were similar to those of STI, primarily "[m]aking officers aware of modern management concepts and tools and showing them how these can be applied in the Service".[17] Courses remained 'free' for public officers; the CSSDI continued to rely on the Finance Ministry's budget to run its training activities.

More significant was a new mapping of the CSSDI programmes with the career development of public officers. This appeared to follow a parliamentarian's feedback, as mentioned in the previous chapter.[18] It is not clear whether this resulted from Conceicao's comments or from ongoing deliberations in the government. Regardless, this was the first time the career development of officers was factored into the planning of training in the Public Service.

Mapping training to career progression was particularly evident at Division 1, especially for the Administrative Service officers. Recruits would attend induction within six months of joining the Public Service.[19] Upon assuming managerial functions, officers would return to the CSSDI for management courses. Deputy Secretaries and Principal Assistant Secretaries would attend advanced management courses. All the AOs would also return for monthly seminars to enhance their understanding of policies and policymaking processes.

The training and career development of Division 1 officers were better developed than that of lower grades. Division 2 officers only had an induction programme and courses in supervision, and financial and personnel administration.[20] The greater attention to the higher grades was magnified when examining the course-career development mapping for officers below Division 2; there was none.

This emphasis on Division 1 arose from the bureaucracy's inherent focus on developing its elite. From the outset, the government concentrated on cultivating the premier Administrative Service as its

---

[17] *Training Programme 1976*: I.1.
[18] "Interview with Mr. J. F. Conceicao," *MD* 11 (March 1976): 6.
[19] *Training Programme 1976*: I.1 and III.1; *ST* 12 April 1976: 13.
[20] *Training Programme 1976*: I.2.

'Praetorian Guard'.[21] The Administrative Service, as mentioned in earlier chapters, was raised originally in the colonial bureaucracy. Since self-government, the AOs had been recruited from among the best and brightest of Singapore society, typically identified from those who aced pre-University examinations and awarded government scholarships for undergraduate studies. The elite status of the Administrative Service was fuelled by its exclusivity; while Executive Service officers in Division 2 could be promoted into the Administrative Service up to the 1970s (*see* previous chapter), political scientist Thomas Bellows asserted that "there is little movement from Division II to Division I" in the 1980s.[22] The priority accorded by the government to the Administrative Service was reiterated in 1979: "whatever the changes to the professional or other services, the pre-eminence of the Administrative Service will be the cornerstone of all services."[23] The CSSDI's focus on the highest echelons of the bureaucracy was thus driven by the government's long-standing focus on cultivating the elite Administrative Service.

In reality, the training–career development mapping appeared more aspirational. Some of the courses prescribed to various levels of officers' career progressions were already in place or could be readily rolled out, such as induction and seminars for Administrative Service officers. However, some courses could not be carried out easily, such as the advanced management courses for Deputy Secretaries. The need to rely on foreign trainers, as it eventually did, hinted at the lack of expertise within the CSSDI to carry out management training beyond its existing suite of courses for the mid-level AOs.[24] Three academics from the University of Southern California were eventually brought in, through the personal efforts of Evelyn Chew, to run advanced management courses

---

[21]Ngiam Tong Dow, Interview with Author, 10 January 2013.
[22]Thomas Bellows, "Bureaucracy and Development in Singapore," *Asian Journal of Public Administration* 7.1 (June 1985): 61.
[23]Ministry of Culture, "Singapore Government Press Release: Ministerial Statement on the Singapore Administrative Service made by the Minister for Trade and Industry on behalf of the Prime Minister in Parliament on Thursday, 15 May 1979," NAS Microfilm No. NAS 553/4.
[24]*Training Programme 1976*: III.5–III.6.

between 1975 and 1977.[25] However, the high costs involved required sponsorship from the Asia Foundation, and when that funding dried up, the gap in the CSSDI's capacity in senior executive development curriculum was once again starkly exposed.

4.1.3 *Overnight name change: From the CSSDI to the Civil Service Institute*

On 27 February 1979, the Prime Minister called a meeting that was to affect the CSSDI. Lee Kuan Yew was unhappy with the verbose language of memoranda reaching his desk. "[This] steady deterioration over the last 20 years," he warned ministers and civil servants that "[i]f we do not make a determined effort to change, the process of government will slow down. It will snarl up."[26] The transcript of the discussion thereafter recorded his response to a reference to the CSSDI; "Prime Minister: Can't we find a better name for CSSDI. Find a word that conveys the meaning instead of an acronym which does not convey any."[27]

Overnight, Kirpa Ram Vij, who took over as the CSSDI Director earlier in the year, recalled that the Civil Service Staff Development Institute became the Civil Service Institute.[28] However, its objectives, as with other aspects, were similar with those of the CSSDI:

(a) Orienting newly-recruited officers to the Service;
(b) Equipping officers with basic administrative skills; and
(c) Making officers aware of modern management concepts and tools, and showing them how these can be applied in the Service.[29]

A more significant development was the establishment of a Training Advisory Council (TAC) "to advise the CSI on the development and management of its training programmes, and to review periodically

---

[25] Ewing-Chow, Interview with Author, 28 December 2011; *Training Programme 1977*: II.5 and III.3; CSSDI; John Ewing-Chow, Secretary, Task Force, "Paper on the Background to the INSEAD Report," undated, JEC Papers.

[26] "PM: Improve your English," *MD* 24 (June 1979): 3.

[27] *Ibid.*

[28] Kirpa Ram Vij, Director, CSSDI, 1979–1981, Interview with Author, 22 January 2013.

[29] Civil Service Institute, *Civil Service Institute Training Programme 1980* (Singapore: CSI, 1980) 1.

Table 4.2: CSSDI and Civil Service Institute, 1979[30]

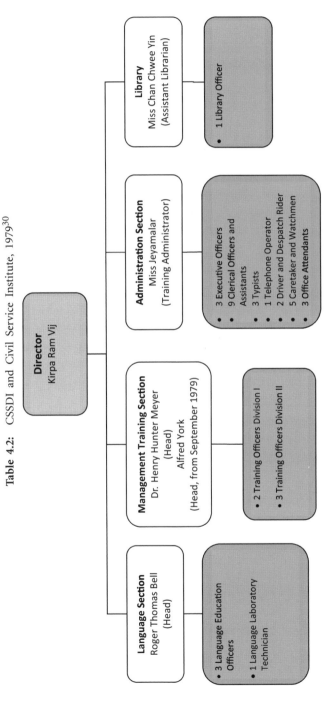

[30]Developed from information gathered from *Govt Directory 1977*: 144–145 updated 1 January 1979; *Training Programme 1979*: 1; Bell, "Teaching Communication Skills: The Grammarian's Funeral," *MD* 24 (June 1979): 15–18; Bell, "Investigating Language Training Needs in the Civil Service," *MD* 30 (January 1981): 9. Evelyn Chew was posted to the Ministry of Health in June 1977: see ASAS *Newsletter* 16 July 1977: 2.

its activities and progress."[31] The TAC comprised the Head of the
Civil Service, Permanent Secretaries from the Prime Minister's Office
and Finance Ministry, Secretary of the Public Service Commission,
and Director of the CSI. While reminiscent of the earlier STI Steering
Committee, the work of the TAC was to be much more significant.

4.2 Leadership Development, Foundational Building, and Remaining Relevant

4.2.1 *The administrative staff college proposal*

Among the Training Advisory Council's first tasks was to review a
recommendation to upgrade the CSI into a Singapore Administrative Staff
College (SASC). This was tabled by two professors from the European
Institute of Business Administration (INSEAD), arising from a French
government offer to help train Singapore's public officers: "a high quality,
prestigious SASC should be set up to provide continuing education in
public administration and management to senior officers in the Civil
Service."[32] This SASC should be structured under a new ministry or
department of Public Service, and guided by a high-powered Board of
Governors. In the long term, the INSEAD team envisioned the SASC to:

> ... play a leading role in providing ideas, promoting concepts, methods and
> organising talks given by visiting scholars or foreign personalities. If the
> College is successful in reaching excellence, it could ultimately play a regional
> role in opening its doors and facilities to neighbouring countries.[33]

A key element of the proposal was a faculty team: selecting
from among the Administrative Service, six officers with a minimum
of six years of service and Principal Assistant Secretary or Deputy
Secretary-grade. After one year of training at INSEAD, the six AOs
would devote four years to developing programmes at the Staff College.
The Training Advisory Council's interest in the INSEAD proposal was
particularly piqued by the need to fill the gap of senior-level executive

---

[31] Ewing-Chow and Teo (1982) 7.
[32] "A summary of the report of the study of the training needs of the higher echelons
of the Singapore Civil Service," undated, p. 3, JEC Papers.
[33] *Ibid.*

training. Except for a few advanced management courses by visiting academics some years ago, the CSI had not provided appropriate training for Administrative Service officers above the Assistant Secretary-grade. This gap in the CSI's leadership development capacity was, as mentioned earlier in the chapter, begging to be filled.

For a more in-depth review of the Administrative Staff College proposal, the TAC set up a dedicated task force. Kirpa Ram Vij, the CSI Director, was also sent to evaluate the British Civil Service College, the French École Nationale d'Administration and INSEAD.[34] This was the furthest Singapore had gone to entertain foreign models of bureaucratic training.

The Political Study Centre, set up after self-government to socialise civil servants towards a closer appreciation of their political context, had no precedent, overseas or locally. The Staff Training Institute was not modelled after any foreign training schools, based on available archival records and on the knowledge of officials interviewed. The CSSDI/CSI, though a progression in training, continued in not taking any reference from overseas models. Against this background, the deliberations of the INSEAD proposal and the studies of the British and French civil service schools indicated the lengths the Singapore Public Service was venturing to fill the gap in the development of its leadership.

On his return, Kirpa Ram Vij recommended support for the INSEAD proposal, and this was taken into consideration by the task force. After deliberations, the task force also endorsed the INSEAD proposal. Suggesting that the most optimal approach was upgrading the CSI into the Administrative Staff College, the task force detailed a possible organisational structure for the SASC (*see* Table 4.3).

Rather than a faculty team of six Administrative Service officers, the task force projected that four AOs would suffice. It saw the Principal of the College and the Director of Studies (Staff College) to be the same officer, and three more AOs to staff the Advanced Management Training section. Two CSI staff would be responsible for Foundational Training and to provide the continuity when the AOs would be posted out after the expiry of their term. Another slight deviation from the

---

[34]Vij, Interview with Author, 22 January 2013.

Table **4.3:**   Proposed Structure of the SASC[35]

INSEAD report was the task force's recommendation for the four AOs to be super-scale officers at least, i.e., Deputy Secretary-grade and higher than the Assistant Secretary and Principal Assistant Secretary-grades in the original proposal. Further, the task force asserted that the four AOs forming the faculty team should possess "relevant post-graduate degree (which should not be restricted to just an MBA/MPA or its equivalent)".[36] The task force thought that training at INSEAD for the four Deputy Secretaries could be reduced from one year to nine months. The Advanced Management Course, which was to be the main SASC course, was envisioned to span over four months, and comprised 20 to 39 participants per course.

Kirpa Ram Vij recalled that the Training Advisory Council spent a long time deliberating over the Administrative Staff College, and the CSI waited for a decision regarding the six or four Administrative Service officers needed to form the faculty team.[37] The proposal was eventually not agreed to, because the Public Service senior leadership did not want to forego experienced AOs from line operational positions for such long periods of time. However, that decision would take some time to emerge,

[35]"Second Discussion on the INSEAD Report," undated, p. 2, JEC Papers.
[36]*Ibid.* MBA referred to the degree of Masters in Business Administration, and MPA to Masters in Public Administration degree.
[37]Vij, Interview with Author, 22 January 2013.

as the TAC and the Public Service leadership continued to consider the proposal.

4.2.2 *Leadership development*

Meanwhile, the TAC completed a review of the training of Administrative Service officers. A four-phase AO training plan was introduced, beginning with a Foundation Course for recruits, management seminars for mid-ranking officers, and finally, seminars for Permanent Secretaries.[38] Current management courses could then accommodate more Executive Officers and other Division 2 officers.

The Foundation Course was most comprehensively developed. Its aim was to foster *esprit de corps* among new Administrative Service officers and "expose the trainees to the political, social, economic, cultural, and administrative environment of Singapore and the neighbouring countries."[39] John Ewing-Chow who helped conceptualise the course explained that "[m]any of [the young AOs] still hankered after the Western, basically British experiences, like the musicals and concerts in London. ... I felt they needed to be brought back to reality. So they had to spend some time in Meet-the-People sessions."[40] Observing Meet-the-People sessions, which were essentially clinics where parliamentarians met residents appealing for help, returned scholars could appreciate the "problems and issues that affect the ordinary citizen, and become more sensitive drafters of policies during their careers".[41]

The daytime formal curriculum was made up of Induction, Management, and Written English modules.[42] Teaching methodology emphasised practicality; in between lectures and discussions were problem-solving exercises, case studies, role-plays, and management games aimed at knowledge application.[43] The curricular was remarkable in the devotion to nurturing these cadets, such as learning — at a

---

[38] Ewing-Chow and Teo (1982) 11, also 7.
[39] *ST* 17 December 1981:.11–12; *Training Programme 1980*: 10.
[40] Ewing-Chow, Interview with Author, 28 December 2011.
[41] Ewing-Chow and Teo (1982) 12.
[42] *Training Programme 1981*: 10.
[43] Sim (1985) 50.

modelling agency — "table manners, how to sit, stand, dress, open and shut doors, and make formal introductions."[44] Classes also visited every Permanent Secretary:

> ... so that the trainees can understand each Permanent Secretary's thinking and style of working (the trainees will have to work closely with the Permanent Secretary during their careers) and can understand each Ministry's policies and functions and so see their own work in relation to that of the whole civil service.[45]

Capping the Foundation Course was a tour of the capitals of the Association of the Southeast Asian Nations (ASEAN) to expose the AOs to these countries.

The Foundation Course represented the Public Service's investment in nurturing its leadership at a very early stage of their careers. For the bureaucracy to forego three months of deployable manpower and having funded these officers through four years of overseas education was a determined commitment towards the long-term development of these officers. The costs of the ASEAN tour were considerable, as Ewing-Chow related that Singapore embassies in the region "looked after us, provided the logistics, hotels, transport, visits to our counterparts."[46] The Civil Service College today continues to run the Foundation Course along the same format, with some updates, which attests to the usefulness of this concept developed by the CSI in the 1980s.[47]

A programme tested out at this time, rather than deliberately planned, was the Organisational Management (OM) seminars by Moneim El-Meligi.[48] A professor from Rutgers University, El-Meligi had put his years of worldwide consultancy into a series of OM seminars. In 1981, the CSI organised a test-run where Public Service leaders were billeted into hotels for seven days which insulated them from any disruptions, to

[44]*ST* 17 December 1981: 11.
[45]Ewing-Chow and Teo (1982) 12.
[46]Ewing-Chow, Interview with Author, 28 December 2011.
[47]CSC, "Milestone Programmes," Web 6 June 2011: http://www.cscollege.gov.sg/page.asp?id=55&pf-=1.
[48]"Speech by John Ewing-Chow, Director, CSI, at the opening of the CSI–INTAN Joint Course on Leadership and Organisational Management for Senior Officers of Malaysia and Singapore Civil Services," 21 May 1984, p. 4, JEC Papers.

focus on issues of leadership and management. The permanent secretaries and chief executives were so impressed that El-Meligi's OM seminars became a regular CSI feature. Ewing-Chow recalled: "When else can you get busy PSs and CEOs to take one week off and live-in without going back to the office and interrupting their sessions?"[49] For the moment, Moneim El-Meligi's OM seminars filled the gap in executive training for senior officers in the Public Service.

4.2.3 *Improving language: Strengthening command, control and communications*

The Prime Minister's 1979 meeting resulted in a preoccupation on clear and concise communication by the CSI and Public Service: "The written English we want is clean, clear prose ... not elegant, not stylish; just clean, clear prose. It means simplifying, polishing, and tightening."[50] Panels were set up to help civil servants write 'proper English'. Guidelines on writing memoranda were incorporated into the Instruction Manual regulating government procedures.[51]

The CSI was directed to intensify its language courses. The first programme was for 180 top Administrative Service officers which, CSI's Head of Language emphasised, was not grammar remedial but for the AOs "to learn simple, clear and precise styles of writing."[52] Courses were also rolled out for officers down the hierarchy, including Division 2 officers, police inspectors, and others. The increase in the number of courses CSI had to conduct did not correspond with an increase in resources, though part-time staff were engaged to assist existing trainers.[53]

In retrospect, these efforts to improve language helped professionalise the Public Service. Despite adapting itself to lead Singapore from a self-governing to a developmental state in 20 years, the bureaucracy

---

[49] Ewing-Chow, email correspondence with Author, 21 February 2013.

[50] "PM: Improve your English," *MD* 24 (June 1979): 3.

[51] Language Section, CSI, *Handbook on Written Communication* (Singapore: CSI, undated); *ST* 13 April 1979: 1.

[52] *ST* 12 July 1979: 8. Also *Training Programme 1980*: 33–38.

[53] A notable instructor engaged to help the CSI in English courses was Mrs Joanna Hennings, the wife of the UK High Commissioner to Singapore and a former UK civil servant and English teacher. *ST* 4 January 1979: 7.

was bogged down by communication. The severity of the problem, amplified by the Prime Minister's personal intervention, begged the questions — was the Public Service's leadership not aware of the problem, and had they not attempted to address this earlier? The language drive resulted in a consciousness for clearer communication among public officers. Ewing-Chow, reflecting on this episode 30 years on, assessed:

> I will put this down as another important accomplishment that is often forgotten, that communication up and down the ranks, if it's clear, concise, crisp … I think that's an important aspect. That's why they are still at it. The job is never done. How many years later, through our education system, the people are still not writing the way they should write. So that's important.[54]

In a population where the majority's mother tongues are not English, the language environment even for those speaking English as the first language can be corrosive. Despite English-education replacing Chinese-medium schools over the years, the Civil Service College still teaches written communication to facilitate the Public Service's communication, command, and control.[55] This may be taken for granted in the bureaucracies of English-speaking countries or civil services of homogenous societies such as China, France, Japan or Korea. However, clear communication in a multilingual society may require deliberate and determined efforts. In the case of the Singapore Public Service, recognition of the importance of clear communication began with the CSSDI's transformation to the CSI.

4.2.4 *Remaining relevant: Productivity, computerisation and even matchmaking*

Meanwhile, changes in the economy and bureaucracy shaped the CSI's evolution. In 1979, Singapore faced global recessionary pressures that was triggered by an oil crisis. The People's Action Party government, empowered by a 78% electoral landslide, restructured the economy towards high-value products. To raise labour productivity, a national

---

[54] Ewing-Chow, Interview with Author, 28 December 2011.
[55] CSC, "Writing Reports and Proposals," Web 28 January 2013, http://www.cscollege.gov.sg/programmes/pages/display%20programme.aspx?PID=2590; "Written Dynamics," http://www.cscollege.gov.sg/programmes/Pages/Display%20Programme.aspx?PID=2579.

committee concluded that "for the productivity movement to gain momentum, the public sector in Singapore should set an example in improving productivity, work attitudes and human management."[56]

At about the same time, several studies within the Public Service were looking into how to attract and retain capable staff, focusing on the personnel systems of the Shell Oil Company and the French and Japanese civil services. This led to the adoption of an 'employee-centred management philosophy', with its aims matching those of the productivity movement — improving work attitudes and efficiency.

The CSI was tasked to operationalise the productivity movement in the Public Service by starting-up Work Improvement Teams (WITs). WITs aimed to enhance efficiency by engaging civil servants to improve their daily work.[57] For a quick multiplier effect, CSI adopted a train-the-trainers approach, training up WITs leaders who would return to their ministries to "spread the Gospel" by setting up more WITs and training more WITs leaders.[58] By 1983, the CSI had trained 757 WITs leaders and 885 WITs were established throughout the bureaucracy. WITs Conventions and *Management Development* were other channels CSI used to propagate the productivity movement across the Public Service.[59] The 1985 economic downturn — when per capita incomes fell for the first time since independence — gave WITs the impetus to expand further across the bureaucracy.[60] By the end of the 1980s, the number of officers involved in WITs rose to 76,000 or 45% of the Public Service workforce. While it later "went off into a numbers game",[61] WITs laid the foundation for future waves of public sector reforms.

[56] *SAR 1983*: 41. Also Turnbull (2009) 327 and 333.
[57] "Country Paper: Singapore: Towards improving the productivity of the Civil Service", Second ASEAN Conference on Reforms in the Civil Service, 22–26 August 1983, Kuala Lumpur, pp. 5–7, JEC Papers; *SAR 1986*: 44.
[58] *ST* 9 August 1982: 13. Also "Country Paper: Singapore: Towards improving the productivity of the Civil Service," 9; "Country Paper: Singapore: Productivity improvement in the Singapore Civil Service," Second ASEAN Conference on Reforms in the Civil Service, 22–26 August 1983, Kuala Lumpur, 7, JEC Papers.
[59] Examples of WITs related issues included *MD* 32 (July 1981); *MD* 37 (October–December 1982).
[60] Lee Soo Ann, "1985: A watershed year for the Singapore economy," *SAR 1986*: 1.
[61] Ewing-Chow, Interview with Author, 28 December 2011.

Another example of how training was used to introduce change in the Public Service was computerisation. Computerisation spun off from the national productivity movement and the bureaucracy was again asked to lead the way: "To stimulate computer utilisation in Singapore, it is important for the Government to take the lead and demonstrate its willingness to computerise."[62] The CSI started with computer 'appreciation' courses for senior public officers to familiarise the leadership with impending changes.[63] At the same time, it launched various computer-related courses. The computerisation drive was later taken over by the specially-created National Computer Board, but the CSI played an instrumental role with the initial training to start off the computerisation programme across the Public Service.

The CSI even went into matchmaking. In 1984, Prime Minister Lee Kuan Yew expressed concern that women with university-degrees were deferring or foregoing marriage and procreation.[64] The PM feared that if female-graduates failed to pass on their superior genes, the quality of Singapore's already shrinking population would deteriorate. The uproar opposing this sentiment, together with other issues, resulted in the PAP suffering its worst electoral showing. Nevertheless, Ewing-Chow recalled that the Public Service Division at the Ministry of Finance decided that "training would be an important activity to bring romance" and the CSI was tasked to play its part:

> Lim Ang Yong [CSI trainer] and I designed the curriculum and did the training... 40 guys and 40 girls met at the Bukit Timah campus. ... Taught them how to dance, we made them dress [up], bring a suit and gown, made the guys go to the door, carry a rose and invite the girls to go down on the last day for the end of course celebration, big dinner, dancing, learning cha-cha.[65]

[62]Tony Tan, Minister of State for Education, Chairman of Committee for National Computerisation, quoted in National Computer Board (NCB), *Connected Government — Using IT in the Singapore Civil* Service (Singapore: NCB, 1998) 43.
[63]"Country Paper: Singapore: Towards improving the productivity of the Civil Service," 16; *ST* 28 October 1981: 1; *MD* 26 (January 1980): 5; M. Logandran, "Microcomputers in the Civil Service," *MD* 34 (January 1982): 6–10.
[64]Turnbull (2009) 334.
[65]Ewing-Chow, Interview with Author, 28 December 2011.

With sensitivity revolving around what the government termed 'social development' policy at that time, not much publicity was allowed on the CSI's efforts: "I am sorry the press cannot quote this", Ewing-Chow apologised to reporters, "as there is a moratorium on this subject but in the lighter vein, this course must be the ultimate in promoting reproductivity among graduate civil servants."[66]

The CSI also proved useful in foreign policy. In 1982, Prime Minister Lee Kuan Yew and Malaysia's premier, Mahathir Mohammad, directed "INTAN [Malaysia's National Institute of Public Administration] and CSI ... to work together and through joint activities promote closer ties between our two countries' civil servants."[67] Kirpa Ram Vij, then-Director of the CSI, recalled: "[It] so happened that in [Kuala Lumpur], the guy who was running the show was a guy by the name of Talib. He was my classmate in University! So that helped a lot with INTAN."[68] The CSI–INTAN cooperation resulted in joint programmes on Leadership and Organisational Management, which saw participants from both the Singaporean and Malaysian civil services.[69] *Management Development* also devoted an edition on Malaysia.[70] The cooperation between the CSI and INTAN fluctuated with the ups and downs in relations between Singapore and Malaysia. In the context of this study, the CSI had once again proven its usefulness.

4.2.5 *Some comparisons*

Comparison with INTAN and other civil service schools is timely at this juncture to locate the state of the CSI's development. By the 1980s, INTAN had developed considerably to wield significant influence in

---

[66]"Speech by Director, Civil Service Institute, Mr. John Ewing-Chow at the Presentation of CSI's Programmes for FY84," 19 April 1984, p. 3, JEC Papers.

[67]"Speech by John Ewing-Chow, Director, CSI, at the Opening of the Second CSI–INTAN Joint Course on Leadership and Organisational Management for Senior Officers of Malaysia and Singapore Civil Service, 15–19 October 1984 at Civil Service Institute," 15 October 1984, JEC Papers. Also *SAR 1982*: 7–8; *SAR 1983*: 60.

[68]Vij, Interview with Author, 22 January 2013.

[69]*ST* 6 February 1983: 16; *ST* 8 May 1984: 10; "Speech by Ewing-Chow at the Second CSI-INTAN Joint Course," 15 October 1984.

[70]*MD* 40 (July–September 1983): 1.

the Malaysian civil service. As one of eight divisions in the Public Services Department, INTAN reported to the Prime Minister through the department's Director-General, equivalent to the Permanent Secretary, and the Chief Secretary, the highest civil service appointment.[71] INTAN had four functional departments: Management Studies, Development Studies, Research and Consultancy, and Employee Department Centre.[72] Under Management and Development Studies departments were several schools responsible for running courses on subjects like development administration, community development, land administration, and so on. INTAN also conducted courses on supervisory and clerical training, basic management training, and 'Top Management Seminars'. While the main mode of delivery was lecture, INTAN also adopted syndicate discussions, site visits, research projects, and other learning methodologies.

INTAN played a strategic role in the personnel management of the leadership cadre. All applicants into the Administrative and Diplomatic Service, the premier scheme of service in the Malaysian bureaucracy had to undergo a one-year diploma course at INTAN.[73] Although the Public Services Department was responsible for the posting of ADS cadets, INTAN's views contributed towards the posting order.[74] The performance of senior officers at mandatory INTAN courses also influenced their promotions to Superscale G-grade. Occupying such central position in the selection and promotion of the leadership, INTAN naturally commanded strong support across the civil service, particularly its leadership.[75]

The CSI obviously did not enjoy the same influence wielded by INTAN. Although the CSI was responsible for the induction of the Administrative Service cadets, the two or three months of Foundation Courses at CSI were not equivalent to the one whole year Malaysian ADS cadets spent at INTAN. Singapore's AOs neither sat for pre-promotion

[71]Teo Hee Lian, "The Civil Service in Malaysia," *MD* 40 (July–September 1983): 4.
[72]Dr Mohd Shahari bin Ahmad Jabar, Director, INTAN, *MD* 40 (July–September 1983): 28.
[73]Marican (1979) 11–13.
[74]Teo Hee Lian (1983) 5.
[75]The 2,000 strong ADS occupied all top leadership positions in the Malaysian civil service, including Chief Secretary and Secretaries-Generals, and administrative posts in central agencies. Teo Hee Lian (1983) 4.

courses at the CSI nor depended on the CSI's appraisal for their promotion. The level of identification with the CSI among AOs was probably not strong, compared to the support INTAN would enjoy among the Malaysian leadership corps, and this would prove critical in the subsequent evolution of the CSI.

In Hong Kong, the Government Training Division was renamed the Civil Service Training Centre in 1975.[76] Staff doubled to 119 from the original 50 officers.

The Civil Service Training Centre provided Hong Kong's administrative officers, modelled after Britain's Administrative Class, with induction and short courses on basic requisite skills.[77] These included topics like staff appraisal, selection interviews, committee chairmanship, and others. However, the centrepiece of the administrative officers' training appeared to be a year of academic studies at the prestigious Oxford or Cambridge universities. Subjects covered included comparative governments, international relations, public administration and urbanisation, as well as electives ranging from economics, sociology, administrative law, constitutional law, history, and others.

For departmental officers at directorate grades, which were the upper echelon of the hierarchy, the Civil Service Training Centre organised seminars on new management concepts while intermediate grade officers could attend Administrative Course on management procedures and practices.[78] Officers with supervisory responsibilities at the lower rungs of the bureaucratic hierarchy could attend courses at the Training Centre on principles of supervision, communications, motivation, and others.

In comparison to Hong Kong's Civil Service Training Centre, Singapore's CSI had a smaller complement of staff directly engaged in training duties. Numbers apart, both Hong Kong's Civil Service Training

---

[76]Civil Service Training Division Internal Circular No. 15/79. 12 June 1979, HKRS 822-1-3; Civil Service Training Centre, *Prospectus 1983–4* (Hong Kong: Civil Service Training Centre, 1983) 4–6, HK PRO; Scott and Burns (1988) 120–125.

[77]Miron Mushkat, "Staffing the Administrative Class," *The Hong Kong Civil Service* eds. Scott and Burns 97–98 and 107.

[78]Scott and Burns (1988) 132–133.

Centre and Singapore's CSI had developed in sophistication over time, evident in the gradual devotion of resources in specialised subjects, especially management programmes for higher echelon officers.

In Britain, the Civil Service College set up in 1971 offered more lessons than yardsticks for comparisons. While the Civil Service College's establishment brought to fruition arguments for formal centralised training, strong beliefs remained in 'sitting by Nellie' on-the-job training.

Against this background, the performance of the Civil Service College was less than spectacular. Rodney Lowe, the official historian of the British Civil Service, remarked that the quality of teaching was poor: "Students' enthusiasm for the majority of courses and their willingness to return ... were both noticeable by their absence."[79] Even after several years of operation, the College was only able to train 6% of the Civil Service, while departments and external providers accounted for the overwhelming majority of training in the bureaucracy.[80] The 1974 Heaton-Williams Committee found the training at the Civil Service College to be "over-academic" in nature.[81] In trying to develop civil servants fast-tracked for leadership positions and simultaneously providing technical education to the broader strata of the bureaucracy, the College was deemed to lack clarity in its objectives. Lacking involvement in the work and life of the Civil Service, the College could not win the confidence of the Civil Service leadership in Whitehall.[82] Unable to rise up to its remit, the newly-appointed principal in 1979, Brian Gilmore, was instructed to either "[k]ill it — or cure it."[83]

Despite a "revival of sorts" in the 1980s under Gilmore, Whitehall's continuing preference for practical experience over formal training

---

[79]Lowe (2011) 314. Also Keith M. Dowding, *The Civil Service* (London: Routledge, 1995) 20.

[80]Kevin Theakston, *The Civil Service since 1945* (Oxford: Blackwell, 1995) 105.

[81]R.N. Heaton and L. Williams, *Civil Service Training,* Civil Service Department, 1974, para 55, quoted in Lowe (2011) 315.

[82]Theakston (1995) 102; Barry O'Toole, *The Ideal of Public Service: Reflections on the higher civil service in Britain* (London and New York: Routledge, 2006) 106.

[83]Peter Hennessey, *The Times,* 11 November 1980, quoted in Lowe (2011) 315.

meant that the Civil Service College remained at the periphery of the bureaucracy.[84] The advent of New Public Management turned the College into an Executive Agency in 1989, having to compete with the private sector for the training-dollars of government departments. Pyper observed: "The implications of this are important ... There is a marked, and increasing, diffusion of responsibility for training within the civil service."[85] Looking back years later, the official account remarked that "the pressure of ... remaining commercially competitive had driven it [the College] towards middle management training and away from strategic organisational and senior leadership concerns."[86]

The travails of the British Civil Service College through the 1970s, 1980s, and into the 1990s epitomised the dilemmas of training across most bureaucracies, not least the Singapore Public Service. Should training be formal and centralised, or decentralised and learning-by-doing? Should curriculum be academically-rooted or practitioner-oriented? Would scholars or civil servants make the best instructors? Should emphasis focus on developing leadership or should resources be distributed evenly to skilling up civil servants across the hierarchy? The tension between leadership development and broad-based training, in particular, would dominate deliberations and events in the Singapore Civil Service Institute soon enough.

4.3 Institutionalisation and a Question of Relevance

In Singapore, the Civil Service Institute was to witness several significant changes as it awaited a decision on the Administrative Staff College proposal. With contracts of the expatriates expiring, local CSI staff began taking over as Heads of Language and Management Training, namely

---

[84]Theakston (1995) 103 pointed out that the 'revival' was also partly due to new emphasis on personnel management.

[85]Pyper (1995) 45.

[86]National School of Government, *Annual Report and Resource Accounts, 2006–2007* (London: Stationary Office, 2007) 5. Efforts to return it to the centre of the bureaucracy, and relevance, saw the Civil Service College restructured as the National School of Government in 2004, but this did not prevent it from closure eventually in 2012. Cabinet Office, *Annual Report and Accounts, 2011–2012* (London: Stationary Office, 2012) 37.

Teo Hee Lian and John Ewing-Chow respectively.[87] In 1981, the CSI was transferred from the Ministry of Finance to the Public Service Commission to centralise the management of Division 1 officers.[88] By mid-1981, it had become clear that the Administrative Staff College would not materialise. Kirpa Ram Vij, who saw his CSI posting as a tasking to set up the Administrative Staff College, left the CSI.

Looking back, Vij recognised that "we were short of experienced staff to become the faculty members".[89] Foregoing six experienced Administrative Service officers from operational posts for five years to undertake training positions, as the proposition appeared in the eyes of the senior Public Service leadership, was simply not tenable. Ewing-Chow concurred: "Though I envied INTAN where they had the pick of the returning postgraduate MBA and PhD AOs to teach a few years before getting promoted to operating departments and ministries, I agree that such a scheme would not be appropriate for Singapore."[90] With the Administrative Service cadre only 250-strong and "extremely busy fighting to survive. INSEAD's proposal was a luxury and an overkill, and it did not take into account the reality of the size of the potential students."[91]

At the same time, training was not a priority, despite all the rhetoric. Tan Boon Huat, who was responsible for posting the AOs, remembered:

> To put it bluntly, at one time, the people who were posted to CSI or CSSDI, were people who were in trouble. The people who got [into] trouble in HQ or somewhere else. Problem, so exiled. That mentality! That was the mentality of the top leaders then: training not important.[92]

With some permanent secretaries refusing to release capable staff and CSI's reputation as a 'sin bin', AOs themselves were understandably

---

[87]Roger Bell, "Investigating Language Training Needs in the Civil Service," *MD* 30 (January 1981): 9 and 16; *ST* 14 August 1981: 18; Public Service Commission, *Annual Report 1981 (PSC 1981)* (Singapore: PSC, 1982) 25.

[88]*PSC 1981:* 21; *Training Programme 1983/84*:1. The Establishment Unit in the PMO came under PSC.

[89]Vij, Interview with Author, 22 January 2013.

[90]Ewing-Chow, email correspondence with Author,18 February 2013.

[91]*Ibid*

[92]Tan Boon Huat, Head, Establishment and Discipline Section, PSC, Interview with Author, 14 January 2013; *PSC 1981*: 25.

reluctant to be posted to the CSI. Tan conceded: "We couldn't get Admin Officers to go [to CSI]."

> ... the individual said, 'You want me to go training? Training is a dead-end place!' They didn't see that going into training is part of their career development. But I supposed it's chicken and egg. Part of it was the curriculum was not developed, and the value was not seen. The evolution took a long time.[93]

CSI's development was also hampered by constant changes. The heads of the two training sections were typically changed within one to two years. In this circumstance, how much attention was available to develop rigorous curricula? Was there supervision over the implementation of these curricula; were there reviews and improvements over training activities? Was there capacity to project and draw up longer term plans?

The changes continued with Vij's departure. The position of Director of the CSI was assigned to Teo Hee Lian. She was only 29 years old. Teo recalled:

> I took over from Kirpa Ram Vij. The understanding was that it was an interim thing. I had no interest in administration. That was one of the reasons why I left the Administration Service. I had no interest in management or administration. So after a year or two, when John was definite that he would stay, I actually wrote to PSC and said I'm stepping down and he can take over.[94]

John Ewing-Chow thus became the first Director of the CSI who did not hail from the Administrative Service.[95] Teo was Deputy Director while remaining as Head of Language. The Head of Management Training post went to Lim Ang Yong.[96]

A very important change took place in 1983. In that year, the CSI was transferred to the Public Service Division (PSD), newly created within the Ministry of Finance.[97] The PSD arose from a consolidation

---

[93]Tan Boon Huat, Interview with Author, 14 January 2013.

[94]Teo Hee Lian, Interview with Author, 3 January 2012. Also Teo, email with Author, 16 January 2013; *ST* 14 August 1981: 18.

[95]All the preceding heads of the Public Service training schools had been Administrative Service officers, from Evelyn Chew, to Kirpa Ram Vij, to Teo Hee Lian.

[96]*SAR 1984*: 45; *PSC 1983*: 2.

[97]*Training Programme 1983/84*: 1.

of all personnel management functions, including the Public Service Commission's responsibility over the Administrative Service officers and the jurisdiction of MOF's Personnel Administration Branch over Divisions 2, 3, and 4 officers. Although the PSD was a division within the Finance Ministry, the establishment of a Permanent Secretary at its head, and the Head of the Civil Service as Permanent Secretary, meant that it was effectively a full-fledged ministry and one of higher standing than the rest.[98] This change in the CSI's reporting lines to the PSD would finally be more enduring, with the CSI's succeeding agencies continuing to report to the PSD.

As part of the centralisation efforts, the CSI was eyed to take over more responsibilities, beginning with the jurisdiction of all civil service examinations. Until then, examinations ranging from probationary to promotion were variously under the charge of the Public Service Commission and the Finance Ministry. The CSI demurred: "CSI's present staff cannot cope with this new workload."[99] Nevertheless, the CSI took over responsibility of civil service-wide examinations from 1984.[100] The CSI was also tasked to train civil servants, particularly clerical officers, for their probationary and promotion examinations. As Sim observed, with 17 CSI staff performing training functions and the public service totalling 147,383, the trainer to public officer ratio was 1:8670.[101]

In 1984, the CSI Director took the unusual step of convening a 'Presentation of CSI's Programmes' to Permanent Secretaries and Heads of Departments. Members from the media were also invited to the session, which was remarkable considering that Ewing-Chow's presentation might not reflect well on the Public Service. After presenting the CSI's highlights, he appealed to the Permanent Secretaries and department Heads to release staff for training. He also asked senior officers to support CSI's invitation to lecture because it still lacked sufficient number of trainers

---

[98]Veronica Quek, "The Public Service Division," *MD* 38 (January–March 1983): 3.

[99]Paper No. 10/10/82, "Proposal to Integrate Service-wide Examinations at CSI," undated, circa 1982, pp. 3–4, JEC Papers.

[100]*Training Programme 1984/85*: 10; *ST* 17 February 1984: 13.

[101]Only 17 of CSI's total strength of 51 staff conducted training. The Public Service then comprised 83,031 civil servants and an additional 64,352 employees from various statutory boards. Sim 24.

to meet the range of training needs. With external lecturers costing up to $4,000 per day, Permanent Secretaries, and department Heads would be more effective and efficient. Finally, Ewing-Chow asked senior officers to counsel staff attending training: "Some come to CSI courses without knowing why they are here. Others came and realise that they are in the wrong course. Still others come for a break from their routine work."[102]

If public sector training was overlooked in the 1970s when priorities focused on the economy, housing, education, and defence,[103] the CSI's difficulties did not appear to have improved a decade later. A young Administrative Service officer at that time remembered that "I didn't even go for Foundation Course, because my boss didn't allow me to go."[104] From reluctance in releasing officers to attend training or to staff the CSI, from individuals' unwillingness to take up the CSI postings to their tentativeness towards training, these attitudes did not appear to have abated over the years. The persistence of such attitudes could no longer be excused away by the priorities of state-building. Perhaps a culture that prioritised nation-building goals at the expense of training and development had developed.

For the CSI, the constant changes and state of flux did not help its development. Adjustments necessitated by regular changes in superior departments, reporting lines, organisational leadership, and expanding scope of activities prevented the CSI from drawing up longer-term plans to remain relevant to the Public Service.

4.3.1 *The institutionalisation of a civil service training school*

By the mid-1980s, the CSI had evolved into an established institution of training for the Singapore Public Service. From 1981, Singaporean civil servants began to take over the leadership positions within the CSI. These positions had required external help since the setting up of the Staff Training Institute. The Heads of Language and Management training were respectively an expatriate specialist and a seconded academic. When

---

[102]"Speech by Director, CSI, Presentation of CSI's Programmes for FY84," 19 April 1984, p. 8. JEC Papers.

[103]Ewing-Chow and Teo (1982) 3.

[104]Lim Soo Hoon, Interview with Author, 15 June 2012.

their contracts expired, these posts were left vacant for some time before other overseas expertise could be secured to fill these posts. In 1981, Singaporean civil servants were finally assessed to be capable of taking over the positions of Heads of Language and Management training.

Parallel with this was the gradual filling up of the CSI's established capacity. Since the setting up of the STI and throughout the period of the CSSDI, the civil service school had long faced difficulties in recruiting staff with the requisite skills to take up training positions. Up till 1983, the CSI had never managed to achieve its full complement of training officers. Although the establishment of the training sections provided for 20 trainers, the personnel strength averaged between eight and 10 at any one time.[105] By 1984, the CSI was finally able to fill 13 of the 14 training positions.

The growth in capacity allowed the CSI to increase its courses, including for Divisions 3 and 4 officers. Until then, the CSI "channelled most of its efforts towards training Division 1 officers because it could not get enough trainers."[106] Ewing-Chow, who was Director of CSI from 1981 to 1985, took the 'public sector' clientele in the Institute's formal objective seriously: "I viewed the whole Public Service as my boss and the CSI and I responded to requests that had national and public service wide impact."[107] The number of courses for Divisions 3 and 4 officers grew from 12.5% of the school's overall offerings in 1976 when the CSSDI was set up, to 19% in 1985.

Events in the mid-1980s had dramatic effects on Singapore and its Public Service but did not affect the growth of the CSI. The 1984 election saw the People's Action Party securing 64% popular votes but losing two parliamentary seats to the opposition.[108] While this would have been a landslide victory in other democracies, it was shattering for the PAP, which had had a complete parliamentary monopoly and more than 75% popular votes since independence. To echoes of government

---

[105]"Information on the Civil Service Institute," undated, p. 1, JEC Papers; *Training Programme 1984/85*: 2.

[106]*ST* 17 February 1984: 13.

[107]Ewing-Chow, email correspondence with Author, 18 February 2013. Also Ewing-Chow, Interview with Author, 28 December 2011.

[108]Turnbull (2009) 335.

not sufficiently heeding citizens' voices as a cause of electoral setback, the Public Service faced "increased pressures to be more attentive to ground feedback ... to be more responsive to citizens and to view them as stakeholders with a legitimate interest in government rather than agents to be controlled."[109]

At the same time, the 1985 worldwide recession and Singapore's economic review that followed led to large-scale corporatisation of government functions.[110] Accompanying the strains of 'small government' and new public management was the shift towards viewing citizens as customers. In response, a Public Contact Improvement Programme was developed to train frontline counter staff to "serve the public with a friendly, polite, helpful, and attentive manner."[111] A Public Relations Planning course was also designed to train Division 1 managers in "Creativity and PR Planning, ... Marketing and PR Interface, The Customer Relations Process".[112]

The growth in the CSI was particularly evident in the improvement to training for the lower strata of the Public Service. Under the leadership of David Ma Kok Leung, who became Director in 1986 after Ewing-Chow left for the private sector, the CSI launched the COSEC programme. Short for Core Skills for Effectiveness and Change, COSEC was a suite of courses put together for Division 3 officers to build up their "skills in communicating better, getting along with others, solving problems that arise on the job, knowing the importance and quality needs of the job, and using the computer."[113] By the time Teo Hee Lian resumed as Director after Ma was posted out, courses for Divisions 3 and 4 officers grew to 26% of the CSI's overall offerings.[114] Setting aside resources to address the needs of lower-rank officers reflected a recognition, at least

[109]Chua (2010) 149 and 158.
[110]Turnbull (2009) 336–337.
[111]*Training Programme 1990/91*: 63.
[112]*Training Programme 1990/91*: 32.
[113]*Training Programme 1988/89*: 135. Also David Ma, Director, CSI, 1986–1989, Interview with Author, 8 March 2013.
[114]*Alpha Soc Newsletter* 1.6 (August 1986): 7; *Alpha Soc Newsletter* 1.12 (September 1989): 8; Teo Hee Lian, Interview with Author, 3 January 2012; David Ma, Interview with Author, 8 March 2013.

on the part of the CSI, that frontline staff were equally important and worthy of investment as the leadership cadre.

The quantitative and qualitative growth in rank-and-file training was in tandem with that for the Division 1 leadership and the overall course offerings for the Public Service. Courses for Division 1 officers rose steadily from 13 in 1976, or 41% of the CSSDI's total of 32 courses, to 19 or 51% in 1985. From 1992, while the share of Division 1 courses remained largely at about half of the CSI's expanding offerings, the absolute number of Division 1 courses swelled exponentially to 50 in 1992 and 73 in 1994. In comparison, courses for Division 2 officers lagged behind those of their senior and junior counterparts, but only in terms of proportion of the CSI's overall figures. The absolute number of courses for Division 2 officers actually grew to 24 in 1992 and 40 in 1994. A significant point worth emphasising is that the CSI's efforts in expanding broad-based training were not at the expense of elite development. The evidence in Table 4.4 showed that Division 1 training had consistently constituted around half of the Institute's overall offerings of courses in the 20-year period.

The rising tide of the CSI's overall number of courses was lifting figures in all the groups, benefitting large sections across the Public Service. By 1990, the total number of courses offered by the CSI had increased to 46, from 32 when it first started as the CSSDI. That year also witnessed the CSI training 31,547 civil servants, the highest figure

Table 4.4: Number of CSSDI/CSI Courses by Divisions, 1975–1996[115]

Year	Division 1	Division 2	Divisions 3 and 4	Total
1976	13 (40.6%)	15	4 (12.5%)	32
1980	14 (50%)	10	4 (14.3%)	28
1985	19 (51.4%)	11	7 (18.9%)	37
1990	19 (41.3%)	15	12 (26%)	46
1992	50 (55.6%)	24	16 (17.8%)	90
1994	73 (50.7%)	40	31 (21.5%)	144
	Division 1	**Divisions 2 and 3**		**Total**
1996	73 (48%)	79 (52%)		152

[115] *Training Programme 1976; 1980; 1984/85; 1990/91; 1992/93; 1994/95; 1996/97.*

attained by the Institute. On average annually in the 1990s, the CSI was training 20,000 officers. With the Civil Service totalling 90,246, the CSI was reaching out to 22% of the bureaucracy.[116] In 1992, the number of CSI courses doubled to 90, and expanded further to 144 by 1994. By 1996, before the CSI was reorganised, the CSI was running 152 courses.

Amid attaining optimal staff capacity and improvements in course offerings was an apparent sense of rising confidence within the CSI. Most evident was its 1984 engagement of the Public Service's leadership before the eyes of the mass media. The CSI's difficulties did not arise overnight, and these would have been discussed regularly with superior and other stakeholder agencies through the bureaucracy's routine communication channels. That the CSI chose to canvass the support of the Permanent Secretaries publicly hinted at a tinge of frustration with the impasse, even when the occasion was couched as the Institute's report to stakeholders. More importantly, inviting the press to witness their accounting to and engagement with their leadership pointed to a level of boldness among the CSI's management team, definitely not representative of the typical media-shy civil servants.

The CSI's institutionalisation did not mean it was not without shortcomings. One study pointed out that the agencies responsible for training public officers had not developed a standardised conceptualisation of 'training'.[117] Training methods and evaluation lacked formalised procedures, compounded by poor supervision. These weaknesses though did not detract from improvements in institutional organisation.

4.3.2 *Ending in tears: Questioning the relevance of the CSI*

By the mid-1980s, the CSI's trajectory of development was pulling it away from the government's longstanding focus on cultivating the Administrative Service elite. Some of its programmes were geared towards the leadership cadre, but the CSI was not rising up to become the AOs'

---

[116]The average Civil Service establishment in the 1990s was 90,245. *Training Programme 1990/91*: iii; *Training Programme 1991/92*: 1; *Training Programme 1994/95*: 1; Ministry of Finance, *The Budget for the Financial Year 1995/96 (Budget 1995/96)* (Singapore: Ministry of Finance, 1995) 81; *Budget FY1997/98*: 66.

[117]Sim (1985) 52.

development centre. To be fair, the Staff College was curtailed not because of the CSI's failing, but the Public Service leadership's unwillingness to divert the AOs away from policymaking posts to start the faculty team.

The CSI actually recognised the importance of developing the AOs and had prioritised resources — at the expense of training rank-and-file officers — towards training the Praetorian Guards.[118] However, the Foundation Course and other CSI programmes for the AOs were "only up to that level" and poor cousins to post-graduate courses at prestigious overseas universities in the eyes of many among its audience:

> I think there [overseas universities], your exposure is different, the people who are with you, your classmates, are all very different, usually upper level. Anyway, it's international, very multi-faceted so it's quite different. The Admin Officers, you also don't want to go the local MPA.[119]

Comparing the MPA programmes at Harvard University, for example, with in-service training at the CSI was unfair, but such was the impression in the minds of many AOs and Public Service leaders,[120] and perceptions shaped policy.

As the CSI sought to improve its relevance to the Public Service, its reputation among the leadership corps was suffering. The CSI's responses to the national call in spearheading productivity, computerisation, and even 'social development' drives, were regarded by some among the Public Service leadership as 'miscellaneous':

> … [the Chairman] felt that at present CSI was conducting too many *miscellaneous* courses and had disproportionately few management development courses for Administrative Officers and senior departmental officers. He was of the opinion that if CSI concentrated on the training for this group of officers instead, there would be benefits and spin-offs for the whole of the civil service.

---

[118]In a paper tabled before the CSI Executive Committee in 1982, the first of four aims listed by the CSI was "Training and development for Administrative Officers," Paper No. 8/10/82, "The Civil Service Institute — Discussion Paper," undated, p. 2, JEC Papers. In a 1984 media interview, the CSI admitted to channelling all its resources to training Division 1 officers, i.e., the AOs, when resources were not available to train all public officers. *ST* 17 February 1984: 13.
[119]Tan Boon Huat, Interview with Author, 14 January 2013.
[120]Mid-career AOs also headed to University of London and Stanford University but Harvard University was the most well attended. *Alpha Soc Newsletter* 1.3 (September 1984): 12; 5 (July 1985): 10; 6 (December 1985): 10; 8 (December 1987): 12; Sim 41.

> The emphasis, therefore, should be on courses to improve the management skills of the Administrative Officers, and senior departmental heads.[121]

Ewing-Chow related the perception of a very senior Public Service official: "I wrote it down: CSI, image of CSI — Division 3 training."[122] Tan Boon Huat verified the impression among public officers: "[I]t's okay up to that level, for the clerical, the EO [Executive Officers] level kind of training. For the real intellectual, more challenging kind of training, you know … [trailed off]."[123] The harder the CSI tried to be the training centre for the whole Public Service, the stronger the perception that it was a training centre for Divisions 2, 3, and 4 officers, i.e., not the leadership. The general impression of the CSI — as early as the mid-1980s — was that it was a school for the *hoi polloi* and was not capable of training the AOs.

The CSI's reputation as a broad-based training school, rather than a leadership development centre, must have further contributed to its difficulties in attracting personnel with the requisite qualities. Over time, the CSI had grown from being an 'exile' for officers in trouble to an established institution of training for the Public Service. Despite this, the challenge of securing talented officers to an instructional stint at the CSI persisted till the late 1980s. In particular, the Administrative Service leadership cadre of the Public Service were reluctant in taking up any CSI posting. David Ma lamented:

> Not many people would like to go to CSI, maybe, as a career. Unless you like training, otherwise you may not want to be there for long. So at one point in time we actually were thinking of getting those returned scholars to be posted to CSI for a short while. Somehow CSI still failed to attract people there.[124]

In 1991, local newspapers disclosed that a new Civil Service College for training the Administrative Service corps was being planned. Citing

---

[121]"Minutes of the 1st Meeting of the CSI Executive Committee," 16 October 1982, p. 6, JEC Papers.
[122]Ewing-Chow, Interview with Author, 11 June 2012.
[123]Tan Boon Huat, Interview with Author, 14 January 2013, left unsaid that CSI was not seen to be capable of highlevel training.
[124]Ma, Interview with Author, 8 March 2013.

a "well-placed civil service source", the *Straits Times* revealed that this proposed institution would be "distinct from the Civil Service Institute."[125] That same year, a Deputy Secretary had been designated as Dean of the eventual college.[126] In the following year, an Administrative Service officer was appointed Deputy Dean and visited several civil service training institutions in North America. A separate study examined the British Civil Service College and several other foreign civil service schools.

The new Civil Service College was formally inaugurated in April 1993.[127] The Foundation Course, conceptualised and run by the CSI for the past two decades, and all training programmes involving the AOs, were transferred to the CSC, thereby removing the CSI's role in training the Praetorian Guards. The monopoly of central training in the Singapore Public Service by the CSI, initially as the STI from 1971 and then the CSSDI between 1975 and 1979, had finally come to an end. From 1993 to 1996, the CSI effectively became a provider of vocational training. In 1996, the CSI ceased to be an independent entity following a broader reorganisation, which will be discussed in greater depth in a subsequent chapter.

In the longer term, a brand-new complex housing the new CSC and several think tanks was to be built at the CSI's existing Heng Mui Keng Terrace's premises. As the CSI was perceived as a training centre for Divisions 3 and 4 officers, Teo Hee Lian who had resumed as Director of the CSI since 1988, recalled:

> ... we [the CSI] were seen as not compatible. So you can imagine how that comment went down with my colleagues. They were furious. And we were just told: make way. Some of my colleagues tried to point out that there was space there enough for everybody. But we were told: move out, because we were not compatible. ... We were even told to go and look at a school. I

---

[125] *ST* 24 May 1991: 30.
[126] Kishore Mahbubani, Dean, Civil Service College, to Col (Res) Ho Meng Kit, Principal Private Secretary to Senior Minister, "Civil Service College (CSC)," 6 February 1993, p. 2, CSC Records.
[127] "Towards a More Professional and Cohesive Administrative Service: Inauguration of the Civil Service College and launching of the Public Policy Perspectives Seminar, 29–30 April 1993," *Apha Soc Newsletter* 1/93 (June 1993): 3.

blew my top when they told me to move to a school. I said, 'We are not moving to an abandoned school!'[128]

The strong sentiments brought into focus the manner in which this reorganisation was approached. The government was effectively creating two centres of training — one set up for leadership development and the proposition for the CSI could be positioned as a specialised centre for functional training. Indeed, one senior official at the Public Service Division reportedly described the CSC and CSI as "strategic" and "tactical" in their respective places in training and development.[129] They did not need to be mutually exclusive or competitive, with each catering to different genres, and could be seen as complementary. With hindsight, requiring the CSI to vacate its long-standing premises for a new entity, following closely on the directive to transfer all the AO training programmes it had developed and run to the new college, came across as hurried and could have been more empathetic. It reflected the establishment's emphasis on developing the AO elite, without addressing the impacts on the CSI. To belabour the point, while the CSI was allocated $5 million from the 1995 budget for the bureaucracy, this was catering to the training of more than 20,000 civil servants. In contrast, the CSC's seemingly lesser $2 million allocation was only covering about 300 AOs and leaders in the Public Service.[130] Greater levels of engagement and sensitivity, and more time, could have been employed to explain and carry out the organisational changes affecting the CSI and its staff.

Eventually, seemingly to sweeten the bitter pill, the CSI was offered a plot of land. Teo found some satisfaction in the design of the North Buona Vista building:

> I told the architect the new building cannot look like a school, it cannot look like an office building … I gave him a brief for the new building, I said, 'The moment you step into the building, there must be openness, there must be

---

[128]Teo Hee Lian was reappointed as Director of the CSI in 1989 when David Ma was posted to the Ministry of Communications. Teo Hee Lian, Interview with Author, 3 January 2012; *Alpha Soc Newsletter* 1.12 (September 1989): 8.

[129]Tan Boon Huat, Deputy Secretary, PSD, quoted in Lai 44.

[130]Lai pointed out that CSI's budget also had to cover a much larger headcount and other overheads such as estate management, compared to the CSC; *see* Lai (1995) 51–52.

Table 4.5: Internal Structure of the Civil Service Institute, 1996 [131]

(Depicting organisation structure just before reorganisation into the Civil Service College)

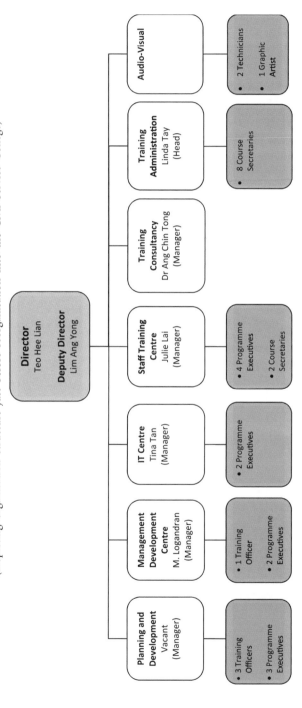

[131] Chart depicts the CSI just before it was reorganised into the Civil Service College in 1996. Developed from information gathered from *Govt Directory January 1996*: 650–651. Lai reported that CSI had 60 staff, with 40% of them performing the dual function of trainer and course administrator; Lai (1995) 24.

air, there must be feeling you are liberated, things are possible.'…We even built in space in that building for future development. We were specifically told we cannot have more [space] than we had in Heng Mui Keng Terrace. We knew we needed more. So we built that in surreptitiously.[132]

Even before the CSI moved into the new building, scheduled to be completed in 1998, events in the broader Public Service further affected the CSI. The Public Service Division which the CSI reported to was transferred to the Prime Minister's Office in 1994. In 1996, the CSI was renamed the Institute of Public Administration and Management (IPAM) and merged with the Civil Service College, renamed the Institute of Policy Development (IPD), to form a new Civil Service College (CSC). Miss Lim Soo Hoon, appointed Dean of the new CSC, remembered:

… bearing in mind that IPD was then called CSC, so CSI people were very upset. They said, 'Why should we, we are twice the size of IPD, have to use the CSC name?'…The real reason was because CSI had baggage. As I told you previously, CSI was doing all these broad-based training, the levels of people they were covering, super-scale [officers at the highest grades] all the way to Division 4. There was a certain baggage, certain brand name.…If we still called it CSI, people would still have the perception that it was the same thing. So we had to refresh it, re-brand it. And we thought that CSC was a very good name.[133]

Twenty years since moving to the new Heng Mui Keng Terrace building as the CSSDI, the CSI ended its existence as an independent civil service training organisation.

4.4 Conclusion

The CSI was a focal point through which changes were introduced across the Singapore Public Service between 1975 and 1996. The CSI expanded upon the foundation laid by the preceding Staff Training Institute to extensively build up the technical competencies of officers across the rank-and-file of the bureaucracy. As the volume and sophistication of its

---

[132]Teo Hee Lian, Interview with Author, 3 January 2012.
[133]Lim Soo Hoon, Dean, Civil Service College, 1995–1998, Interview with Author, 15 June 2012.

programmes grew and it was training an increasing number of public
officers, the CSI grew into an institution of reform for the Singapore
bureaucracy.

The CSI's two decades, the longest period of any training initiative
thus far, comprised several phases. The first few years as the CSSDI laid the
foundation for subsequent growth, such as integrating modern facilities,
developing staffing capacities, and mapping training courses to career
development of public officers. Although the overnight name-change to
the CSI had no material changes in organisational goals or structures,
it demarcated a point when the Public Service's central training school
began to develop. *The CSI, through its roles in offering language and
communication courses and training in WITs and computerisation, was
evidently the focal point through which reforms were introduced into and
across the Singapore Public Service.* By helping to improve the language and
writing of public officers, communications up and down the hierarchy
and across the bureaucracy was enhanced, thereby facilitating command
and control throughout the government machinery. The provision of
requisite training seeded the productivity and computerisation drives
across the bureaucracy, which eventually propagated across the whole
country.

By the early 1980s, the CSI was evolving into an established institution
of training for the Singapore Public Service. The initial difficulty with
recruiting personnel with the necessary expertise was gradually overcome,
as seconded academics and foreign experts bought time for the CSI to
develop its own staff. From 1981, officers who rose up the CSI ranks and
were groomed by the Institute, such as John Ewing-Chow and Teo Hee
Lian, began taking over leadership positions, including as Director of
the CSI. Gradually, the CSI was able to fill up its staffing establishment,
providing it the capacity to improve its inventory of courses over the
years. By the early 1990s, the CSI had doubled its total number of courses
from its initial years as the CSSDI, and reaching out to more public
officers across the various hierarchical strata of the bureaucracy. The CSI's
role in leading the productivity and computerisation drives across the
Public Service was an acknowledgement of the CSI's maturing capacity
by the leadership of the Public Service. The most credible recognition
of the CSI's institutionalisation was the government's deployment of the

CSI as a foreign policy instrument in strengthening bilateral relations with Malaysia.

The CSI's institutionalisation also manifested through the rising levels of confidence among its leadership team, the emergence of particular organisational interests, and the identification with these interests by its staff. The decision by the CSI leadership to engage Permanent Secretaries on the Institute's difficulties, especially before the gaze of the mass media, was particularly bold and pronounced. However, even away from the public domain, John Ewing-Chow and Teo Hee Lian were also active in pursuing the interests of the CSI during their respective tenures as Directors. When he was Director, Ewing-Chow strove to uplift the image of the CSI as a school for training the whole Public Service. In turn, Teo represented the sentiments of the staff in holding onto — metaphorically but also literally — the CSI's ground as the central training school of the bureaucracy. Thus, the forging of such close identification among the staff with the organisation and its peculiar interests, together with its capacity to train large sections of the bureaucracy, pointed to the CSI's development into a recognised institution of training in the Singapore Public Service.

The dilemmas and tensions faced by the CSI, and the bureaucracy, should not be understated. Like the civil services of other countries, the Singapore Public Service also faced quandaries associated with training. Seeking the optimal balance between on-the-job training and formal training appeared to be sorted out with the setting up of the STI, and was definitely resolved by investing in modern facilities for the CSSDI. The debate between an academic-oriented curriculum and a practitioner-based approach did not appear to be an issue from the start. Although academics enlisted in starting up STI continued into the transition to the CSSDI, their contracts were short-term from the beginning, and the curriculum they helped to draw up bent towards applied — rather than theoretical — training.

The real tension for the CSI, as well as the bureaucracy, was between broad-based training and elite development. On the formal organisational level, the Public Service appeared to aspire towards training up the whole bureaucracy. This goal was repeatedly stressed by the Minister for Finance during the STI period described in Chapter 3. Indeed, broad-based training seemed to be the *raison d'être* for the establishment of the CSSDI and the CSI, i.e., "[t]he objective of the Institute is to enhance the effectiveness of the *public sector*".[134] The team of public officers managing the CSI certainly took this formal organisational goal seriously. During their respective terms as Directors, John Ewing-Chow, Teo Hee Lian, and David Ma led the CSI to improve the training programmes for the rank-and-file of the bureaucracy, without diverting attention away from developing the leadership corps. As the overall inventory of programmes grew, so did the number of courses for the elite, allowing leadership development to consistently constitute half of the CSI's total course offerings. The Permanent Secretaries and Chief Executives who collectively formed the leadership of the Public Service seemed to support this goal of training the whole bureaucracy, at least at the formal organisational level.

Informally, the leadership of the Public Service evidently rooted for an emphasis on developing the Administrative Service elite. In all purposes, these Permanent Secretaries and Chief Executives heading government agencies could be reflecting the position of the political leadership. The decision by then Prime Minister Lee Kuan Yew and Finance Minister Dr. Goh Keng Swee immediately after self-government to concentrate on cultivating a corps of Administrative Service leadership elite — the Praetorian Guards — did not appear to have changed over the years. The fact that these Permanent Secretaries and Chief Executives were predominantly AOs themselves should not be overlooked, even though not all of them would be driven by provincial outlooks. To be sure, many among these senior officers would have been very conscious of their responsibilities over their respective ministries and agencies, as well as their responsibilities over the whole Public Service, and even the Singapore state. Many of these Public Service leaders were involved in leading the bureaucracy in steering Singapore through the phases of state-formation and developmental state. In the eyes of some of these Public Service leaders, the best interests of the bureaucracy and the state was to focus on grooming scarce talents, and to sustain and expand the training of the AOs. While not all of them might be completely like-minded, the

---

[134] *Training Programme 1979*: 1; *Training Programme 1980*: 1.

prevailing consensus by the 1980s was to raise a dedicated centre for developing the AO leadership, and which should be set apart from the CSI. Thus, while at the formal organisational level, the Public Service leadership supported the CSI's drive towards broad-based training; at the informal level, that endorsement was conditioned upon continued and sustained heavy emphasis on developing the AO leadership elite.

Ironically, the CSI's development into an institution of broad-based training, seemingly fulfilling its mission in the eyes of its staff, highlighted the CSI's lack of capacity in leadership development from the perspectives of the Public Service leadership. The possibility of positioning the issue as flourishing the CSI as a centre of functional training on the one hand, and filling a gap in leadership development on the other, was lost with the awkward handling of the CSI amid the reorganisation. The interest of the Public Service leadership and the government towards cultivating the AOs was demonstrated by the rush to set up the new Civil Service College. From the viewpoints of those in the CSI, this was a marginalisation — a literal displacement with the mandatory move away from Heng Mui Keng Terrace — of the CSI. The CSI's tenure as the sole central civil service training organisation finally came to an end with its renaming and subordination as a department under the banner of the Civil Service College in 1996.

Chapter 5

The First Dedicated Leadership Training Initiative: The Civil Service College (1993–1996)

In 1993, the Civil Service College (CSC) was set up to improve policymaking and leadership development in the Singapore Public Service. By locating the context against which the CSC was established, this chapter begins by highlighting the significance of the College: that not only did the CSC realise the bureaucracy's long search for a credible leadership development scheme, strong political impetus drove — indeed provided the *raison d'être* for — the establishment of the CSC.

The chapter proceeds then to highlight the importance of personnel selection in setting up the bureaucracy's latest training initiative. Selecting leaders with the vision and competence not only helped to overcome potential resistance against the CSC venture, it allowed the College subsequently to produce remarkable programmes. The CSC's milestone programmes were by far its most notable accomplishment as they offered, for the first time, a comprehensive set of leadership development programmes for the bureaucracy's Administrative Service and upper leadership echelon. More significantly, an examination of the CSC's staffing and activities also reveals the high level of political attention accorded to the institution. This high level of support from the political leadership made possible the creation of the CSC as the platform through which reforms were introduced into the leadership echelon of the Singapore Public Service.

5.1 The Bureaucratic Imperative

The first public inkling of the pending establishment of the CSC came from a planted 'leak' in the national broadsheet. On 24 May 1991, *The Straits Times* quoted a "well-placed civil service source" revealing that a new institution for training Administrative Service officers was in the works: "[W]e have gone past the study stage and some plans have already been drawn up."[1]

Leadership training had always featured prominently in the Singapore Public Service, as described in the preceding chapters. The Political Study Centre, set up in 1959 when Singapore became a self-governing state, targeted the leadership of the bureaucracy, to socialise them to the tasks of state-formation. Equipping officers of the Administrative Service leadership cadre with the requisite management skills to lead the developmental state was the motivation for creating the Staff Training Institute in 1971. Throughout the 1980s, leadership development continued to preoccupy the Public Service's leadership when contemplating the subject of training. As described in the previous chapter, their dissatisfaction with leadership training efforts in the Civil Service Institute also led to the decision for setting up the CSC. Kishore Mahbubani, then Deputy Secretary at the Ministry of Foreign Affairs, reflected the sentiments of his colleagues and Permanent Secretaries who constituted the leadership of the Public Service:

> I think the Civil Service Institute was always to provide skills-based training; more for lower-level officials; teach them various skills they needed to know to do their jobs. Whereas Civil Service College was always intended for the highest levels of the Service, for the AOs, for the high flyers, to train them, develop them, socialise them.[2]

In 1992, Richard Hu, the Minister for Finance, formally announced plans to set up the CSC: "[T]he Civil Service presently lacks an institutional focal point where tradition is preserved, and values shared and transmitted through generations."[3] Hence, Singapore needed an

---

[1] *ST* 24 May 1991: 30.
[2] Kishore Mahbubani, Dean, CSC, 1993–1995, Interview with Author, 20 June 2012.
[3] *ST* 11 July 1992: 1. Also, *Business Times* 11 July 1992: 2.

equivalent of France's École Nationale d'Administration or Malaysia's National Institute of Public Administration, where public officers could be imbued with common values and traditions.

On 29 April 1993, the CSC was inaugurated at the Treasury Tower, its official mission:

> To foster the development of a strong and vibrant senior Civil Service which will, in addition to the prevailing strengths of competence, dedication, integrity and meritocracy, have a strong sense of tradition, *esprit de corps*, enhanced managerial skills, a sensitive understanding of the new evolving political and economic realities (domestic, regional and global) and commitment to a long-term vision of a secure, stable and successful Singapore.[4]

A key reason for setting up the CSC was to forge a stronger *esprit de corps* among the Administrative Service officers.[5] These AOs, who formed the leadership of the Singapore Public Service and whose role in policymaking was secondary only to the political leadership, had long been heading various government agencies across the bureaucracy. By the early 1990s, the Public Service had evolved from the traditional ministries to include 62 statutory boards; public officers — especially the AOs —'were also deployed to many Government-linked Corporations (GLCs).[6] Kishore Mahbubani, who was appointed the first Dean of the CSC, felt this diversification had led to too much fragmentation of the Public Service.[7] The leadership cadre needed to come together as a strong team. In fact, political scientist Seah Chee Meow observed in the mid-1980s that "the bonds among the civil servants are not strong [and the] external respectability enjoyed by the civil service is not matched by strong intra-organisational cohesion."[8] Peter Ong, who was appointed the College's Deputy Dean, elaborated in an interview

---

[4]"Mission," *Ethos*, First Quarter (1994): 2. Also, *Business Times* 30 April 1993: 2.

[5]Kishore Mahbubani, Dean, Civil Service College and Permanent Secretary, Ministry of Foreign Affairs, "Foreword," *Ethos*, First Quarter (1994): 3–4.

[6]*SAR* 1992: 236–241; Lee Boon Hiok (1975) 6 and 30; Linda Low, *Rethinking Singapore Inc. and GLCs* (Singapore: NUS Business School Research Paper Series, 2002).

[7]Kishore Mahbubani, Dean, CSC, to Col. (Res) Ho Meng Kit, PPS to SM, "Civil Service College (CSC)," 6 February 1993, CSC Records.

[8]Seah (1987) 109.

years later:

> ...getting a group of folks...the PWD [Public Works Department] engineer, the SAF [Singapore Armed Forces] pilot, the Admin Officer, to come together, to have a collective instinct of what it will take for Singapore to survive and to grow to the next stage. We didn't have that; we had functional training — write good English, leadership management training, supervisory skills. But not quite, we didn't use 'Whole-of-Government' then, not quite getting the whole group of leaders together. So, a sense that the senior people in the system would progress through the system together, knowing each other, and having the collective instincts of what make this place tick and what would be needed to make this place continue to grow and develop into the next phase.[9]

Another rationale for establishing CSC was to create a focal point for the *élan* of the Singapore Public Service. As early as 1975, Seah had warned that:

> ...the bureaucratic ethos (such as pride in serving in the bureaucracy) is not effectively instilled among the bureaucrats who tend to be more susceptible to purely monetary considerations...due to the fact that many of the bureaucrats (especially those in the senior or division one grade) have not been in the bureaucracy for a long time. They have yet to internalise many of the norms of the bureaucracy.[10]

Table 5.1: Manpower Strength of the Administrative Service, 1974–1996[11]

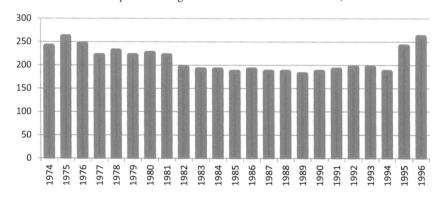

---

[9]Peter Ong, Deputy Dean, CSC, 1993–1995, Interview with Author, 6 June 2012.
[10]Seah (1975) 21. Also, Seah (1987) 109.
[11]Personnel Development Branch, Public Service Division, Prime Minister's Office, in Anthony Tan (1997) 23.

Table 5.2: HR Structure of the Administrative Service, circa 1993[12]

	Grade	Corresponding Rank	Monthly Salary
Timescale*	Administrative Assistant	AA / SAA	$2,715 - $3,550
	Senior Administrative Assistant		$4,065 - $4,845
	Assistant Secretary	AS	$5,090 - $6,080
	Principal Assistant Secretary	PAS	$6,980 - $8,155
Administrative Officer	Super-scale G	Deputy Secretary	$10,445
	Super-scale F		$11,390
	Super-scale E	Deputy Secretary/ Higher Deputy Secretary	$12,445
	Super-scale E1		$13,660
	Super-scale D	Higher Deputy Secretary/ Senior Deputy Secretary	$14,970
	Super-scale D1		$17,180
Senior Administrative Officer	Super-scale C	Senior Deputy Secretary/ Permanent Secretary	$20,020
	Super-scale B	Permanent Secretary	$24,020
	Super-scale A	Permanent Secretary/ Senior Permanent Secretary	$28,335
	Staff Grade I		$33,490
	Staff Grade II	Senior Permanent Secretary/ Special Permanent Secretaru	$39,280
	Staff Grade III	Special Permanent Secretary	$46,120
	Staff Grade IV		$54,220
	Staff Grade V		$63,690

*'Timescale' refers to the general scheme of service.

As the Public Service entered into the 1990s, the imminent retirement of a whole generation of officers raised the need to preserve the traditions and values which had emerged from and which had defined

---

[12]"The Administrative Service," Public Service Division, Prime Minister's Office, 1993, in Anthony Tan (1997) 26.

the Public Service. To George Yeo, then-Minister of State for Finance, the bureaucracy needed:

> ... a tradition and a spirit. We needed institutional memory, myths, and heroes. This was how the idea of CSC came about.... I never had formal responsibility for CSC... but always took a close interest in them. At that time, I was probably the minister most convinced of the need for the CSC.[13]

The CSC would cultivate three characteristics Yeo thought were essential for the Public Service's leadership — intellectual leadership, moral leadership, and an awareness of its role in society.

Continuing to recruit from among the best and brightest would ensure that the AOs could command intellectual leadership. However, to George Yeo:

> That leadership is not only intellectual, it must also be moral. That is the second condition for a successful civil service. The moral basis of the civil service of the Roman Church is the Christian Bible. The moral basis of the Chinese mandarinate was and may well again be Confucianism. In Singapore, the moral basis of the Civil Service is gradually taking shape. Some aspects are clear, like intolerance of corruption and commitment to national independence, but others are not. Our national values, when they are settled, must eventually be reflected in the way the Civil Service carries itself. Moral leadership must not only be exercised, it must be publicly and visibly exercised. We cannot succumb to the free-wheeling ways of the private sector. The free market idealised by Adam Smith works only when competition takes place within a moral framework that engenders regard for law and respect for human life and dignity. That moral framework the Civil Service helps to provide. The Civil Service has to be above the fray of the marketplace.[14]

Finally, the AOs needed a "collective self-consciousness of its role in society and of its corporate mission.... As a group, civil servants must always be concerned with the national welfare and proud to be charged with that responsibility."[15]

---

[13] George Yeo, Minister of State for Finance and Foreign Affairs, 1988, email correspondence with Author, 21 June 2012.

[14] "Opening address by George Yong-Boon Yeo, Minister of State for Finance and Minister of State for Foreign Affairs, at MSD's Seminar 'Business management practices for a better public service,'" 2 December 1988.

[15] *Ibid.*

The CSC's chief advocate was thus envisioning CSC as a transmitter of what was essentially the *élan* of the Singapore Public Service. Through telling and re-telling of 'war tales' and even the perpetuation of 'myths' and 'heroes', this 'moral leadership' could be cultivated among new recruits and young officers of the Administrative Service.

5.2 A New Political Context: Development, Democratisation, and Socialisation Revisited

Evidently, the Civil Service College was also meant to develop political acumen among the leadership corps of the Public Service, implicit in George Yeo's vision of Administrative Service officers filled with a 'collective self-consciousness of its role in society'.

The political context was instrumental in the CSC's formation. The 1980s witnessed a dip in the electoral fortunes of the ruling People's Action Party. Following the concession of its long-standing absolute monopoly over the Parliament, after losing a by-election in 1981, the PAP lost another Parliamentary seat in the 1984 General Elections; its share of popular votes fell by 12.6% to 62.9%.[16] The PAP's relatively dismal performance was attributed to the electorate's resentment with the recent slew of unpopular measures and, in connection with that, a greater desire by increasingly affluent and well-educated citizens to be consulted regarding policymaking.[17] In the aftermath, the government responded with various initiatives to solicit feedback from the public; public communications training for public officers intensified, as mentioned in the previous chapter. The 1988 polls again saw the PAP's vote-share dipping to 61.8%, although the party clawed back one Parliamentary seat.[18]

---

[16] *SAR* 1985: 66.

[17] Jon S. T. Quah, "Singapore in 1988: Safeguarding the future, "*SAR* 1989: 2; Diane K. Mauzy and R. S. Milne, *Singapore Politics Under the People's Action Party* (London and New York: Routledge, 2002) 149–150; Yap, Lim and Leong, 364–368; Turnbull (2009) 340.

[18] Quah (1989) 9, thought that the results were a PAP victory but Mauzy and Milne, pointed out continued unhappiness among the electorate to explain the PAP's continued slide at the polls. Mauzy and Milne, 150. See also Yap, Lim, and Leong, 446.

When Goh Chok Tong succeeded Lee Kuan Yew as Prime Minister in 1990, Goh premised his tenure upon an "open and consultative style of government".[19] The population appeared to be drawn to his affable personality and gentler style; with the economy buoyant, Goh decided to seek the electorate's endorsement by calling for early polls.[20] In the 1991 General Elections, the PAP — while returned to power — witnessed its worst ever electoral outing: the loss of four Parliamentary seats and an all-time low of 61% of the popular vote. This might have been a decisive win in other democracies but until the 1980s, the PAP had monopolised all the seats in Parliaments and its vote-share never dropped below 70%.

At around this time, a growing discourse in political economy on development's causality relationship towards democratisation began to turn its lens on Singapore. The theory that economic development, by raising educational levels and social mobility, would raise a middle class seeking greater role in politics was not new and could be traced to Marx and Weber.[21] The spate of political liberalisation in Newly Industrialising Countries (NICs) in the 1980s, from Taiwan and Korea to Thailand and the Philippines, renewed interest in the development-democratisation thesis.[22] The middle class rising from state-led development across these NICs in the 1960s and 1970s, *à la* Chalmers Johnson's developmental state, and then playing influential roles in the democratisation of these countries, appeared to lend credence to the postulation. More significantly, the seeming validation of this theory heralded questions on whether similar democratisation would emerge in other Southeast Asian NICs or near-NICs like Indonesia, Malaysia, and Singapore.[23]

---

[19]Hussin Mutalib, "Domestic Politics," *Singapore: The Year in Review 1991*, ed. Lee Tsao Yuan (Singapore: Institute of Policy Studies, 1992) 71–72.

[20]Bilveer Singh, *Whither PAP's Dominance? An Analysis of Singapore's 1991 General Elections* (Malaysia: Pelanduk Publications, 1992) 32–34.

[21]Anek Laothamatas, "Development and Democratisation: A Theoretical Introduction with Reference to the Southeast Asian and East Asian Cases." *Democratisation in Southeast and East Asia*, ed. Anek Laothamatas (Singapore: ISEAS, 1997) 2.

[22]Kevin Hewison, Garry Rodan and Richard Robison, "Introduction: Changing forms of state power in Southeast Asia," *Southeast Asia in the 1990s: Authoritarianism, democracy and capitalism*, eds. Kevin Hewison, Richard Robison and Garry Rodan (Australia: Allen & Unwin Pty Ltd, 1993) 2; *Ibid.*

[23]Rodan (1993) 52; Hewison, Rodan and Robison (1993) 2; Anek (1997) 15–16.

For Singapore, the PAP's electoral dips from the 1980s into 1991 against the background of an increasingly educated and affluent population appeared to signal a similar trend towards development-induced democratisation. Even with the benefit of a few years of hindsight in the later-1990s, scholars were more circumspect whether Singapore would go the way of Taiwan, Korea or Thailand.[24] However, for the PAP leadership in the aftermath of the 1991 General Elections debacle, the party's future might not have appeared certain. What was apparent amid the intense soul-searching that followed was the need to respond to the changing political milieu.[25]

Among some of the PAP's more public post-electoral reflections which, given the party's introspective nature, were clearly directed at an external audience, were some references to the Public Service. In an address to PAP activists, the Deputy Prime Minister (DPM), Ong Teng Cheong, admitted that some policies had hurt the poor and alienated Chinese-educated sections of the population.[26] However, Ong wondered aloud why there was this perception gap between how the people and the government viewed official policies? While urging party activists to attune themselves to the sentiments among the population, DPM Ong called on civil servants to be "politically astute" in the same breath:

> Sometimes, even the most well-meaning policy can end up a disaster if the Government bureaucracy shows no political sensitivity in implementing it. . . . there is sometimes room for accommodating people adversely affected by our policies. In such cases, there is no need for the bureaucracy to take the clinical view that no exceptions can be made. Government is about people, and rules are made by people.[27]

---

[24]Writing in 1993, Rodan in "The growth of Singapore's middle class and its political significance" argued that while "there is a degree of middle class alienation from the PAP", the government had sufficiently co-opted the middle class to forestall any threat to the PAP. In 1997, Heng argued that the PAP changed to a more consultative governing style and "use . . . the party's considerable experience and power to pre-empt, co-opt or curb dissidence so that they do not undermine the fundamentals of a dominant party system." See Heng Hiang Khng, "Economic Development and Political Change: The Democratisation Process in Singapore," *Democratisation in Southeast and East Asia*, ed. Anek (1997) 135.

[25]Mutalib (1992) 92–93; Yap, Lim and Leong (2009) 460–461.

[26]Yap, Lim and Leong (2009) 461–463; Singh (1992) 119–125.

[27]Ong Teng Cheong (1992) 18.

To the Deputy Prime Minister, younger officers who rose to key positions across government agencies might not wield the political acumen of older civil servants:

> When the PAP took office in 1959, one of the first things it did was to set up the Political Study Centre...to get senior civil servants...aware of the changed political environment...Perhaps the proposed Civil Service College is a good place for the government to inculcate greater political sensitivity among younger civil servants.[28]

Lest this be taken as making a scapegoat of the bureaucracy for the ruling party's electoral woes, the political leadership had already detected a need to sharpen the political sensitivity of civil servants prior to the polls. Two months before the 31 August 1991 General Elections, the Prime Minister, Goh Chok Tong, addressed the Administrative Service officers, the leadership echelons of the Public Service:

> Administrative Officers should have political sensitivity. An understanding of the history of our young nation, and how it has influenced the attitudes and perceptions of the various communities in the population, is necessary. So too is the need to know the thinking and value system of the political leadership and electorate.[29]

The reference to the Political Study Centre draws comparison with the political milieu following self-government — new political elite consolidating their authority amid a bureaucracy disconnected with the population. The PAP leaders recognised the critical role played by public officers in delivering public services, which thus contributed towards their electoral legitimacy. Like their predecessors three decades earlier, the PAP leaders in the early 1990s turned to the 'political education' of the Administrative Service leadership echelon of the Public Service, its 'Praetorian Guards'.[30] This inculcation of 'greater political sensitivity' among the AOs was evidently a role envisioned for the Civil Service College.

---

[28] *Ibid.*

[29] NAS, "Speech by the Prime Minister, Mr Goh Chok Tong, at the Third Administrative Service Dinner, 5 July 1991", Web, 22 June 2014 http://www.nas.gov.sg/archivesonline/data/pdfdoc/gct19910705.pdf.

[30] Ngiam, Interview with Author, 10 January 2013.

5.3 Getting the Right People: Personnel Selection and Organisational Structure

The first task in setting up the CSC was selecting the key personnel. The position of Dean of the CSC was deliberated at the highest political level, Kishore Mahbubani disclosed:

> I was Deputy Secretary of Foreign Affairs when they made me Dean of the Civil Service College. The man who approached me and asked me to become the Dean was George Yeo, who was then 2nd Minister of Foreign Affairs [and Finance]...I wasn't privy to all the thinking that went into it; it was all decided at the *Cabinet* level.[31]

When conferred the discretion to select his deputy, Mahbubani — conscious that his time would be divided between the CSC and the Ministry of Foreign Affairs where he continued concurrently as Deputy Secretary — made sure that the CSC had an effective leader at the staff level. He requested for Peter Ong as his deputy:

> The Deputy Secretary in PSD [Public Service Division] at that time was Tan Boon Huat. Tan Boon Huat gave me two choices, either somebody else or Peter Ong. But he said, '[For] Peter Ong you have to wait six months.' I said, 'Peter Ong is very good, I'll wait six months.' So once Peter Ong came on board full-time, then I just left it to him. I worked with him before, in APEC [Asia-Pacific Economic Cooperation] meetings, I knew how good he was, and so I was very happy to get him back. Because I knew if you have somebody good, you just leave it to them to do it.[32]

Ong, pursuing his Master in Business Administration degree at Stanford University in 1992, revealed another consideration in his selection:

> Kishore called me: 'Would you want to work in CSC?' Because they wanted someone who was familiar with case studies, being business schools, we did case studies. So they thought I could contribute in terms of case studies.[33]

The depth of thinking that went into selecting the appropriate staff at the CSC was further illustrated in the Assistant Dean appointment.

---

[31] Mahbubani, Interview with Author, 20 June 2012.
[32] *Ibid*. Peter Ong will eventually rise to become the Head of Civil Service in 2010.
[33] Peter Ong, Interview with Author, 6 June 2012.

Miss Patricia Lam, a young Administrative Service officer, recognised that while she was left to define the parameters of her role, it was an opportunity for her own development:

> As I was a fresh graduate, it was mainly a training post for me and I was very aware that I had no more experience than any of the MDOs [Management Development Officers, working-level staff].... It was also a very flat organisation so we all did whatever was necessary. I did everything from moving chairs and planning an office move; to writing speeches and later to filling in for Peter as far as I could. As time passed and things became busier, I took on more of the management — interviewing applicants, some staff performance appraisals, ministry-level meetings — and as much of day-to-day stuff as I could so that things didn't have to go to Peter.[34]

The CSC was deliberately set up as a small organisation, having three Administrative Service officers managing a handful of working level staff (*see* Table 5.3). The choice of only three AOs, and a combination of a senior, intermediate, and subaltern, overcame the concerns that stalled the Administrative Staff College proposal in the 1980s — the detachment of four to six AOs from operational positions were deemed

Table 5.3:   Civil Service College, 1994[35]

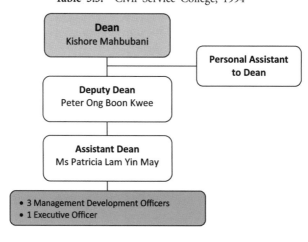

---

[34]Patricia Lam, Assistant Dean, CSC, 1994–1995, email correspondence with Author, 27 March 2013.
[35]"Who's in CSC," *Ethos* First Quarter (1994) 14; *Directory*, January 1994: 254.

too high an opportunity cost for that leadership development venture at that time. Intended as a platform for the transmission of values and political instincts, CSC was also envisioned to draw on senior public officers rather than rely on a large full-time faculty.[36]

The CSC was set up within the Ministry of Finance's Public Service Division, the personnel management agency of the bureaucracy.[37] This reporting line paralleled that of the Civil Service Institute, indicating that training continued to be seen as a subject of human resource management by the government. Originally, an option was to site the CSC as a centre within the CSI, to draw on existing resources, but the final decision was to establish the CSC as a separate institution.[38] Like the CSI, the CSC was funded by the PSD's budget and did not charge participants or their ministries for the courses they attended.

Plans for the CSC also included a Board of Governors to advise the College's executive team. It was mooted by the Deputy Prime Minister, Lee Hsien Loong, revealing the very high level of political attention paid to the CSC.[39] Like earlier counterparts, this board was chaired by the Head of the Civil Service, but for the first time, the CSC board had representation from private corporations, the media, and academia, apart from Permanent Secretaries and senior civil servants.[40] There was no additional information to either assess the effects of this Board of Governors upon the CSC or compare it with earlier predecessors.

In all, the Civil Service College's personnel selection and organisational structure indicated high-level political commitment and long-term planning for the bureaucracy. In particular, with the Administrative Service officers so highly prized for their operational roles, appointing three AOs to head the CSC represented a deep determination to invest in the strategic development of the AO leadership cadre and the broader Singapore Public Service.

---

[36]Lai (1995) 37.

[37]*SAR* 1993: 264–269; *Directory*, January 1994: 243–274.

[38]Lai (1995) 33.

[39]Kishore Mahbubani, Dean of CSC, to Dr. Goh Keng Swee, Executive Chairman, IEAPE, 3 February 1992, CSC Records.

[40]"Board of Governors," *Ethos*, First Quarter (1994): 1.

5.3.1 *Overseas exemplars*

Forming the Civil Service College represented the furthest Singapore had gone in studying foreign exemplars. In the 1980s, an Administrative Staff College proposal led to studies of various European training institutions. Nothing emerged from these studies, not due to the shortcomings of these foreign models but an unwillingness to forego Administrative Service officers from operational posts to form the faculty for the proposed institution.

In drawing up the CSC, well-known centres of leadership training were thoroughly studied but the main consideration was adaptability to the local context.[41] For example, Mahbubani pointed out that while the École Nationale d'Administration was held up as the yardstick for bureaucratic training, it was not practicable in Singapore's circumstances: "ENA is very critical, because the ranking in the class determines which service you go to ... ENA basically was a very powerful institution that determines the career. We were not that powerful, we can't get people for two years."[42] Deputy Dean Peter Ong added: "I don't think it's possible for any senior or high potential officers to be spared three years. If they could be, they cannot be very needed in their workplace."[43] Whether or not they were privy to complications forestalling earlier proposals, CSC's planners avoided the lengthy secondment of the AOs as permanent faculty. Mahbubani said:

> I did visit some institutions, British and so on. But we knew our circumstances, we were small. If you want to have a big institution, you are going to have throughput. Our Administrative Service was only 250, so Civil Service College can't do that much. And we didn't want to have full time faculty, we relied on either current leaders or retired leaders.[44]

---

[41] A study team that included Tan Boon Huat, Deputy Secretary, PSD, and Teo Hee Lian, Director, CSI, visited some notable leadership training institutions in Europe, including ENA. Lai (1995) 33.

[42] Mahbubani, Interview with Author, 20 June 2012. Also, Mahbubani to Goh, 3 February 1992.

[43] Peter Ong, Interview with Author, 6 June 2012.

[44] Mahbubani, Interview with Author, 20 June 2012.

The source of inspiration for the CSC was to be North America.[45] Peter Ong was amid his post-graduate studies at Stanford University in 1992, when he was directed to visit various leadership training institutions in the United States (US) and Canada. He was most impressed by the Canadian Centre for Management Development, convinced that "you need to put leaders across Whole-of-Government together at various milestones of their lives."[46]

5.4 Political Support: Overcoming Doubters

The Civil Service College proposal was not without complications and the project soon encountered a doubter, and an influential one at that. Retired Deputy Prime Minister Dr Goh Keng Swee had expressed concern with the cost of building the CSC complex upon learning of the CSC proposal.[47] The long-time Finance Minister known for his frugality, Goh also had reservations over CSC's ability to match the ENA in turning Administrative Service officers into French *énarques*. Although retired for a decade, Goh continued to be highly respected within the political circle and the bureaucracy. He was instrumental in reorganising the post-colonial Public Service, devising the strategies that led to Singapore's economic development, and setting up the Singapore Armed Forces. For 11 of his 25 years in government, he was Deputy Prime Minister. Fortunately, Goh raised his objections over the CSC in private, though this he did with Lee Kuan Yew.[48] While Lee had relinquished the Prime Minister post to Goh Chok Tong, he remained as Senior Minister in the Cabinet, and ranked second only to the Premier in government protocol. Mahbubani, as Dean of the CSC, quickly found himself fielding high-level queries, and doubts, over the CSC.

The CSC was fortuitous to enjoy some political support. Mahbubani was able to seek advice from George Yeo, who was by then Minister

---

[45] *Ibid.*

[46] Peter Ong, Interview with Author, 6 June 2012.

[47] Gok Keng Swee, to Professor Kishore Mahbubani, Dean, CSC, 23 December 1992, CSC Records; Mahbubani, Interview with Author, 20 June 2012.

[48] Yeo, email correspondence with Author, 21 June 2012.

for Information and the Arts and concurrently Second Minister for Foreign Affairs, and a consistently strong proponent of CSC in the Cabinet.[49] More importantly, the CSC had the support of the Deputy Prime Minister, Lee Hsien Loong. His endorsement of Mahbubani's responses to various objections — the CSC complex was to be shared with other institutions and hence the costs were reasonable, and CSC was not seeking to replicate ENA — helped to assure Dr. Goh Keng Swee. Recounting this episode, Mahbubani credited then-DPM Lee Hsien Loong for saving CSC from a still-birth:

> [DPM Lee's] support was absolutely critical. His support was critical in terms of making sure that Dr. Goh's opposition did not derail the whole process. In fact, the critical thing he did was that he called me in for a meeting. We had a conversation; most of it was what he was telling me. And then the notes of conversation were circulated to all the Permanent Secretaries...send a signal to all the Permanent Secretaries that the Singapore Government and he were strongly supporting the Civil Service College project. And that was how I got very strong support.[50]

5.5 Training Programmes and Activities

Conceptualised as a dedicated leadership development centre, the Civil Service College was able to concentrate its activities on developing the elite Administrative Service officers. Unlike earlier training initiatives, it did not have to put up with the inhibitions and distractions of attending to the other demands of the broader bureaucracy. The outcome of its focus on leadership development was a syllabus the CSC termed as 'milestone programmes'.

5.5.1 *Milestone programmes*

Milestone programmes were designed as training interventions scheduled at various 'critical points', or milestones, in the careers of senior public officers. In the schema developed by the CSC, three milestone programmes would provide the relevant training for Administrative Service officers and other public officers with leadership potential at different phases of their careers — (1) the Foundation Course to induct new AOs, (2) the

---

[49] *Ibid.*
[50] Mahbubani, Interview with Author, 20 June 2012.

Senior Management Programme for mid-career heads of departments, and (3) the Leadership in Administration Programme for senior officers rising to the apex of the Public Service hierarchy.

The Foundation Course (FC) was developed by the Staff Training Institute in the 1970s. It aimed to induct scholars who recently returned from overseas — typically prestigious American and British — universities into their junior Administrative Service posts. The FC's curricula had remained similar as STI evolved into the CSSDI and finally the Civil Service Institute, a remarkable accomplishment considering that the leadership of the Public Service constantly deliberated over the training of the AOs. In fact, it was their dissatisfaction with the CSI's leadership training offerings that led to the decision to set up the CSC.

Now transferred to the CSC, the FC continued to induct the new AOs to the machinery of government, management, and communication skills, and a tour of the ASEAN capital cities.[51] However, in revamping the FC, Patricia Lam recalled that teaching methodologies in graduate business schools served as reference: "A bigger influence on the design of the courses was the MBA approach — it was meant to be intense, cohort-building, mix hard and soft skills, and include leadership training."[52]

The Senior Management Programme (SMP) was a CSC invention, directed at talented public officers "between 30 and 40 years old, and who are typically heading Departments or Divisions in their Ministries."[53] The resultant five-week SMP put participants through panel discussions, case studies, and meetings with senior civil servants and ministers, with the curriculum focusing on principles of policymaking in Singapore. The incorporation of adventure learning activities sought to foster *esprit de corps* among the participants. A final test then dispatched the participants to act as consultants to various ministries, to study potential problems, and offer recommendations, thereby exposing them to "the difficulties of reconciling policy formulation with operational and logistical considerations."[54] Capping each SMP was a study trip aimed at

---

[51]"Year in Review," *Ethos*, First Quarter (1994): 7.
[52]Lam, email correspondence with Author, 27 March 2013.
[53]"Leaders in Administration Programme," *Ethos*, Third Issue (1995): 11.
[54]"1st Senior Management Programme," *Ethos*, Third Quarter (1994): 7–8.

raising participants' awareness of regional issues. A CSC official pointed out that attending SMP did not guarantee participants promotion, but it did prepare them for the eventuality, should they be promoted, to work at the next higher grade.[55]

At the apex of CSC's pyramid of milestone programmes was the Leaders in Administration Programme (LAP) for "officers identified as having the potential for very senior positions in the public sector."[56] The 15 participants in the 1995 pilot run consisted of Deputy Secretaries, Chief Executives of statutory boards, and top uniformed service commanders. Beside meetings with Permanent Secretaries and ministers, discussions among participants probed them to evaluate the principles of policymaking as Singapore developed. Like the FC and the SMP, a key aim in the LAP was to forge cohesion among the participants. Initial feedback from participants appeared to reward CSC and its staff for their efforts — in particular, participants found "experiential learning and sharing of ideas in group discussions are useful learning tools."[57]

While the three sets of 'milestones programmes' appeared neatly pegged to various optimal intervening career points of Administrative Service officers, drawing these up were not without their difficulties. Miss Lim Soo Hoon, who succeeded Peter Ong as Deputy Dean in 1995, pointed out that CSC's small and recent set-up could have limited their capacity in designing an appropriate curriculum: "[the officers] were all very green, first time working in the Civil Service. And here they were supposed to come out with the curriculum."[58] CSC staff held discussions with officials in charge of personnel policies at the Public Service Division and prospective participants and they studied several foreign leadership training programmes for applicable lessons.[59] Their readiness to experiment, in the opinion of Lim Soo Hoon, and some beginner's luck, helped CSC pulled off the whole suite of "milestones programmes":

---

[55] Zee Yong Kang, Assistant Dean, CSC, 1996, quoted in Lai (1995) 39.

[56] "Leaders in Administration Programme," *Ethos*, Third Issue (1995): 11.

[57] *Ibid* 12.

[58] Lim Soo Hoon, Deputy Dean, CSC, Interview with Author, 15 June 2012.

[59] Foreign leadership programmes studied included Hong Kong's Senior Staff Course, the Federal Executive Institute's Leadership for Democratic Society programme, and the CCMD's Career Advancement Programme. "Civil Service College's Senior Management Programme," *Ethos*, Second Quarter (1994): 7.

...the good fortune for us was that we used basically the same template. Because it was so new, nobody had ever gone through any of these programmes. So whatever we gave, let's say LAP, we could replicate and deepen it a bit more or increase the level of people coming to talk to you a bit more. Because none of the participants in LAP had ever been through SMP. So we were able to do that for a few cycles, before people started saying, 'Hang on, the people who are going to LAP are the people who went through SMP, and therefore you cannot replicate.'[60]

Another difficulty was attendance. While the Public Service Division had the power to send officers for "milestones programmes", the task of ensuring officers' physical attendance fell onto CSC staff.[61] This was an awkward challenge, considering that most participants outranked CSC officers. Mahbubani recounted:

...a perpetual challenge in Singapore, is that most senior civil servants think training is a waste of time, so they were very reluctant to come for the courses. And even when they came they would be focused always on their day jobs, and never fully properly immersed into training.[62]

Deputy Dean, Peter Ong, added:

I remember it was very difficult, one of the key challenges, early challenges, was how to get the SAF to cough up their Chief of Defence Force, or Service Chiefs to come for LAP. How to cough up DSes [Deputy Secretaries], Perm Secs, and Managing Directors of Statutory Boards to come?...it would not have been possible if DPM Lee [Hsien Loong] at that time did not personally play a very instrumental role.[63]

In a meeting involving senior civil servants, the Deputy Prime Minister urged supervisors to recognise the importance of training in the career development of their staff; the returns for giving up a key lieutenant for training would inevitably be rewarding.[64] Without the offer by DPM Lee — and other ministers — to meet with participants,

[60]Lim Soo Hoon, Interview with Author, 15 June 2012.
[61]Lai (1995) 36.
[62]Mahbubani, Interview with Author, 20 June 2012.
[63]Peter Ong, Interview with Author, 6 June 2012. Also, Lai (1995) 36.
[64]"Key points of speech by DPM BG (Res) Lee Hsien Loong at lunch hosted by DPM and Minister for Finance for prospective members of the Civil Service College's Board of Governors," 14 October 1993, CSC Records.

securing the attendance of senior officers at the "milestones programmes", in Ong's opinion, "would not be possible."[65]

All milestone programmes underwent rigorous internal reviews. Participants would complete evaluation forms, which were customised to every course, and "elaborate in order to assess their satisfaction with the courses and if refinements are in order."[66] Their feedback were summarised for submission to the Dean, before final reports were presented to the Public Service Division. However, these internal reviews are not available currently. In lieu of such internal records, participants' feedback in *Ethos*, the CSC's newsletter, provided a sampling of their reception towards these "milestones programmes": "the best civil service course I have ever attended, both in terms of learning and the camaraderie built up in the five weeks."[67]

5.5.2 *Case study as modus operandi*

One of the decisions taken in conceptualising CSC was to adopt the case study method. Peter Ong explained that "we didn't want to go back to the Political Study Centre. We didn't want it to be propaganda. And that's why we use the case study."[68] To inculcate *élan* and political instincts among highly-educated and intellectually sharp Administrative Service officers, the didactic style of learning would be counter-productive. In comparison:

> Case study allows you to come to your own conclusions about what should have been done, what could have been done, and evaluate what was done against your own views.... We did that by giving all the raw data that led the policymakers at that time to come to their conclusions. And you use the same source document and decide whether [the] policymakers did the right thing. That is the power of case study.[69]

---

[65]Peter Ong, Interview with Author, 6 June 2012.

[66]CSC staff, quoted in Lai 41. Also, p. 55.

[67]Lee Yuen Hee quoted in "1st Senior Management Programme," *Ethos*, Third Quarter (1994): 10. See also, "Participants' Feedback: Team Building Experience," *Ethos*, First Issue (1995): 9.

[68]Peter Ong, Interview with Author, 6 June 2012.

[69]*Ibid.*

In the academic-field of adult learning or andragogy in Singapore at that time, the case study method was very new. Existing case studies were either business-management types or on foreign public policies. Yet, for the Singaporean Administrative Service officers to be able to engage in realistic discussions and take away real lessons, case studies on public policies in Singapore needed to be drawn up. There were obviously no lack of material to write up case studies on policymaking in Singapore but planners for the CSC recognised the challenge laid in selecting issues suitable for discussion.[70] The guidelines that emerged from discussions on the matter directed topics to cover dilemmas of policymaking, where no final answers were readily apparent. Case studies would aim to point out that policymaking was a continuous process, where policy-issues would evolve over time, and that even the best policies needed to be reviewed constantly in light of changing circumstances. Another objective these case studies would seek to highlight was the importance of the political context in policymaking, and that economically-efficient policies needed to be packaged in politically acceptable ways in order to resonate with the citizenry.

Having decided on writing up case studies based on actual Singapore policymaking, the next challenge was identifying case writers. With the CSC designed as a small set-up, it simply did not have the capacity to write up case studies. At the same time, CSC planners thought that government agencies would be in the best position to write up case studies of topics within their jurisdictional portfolio; being domain owners, these agencies would be familiar with the considerations and constraints of the policies being addressed. However, coaxing government agencies to deviate from their regular writing style advocating specific policy position was a struggle, as Peter Ong recounted:

> It took a long time just convincing ministries how to write case study, keep it open-ended. Because if I'm Ministry of Communications, MinComms, I want to write the COE [Certificate of Entitlement] case study convincing you why COE was the right way.... It was not easy to tell them: 'No, no, no, that's not how.' And we needed MinComms to write the case study, we needed MinComms to provide a lot of data.... MinComms would not want

---

[70]"Notes of meeting between Deputy Prime Minister Lee Hsien Loong and Mr. Kishore Mahbubani, Dean, Civil Service College," 5 April 1993, CSC Records.

to write it this way; they will want to write why COE was the best thing. So we have to convince them. And that was not easy.[71]

Lim Soo Hoon remembered that the ministries needed 'persuasion' from then-Deputy Prime Minister Lee Hsien Loong: "[H]e called all the Perm Secs to a meeting, because we had complaints that ministries were not willing to step up to do case studies for us, he actually chaired a meeting to tell people to do these case studies."[72] Eventually, the case studies that the CSC obtained from government agencies included those on the Certificate of Entitlement, a policy regulating vehicular congestion by requiring prospective owners to bid for eligibility, the policy-dilemmas of healthcare financing, and streaming students according to academic performance.[73] In light of worldwide media attention on the judicial caning of an American teenager convicted for vandalism, a case study was drawn up on dealing with the international press.[74]

Another difficulty was locating facilitators for case studies. So new was the andragogy in Singapore at that time that even local universities had very few qualified case study facilitators.[75] Eventually, senior policymakers led many case studies, injecting realism into these discussions: "The presence of the Ministers and Permanent Secretaries enabled participants to hear from the policymakers themselves the detailed considerations that went into forming the various policies."[76]

Official evaluations on the CSC's use of case studies are not available, but the reflections of one reporter were illustrative. Warren Fernandez, a *Straits Times* correspondent, joined a CSC Public Policy

---

[71]Peter Ong, Interview with Author, 6 June 2012.

[72]Lim Soo Hoon, Interview with Author, 15 June 2012.

[73]Warren Fernandez, *The Straits Times*, "What Would You Do if You Were the Government?" *Ethos*, First Quarter (1994): 6; "Notes of meeting between DPM Lee and Mahbubani," 5 April 1993.

[74]Michael Fay, an 18-year-old American, and several teenagers were convicted of theft and vandalism in 1994. Fay's sentence included six strokes of the cane, a routine penalty in Singapore courts. Despite President Bill Clinton's plea for leniency, Singapore held firm to the sentence on grounds of the sovereignty of its courts. "Public Policy Perspectives Seminar," *Ethos*, Second Quarter (1994): 5–6.

[75]"Notes of meeting between DPM Lee and Mahbubani," 5 April 1993.

[76]"Public Policy Perspectives Seminar," *Ethos*, Second Quarter (1994): 5–6.

Perspectives Seminar in 1994. After labouring over a case study with fellow participants for some time, the reporter lamented: "It came as a disappointment to some, that despite a host of ideas being bandied about, no one could think of a sensible alternative to the dreaded Certificate of Entitlement (COE)."[77] Fernandez opined that the case study method uncovered the constraints of policymaking: "[P]olitical debate in this country is often conducted in a vacuum. Charges are hurled without any clear idea of what the alternative might be. Demands are often made without much sense of their costs."[78] Fernandez, while not representative of all, was sold on the use of case study to examine policymaking:

> Perhaps the case study method, coupled with discussions of the constraints facing policymakers, would make for a fascinating general studies course at our universities as well. It would serve as a good way of focusing young Singaporean minds on the key issues that lie ahead of them.[79]

5.5.3 *Seminars, lectures, talks and publications*

The Public Policy Perspectives Seminar (PPPS) was not listed among the CSC's "milestones programmes", but it was pegged to the career development of the Administrative Service officers. Targeted at scholars who had just returned from overseas universities, PPPS aimed to prepare them for the local policymaking milieu in which they would be serving.[80] Through the case studies of actual policies, PPPS allowed participants to debate and even disagree over these policies.[81] Hence, even before the new AOs attended the Foundation Course, which was a two-month long and much more comprehensive induction programme, in effect, PPPS was a shorter and more concise "milestones programme" preparing the AOs for the FC.

As part of its mission to institutionalise and foster the *élan* of the Public Service among younger officers, the CSC organised a series of

---

[77] Fernandez, "What Would You Do if You Were the Government?" *Ethos*, First Quarter (1994): 6.

[78] *Ibid.*

[79] *Ibid.*

[80] "Year in Review," *Ethos*, First Quarter (1994): 7.

[81] "Key points of speech by DPM Lee," 14 October 1993.

talks entitled 'Reflections at Raffles'. These were 'fire-side' chats with senior leaders of the Public Service, created as a platform to allow the younger Administrative Service officers to meet and learn from the experiences of their 'elders'.[82] Held at Raffles Hotel, hence the series' title, these sessions were styled in an informal setting to encourage dialogue.

'New Insights Lecture Series' sought to keep the Public Service's leadership corps informed of external developments pertinent to their work. It featured speakers like the Chief Secretaries of the Malaysian and Hong Kong governments, and leading thinkers such as Peter Senge who spoke on 'Learning Organisation'.[83] In conjunction with Canada's Institute On Governance, the CSC also ran a "Transforming Public Sector Leadership" workshop involving participants from Southeast Asia and Canada.[84] These CSC programmes — while furthering training objectives — were also used as platforms for fostering relations with foreign civil services and governments.

In 1994, a year after its inauguration, the CSC published *Ethos*. Mahbubani introduced the periodical as a platform for communicating with the CSC's stakeholders: "To reach out to our constituency, we will need a vehicle for communication."[85] Contents focused on reports of the CSC events, such as "milestones programmes", seminars, and lectures. There was usually an article on the "latest issues and politics challenging Singapore's public sector" in each issue, with subjects ranging from budgeting to personnel management.[86] Like *Bakti* and *Management Development*, periodicals of earlier civil service training institutions, *Ethos* occasionally published speeches of ministers and interviews with

---

[82]"Reflections at Raffles," *Ethos*, Second Quarter (1994): 6. Speakers included serving and retired senior civil servants such as J. Y. Pillay, Dr. Andrew Chew, Ngiam Tong Dow, Dr. Kwa Soon Bee, etc.

[83]"New Insights Lecture Series," *Ethos*, Second Issue (1995): 11; "New Insights Lecture Series 1993–1999," *Ethos*, (July 1999): 15.

[84]"Year in Review," *Ethos*, First Quarter (1994): 7.

[85]Mahbubani, "Foreword," *Ethos*, First Quarter (1994): 3–4.

[86]"A Step in the Right Direction," *Ethos*, First Quarter (1994): 11–12; "A look at the Civil Service Personnel Management System," *Ethos*, Second Quarter (1994): 13–15; "A look at the changes to the Administrative staff appraisal system," *Ethos*, First Issue (1995): 13–14.

leaders in the bureaucracy.[87] Unlike *Bakti, Ethos* did not replicate articles from newspapers or other journals. Unlike *Management Development, Ethos* did not publish academically formatted essays. In all purposes, *Ethos* was arguably more a corporate newsletter reporting on the CSC and Public Service activities, as this was the role defined for it.

5.6 Heralding Change, Preparing for Change

In June 1994, the entire Public Service Division was transferred from the Finance Ministry to the direct jurisdiction of the Prime Minister's Office.[88] The government was evidently increasing its attention to the management of public officers, including their training and development, with the Civil Service College and Civil Service Institute remaining under the PSD.[89]

Changes at the broad bureaucracy-level also percolated to the CSC. Around the same time, Kishore Mahbubani was promoted to Permanent Secretary at the Ministry of Foreign Affairs, where he had been serving concurrently to his Dean of the CSC portfolio. At the same time, rotations involving the senior leadership of the Public Service Division would affect the future direction of the CSC. Mahbubani recounted the confluence of factors:

> Once I became Perm Sec, I really wanted to focus on MFA. It was very difficult to be Perm Sec and Dean at the same time. So I handed over. And there was a new [Permanent Secretary, Public Service Division, and eventually] Head Civil Service, Lim Siong Guan. Andrew Chew [preceding Permanent Secretary of PSD and Head of Civil Service] was prepared to leave the CSC alone and say: 'You do whatever you want to do.' He didn't bother me. Siong Guan had a much more clearly defined vision for Civil Service College. So he wanted a Dean that he could work with full time, not a part-time Dean. So he switched and got Soo Hoon."[90]

Staff changes involving the CSC began taking place incrementally, like chess-pieces lining up for a masterful game-changer. In the first

---

[87] For example, "Equipping Tomorrow's Public Sector Leaders," *Ethos*, First Quarter (1994): 9–10; "Interview with Andrew Chew," *Ethos* Second Quarter (1994): 9–12.
[88] *SAR* 1995: 49.
[89] *SAR* 1995: 48–49; *Directory*, July 1994: 715–723.
[90] Mahbubani, Interview with Author, 20 June 2012.

instance, Miss Lim Soo Hoon, an Administrative Service officer, was posted into CSC as Deputy Dean and this allowed Peter Ong to be take up another posting in the Public Service as part of his AO rotation.[91] Another AO, Zee Yong Kang, replaced Patricia Lam as Assistant Dean in the same exercise. In July 1995, Mahbubani relinquished his CSC appointment to concentrate on heading the Foreign Affairs Ministry, and Lim Soo Hoon succeeded as the Dean of the CSC (*see* Table 5.4).[92]

In her first address as Dean, Lim Soo Hoon immediately positioned the Civil Service College as an agent of change: "*As an agent of change for the Civil Service, CSC* is at the forefront of the efforts to create the Public Service for the 21st Century."[93] The Public Service for the 21st Century, abbreviated as PS21, was the set of reforms initiated by the Committee of Permanent Secretaries in May 1995.[94] With a broader aim of keeping Singapore competitive as the country became a developed economy, PS21 sought to orientate the bureaucracy towards a culture of

Table 5.4: Civil Service College, 1995[95]

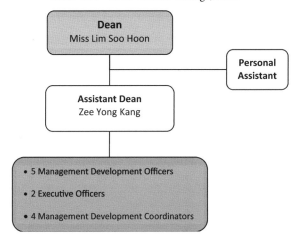

---

[91]"Staff Update," *Ethos*, First Issue (1995): 16; *ST* 16 September 1995: 34.
[92]Ms Lim Soo Hoon, Dean, Civil Service College, "Foreword," *Ethos*, Second Issue (1995): 2.
[93]Lim Soo Hoon, "Foreword," *Ethos*, Second Issue (1995): 2. Emphasis mine.
[94]"Public Service for the 21st Century," *Ethos*, Second Issue (1995): 9–10.
[95]*Directory*, January 1996: 649.

"service excellence" and "continuous change for greater efficiency and effectiveness".[96]

Among the series of follow-up measures was the target for every Public Service employee to receive 12.5 days of annual training by the year 2000. This obviously necessitated mobilising the bureaucracy's training institutions. Indeed, within six months of Lim Soo Hoon taking over the CSC, announcements were made that the Public Service's training centres would be reorganised.[97] The CSC was renamed the Institute of Policy Development, and merged with an Institute of Public Administration and Management, renamed from the Civil Service Institute. The new central training institution that emerged was named Civil Service College, with Miss Lim Soo Hoon as Dean. This reorganisation of the CSC and CSI into the new Civil Service College is discussed in the next chapter.

5.7 Conclusion

The Civil Service College, from its formal inception in 1993 to its reorganisation in 1996, was paradoxically the shortest training initiative in the history of the Singapore Public Service, yet it was the most significant in the growth of training and development in that bureaucracy. The CSC finally brought to realisation a meaningful leadership development centre for the Administrative Service leadership corps after decades of futile experimentation.

In the evolution of training and development, the Civil Service College was a progression in the Singapore bureaucracy's use of training for reforms. Its focus on leadership development and preparing the Public Service for the future sought to build up the strategic capacity of the bureaucracy. Compared with the Political Study Centre producing a dependable bureaucracy and the STI and the CSI equipping public officers with technical competencies, this was a step-up advancement in the continuum of executive development and training in the Singapore Public Service.

---

[96]Lim Siong Guan, "The Public Service," *Singapore: The Year in Review 1995*, ed. in Yeo Lay Hwee (Singapore: Institute of Policy Studies, 1996) 36–37. Also, SAR 1997: 53.
[97]*ST* 28 February 1996: 23; *Business Times* 28 February 1996: 2

From the perspective of the Public Service, the impetus for the Civil Service College, besides raising a dedicated leadership development institute, was the imperative of fostering the values and *élan* that epitomised the Singapore Public Service. From the perspective of the state, a new generation of People's Action Party leaders saw the CSC as necessary to inculcate within the AOs the political acumen and finesse required to formulate and implement public policies. From its conception, thus, *the Civil Service College was envisioned as a point to introduce reforms into the leadership corps of the bureaucracy.*

The realisation of the CSC highlighted the importance of strong political support for the development of training initiatives in the bureaucracy. Besides empowering it to overcome influential detractors, the strong political support allowed a very deliberate selection of the team of AOs whose vision and competence helped set up the CSC. Kishore Mahbubani, Peter Ong, Patricia Lam, and the very small team that made up the CSC at that time deserved credit for their dogged determination in overcoming resistance towards the CSC proposal and for germinating the ideas giving rise to the "milestones programmes". However, reflecting upon their roles, Mahbubani took a long view: "[This was] phase one, I was just foundational, Peter Ong and I were just foundational, putting in place the people, processes, organisation and so on and so forth."[98] More critically, in Mahbubani's opinion, the most important factor in setting up the CSC — indeed for saving the CSC from still-birth — was the high level of political attention accorded to the CSC: "[then-DPM Lee Hsien Loong] took a personal interest, like in the LAP. He was personally interested in checking everything."[99] Peter Ong elaborated on the importance of political attention in helping CSC's programmes:

> ...[then-DPM Lee] himself went through development in milestone programmes in SAF. So he understood what it meant to get Air Force, Army, and Navy to work together, to have a shared sense of *esprit de corps*. When he was Minister for MTI [Ministry of Trade and Industry], we took policies of different agencies and put it together and said that all these required collective sense of understanding, what is micro-economic efficiency of policies, and then reviewing each one across different agencies. So what we

---

[98] Mahbubani, Interview with Author, 20 June 2012.
[99] *Ibid.*

saw in his thinking of CSC reflected his own experiences through the SAF and his own experiences of policy review across the whole-of-government — we never used 'Whole-of-Government' at that time. So he felt something was needed. And he personally chose many of the case studies.[100]

Indeed, a particularly prominent factor in the genesis and development of the CSC and its programmes was the high level of political support devoted to it.

Finally, the most significant accomplishment of the CSC was not just the production of a set of leadership development programmes, but in the enduring timelessness of this framework. For the first time in the history of the Singapore Public Service, there was a comprehensive set of training programmes at various stages in the career progression of the Administrative Service and senior officers. Although it inherited the Foundation Course from the Civil Service Institute, the CSC conceptualised and launched two additional courses — the Senior Management Programme for mid-career officers and Leaders in Administration Programme for senior officers. More important than drawing up these individual courses was the CSC threading together all three programmes into a coherent suite of development interventions that matched the career progression of the AOs. The timelessness of this framework developed by the CSC is demonstrated by the continued usage of these "milestones programmes" in leadership development by the present-day Civil Service College.

The new Civil Service College, resulting from the centralisation of the CSC and Civil Service Institute in 1996 to harness training as a point of introducing the Public Service for the 21st Century reforms, is the subject of the next chapter.

---

[100]Peter Ong, Interview with Author, 6 June 2012.

Chapter 6

Instrument for Reforms: Aligning the Civil Service College for PS21 (1996–2001)

In April 1996, the two existing central training schools of the Singapore Public Service underwent a major reorganisation. The leadership development centre set up in 1993 as the Civil Service College was renamed the Institute of Policy Development; the Civil Service Institute became the Institute of Public Administration and Management.[1] Both institutes were then subsumed under a new Civil Service College. Within four years, the CSC would be further restructured and detached out of the civil service to become a self-financing statutory board.

This chapter shows that the series of organisational changes involving the Civil Service College were a consolidation of the various training functions into a focal point to introduce administrative reforms. The series of restructuring seemed like a myriad of relabelling of the training schools, but in reality, these were part of a broader strategy to align the training institutions to support the reforms agenda. This started off by centralising the different training functions into an umbrella Civil Service College in preparing the transition into the next phase of the strategy. Following on was a controlled experiment, essentially, to compel the alignment of training programmes towards the reforms agenda, by introducing market principles into an institute. The success of this trial emboldened the leadership of the Public Service to then detach the CSC from the Civil Service, and convert it into a self-financing statutory board.

---

[1] *ST* 28 February 1996: 23; *Business Times* 28 February 1996: 2.

Thus, rather than a seemingly arbitrary or piece-meal restructuring of the training institutions, the various changes in names and structures were in fact set-pieces on a chess-board, building up towards the goal of setting up the CSC as a statutory board. However, that was not an end-goal by itself; the ultimate objective of turning the CSC into a statutory board was to orientate the training functions to support the agenda for administrative reforms.

Thus, this chapter argues that the organisational changes between 1996 and 2001 were part of a grand strategy to shape the Civil Service College into a focal point for introducing reforms across the Singapore Public Service.

6.1 PS21: The Emerging Bureaucratic Context

The reorganisation of the central training schools of the Singapore Public Service in 1996 was driven by broader developments in the bureaucratic context, specifically PS21. Launched in May 1995, "Public Service for the 21st Century" was a series of long-term reforms. According to Lim Siong Guan, Permanent Secretary in the Prime Minister's Office, the objectives of PS21 were:

> To nurture an attitude of service excellence... [and] foster an environment which induces and welcomes continuous change for greater efficiency and effectiveness [with the ultimate outcome] a Public Service always on the lookout for improvement, for better ways of doing things, questioning if it should carry on doing what it is doing, asking what else it should be doing.[2]

PS21 coincided with the wave of administrative reforms sweeping across the world in the 1990s: 'small government', decentralisation, and application of private sector managerial techniques on public administration, i.e., New Public Management. The official account of the Singapore bureaucracy noted that "devolution — the loosening of central controls — was a key theme for the Public Service throughout the 1990s."[3] However, in an interview for this study, Lim Siong Guan

---

[2] Lim Siong Guan, "The Public Service," *Singapore: The Year in Review 1995*, ed. Yeo Lay Hwee (Singapore: Institute of Policy Studies, 1996) 37.
[3] Chua (2010) 167.

distinguished PS21 by its quest for 'excellence':

> The whole impetus for PS21 has nothing to do with the idea of 'small government' and so forth. However, there's a lot we learnt.... the things that happened in the times of Thatcher, we studied them a lot. They are good ideas on what can be done to improve efficiency and effectiveness. The most fundamental idea of all [with PS21] is this idea that it is not good enough to be efficient, it is not good enough to look for effectiveness.
>
> There is this whole concept of 'excellence' — and 'excellence' is being the best that you can be, it's a never-ending journey, being the best that you can be — which to me is a different paradigm than just 'efficiency' and 'effectiveness'. I think most of the time when we talk about what happened with 'small government', they are very much confined to the idea of 'efficiency' and 'effectiveness'.[4]

Although the Singapore Public Service was known for its "competence, efficiency, and integrity" by the 1990s, there were areas that needed improvement:

> ...reducing the dependence on rules and precedents in making decisions, fostering a more open attitude to change and innovation, greater empowerment at the lower levels of the Public Service, more emphasis upon performance and outputs to ensure higher quality services, and making public servants in dealing with the public more flexible, courteous and helpful.[5]

Indeed, Lim Siong Guan, who came to be regarded as the chief advocate of PS21, was conscious that the Singapore Public Service should neither rest on its laurels nor be lured into a sense of complacency:

> The reason why the motto [for PS21] was 'Be in time for the future', was because of this sense that the Singapore Public Service already had such a high standing worldwide, it had a high standing for efficiency and competence and integrity. So if everybody in the world say, 'You are already so good,' and the people in the Service therefore also say, 'We are already so good,' then how do we move our people to be thinking about how can we be better?
>
> That's why the motto came out to be 'Just in time for the future.' It is to say, 'Who of you can claim we are good enough for the future?' The future is unknowable, the future is uncertain? And so, who in the Service,

---

[4]Lim Siong Guan, Permanent Secretary (Prime Minister's Office), 1994–1998, Interview with Author, 20 November 2013.
[5]David Seth Jones, "Public Service for the 21st Century — PS21," *Everyday Life, Everyday People*, eds. Chua Fook Kee and Thana Luxshme Thaver (Singapore: Ministry of Education and National University of Education, 1997) 76.

not even the political leadership, can claim to know? And that's why the motto is 'Be in time for the future.' The idea of PS21 is to be able to work in that future and that future is really what we are prepared to imagine, visualise, take initiative, try out and hence, the whole idea about engaging people and imagining the future.[6]

In spite of the already stellar accomplishments of the Singapore bureaucracy, this need for further reforms was recognised by the Committee of Permanent Secretaries — the apex leadership body of the Public Service — which threw its support behind PS21.[7] The operating milieu of the Singapore Public Service, in any case, was already evolving: "[F]irst, a public that is increasingly demanding higher standards of service, and second, an economy that is increasingly outward-oriented."[8]

6.1.1 *The political dimension*

Even though it was a project of the bureaucracy, the political dimension of PS21 cannot be missed. With the Public Service often regarded by the population as 'the government' — everyday citizens do not bother with the legal distinctions between the political leadership and the career bureaucrats in daily discourse — a Public Service that could not measure up to the citizenry's growing demands could have repercussions upon the ruling People's Action Party.

The dipping electoral fortunes of the PAP had led to a framing of the development–democratisation discourse upon Singapore, as discussed in the previous chapter. After its share of electoral votes fell through the 1980s, the PAP suffered its worst-ever performance at the 1991 General Elections.[9] Development-democratisation theorists inevitably wondered if Singapore was heading the way of Taiwan, Korea, Thailand, and the Philippines.[10] The developmental-state, i.e., state-led rapid

---

[6]Lim Siong Guan, Interview with Author, 20 November 2013.
[7]Saxena (2011) 89 also highlighted the 'high-level' structures set up to support and implement PS21, such as Functional Committees and a PS21 Office set up within the Public Service Division.
[8]Lim Siong Guan (1996) 36.
[9]Quah (1989) 9; Mauzy and Milne (2002) 150; Yap, Lim and Leong (2009) 446; Mutalib (1992) 71–72; Singh (1992) 2–34.
[10]Rodan (1993) 52; Hewison, Rodan and Robison (1993) 2–3; Anek (1997) 15–16; Heng (1997) 135.

economic development as espoused by Chalmers Johnson, had expanded a middle class whose rising educational levels and affluence were leading them to seek greater participatory roles in the political system. While the development-democratisation nexus unfolded in several East Asian Newly-Industrialising Countries, scholars refrained from plotting the trajectory of Singapore.

The PAP leadership was naturally not unaffected by its electoral performance, whether or not they were informed of the development–democratisation theory. Political considerations evidently figured in the ruling party's interactions with the bureaucracy in the aftermath of the 1991 polls. The political leadership certainly felt that there were occasions when the government's "most well-meaning policy" was undermined by civil servants taking the "clinical view" in the implementation stage.[11] Part of the *raison d'être* in setting up the Civil Service College in 1993 was to sharpen the political acumen of the Administrative Service leadership echelons of the Public Service.

With a focus on greater efficiency and effectiveness in policymaking and service delivery, PS21 could not be divorced from the political context at that time. While it was an initiative of the Public Service, PS21's drive to raise service standards among public officers could reasonably be expected to also aim at arresting further electoral slippage, following the 1991 electoral setback.

However, Lim Siong Guan, who led PS21 clarified that PS21 was wholly a project of the Public Service; the political leadership did not play any part in the administrative reforms. In an interview for this study, Lim explained that:

> We [the Public Service] never cleared the [PS21] initiative with the political leadership. I took a position like this: political leadership makes policy decision, PS21 is about delivery. 'How well do you deliver policy?' That's a specific, to my mind, a specific responsibility of the Public Service. It's got nothing to do with the political leadership, that's why it was never cleared with the political leadership.
>
> Basically, to my mind it's like this, there's no need to ask for permission for these things. You are doing something which is good, you are doing something which is your responsibility, you are doing something which

---

[11]Ong Teng Cheong (1992) 18. Also, "Speech by the Prime Minister, Mr Goh Chok Tong", at the Third Administrative Service Dinner, 5 July 1991.

intends to really raise the capabilities of the Public Service and raise the standards as well as the achievement and capabilities of Singapore, why do you need to ask for permission, just carry on.

   To be quite frank, I took the position that PS21 is the responsibility of the Civil Service. [12]

6.1.2 *PS21 and the review of training in the public service*

PS21 was "the most comprehensive administrative reform to be introduced in Singapore." [13] Indeed, PS21 is a topic deserving dedicated study [14] but to provide a brief context for the current discussion, PS21 constituted four focal areas:

- staff well-being, focusing on the individual public officer;
- service quality, focusing on the customer, i.e., the citizenry;
- Work Improvement Teams (WITs) and Staff Suggestion Schemes (SSS), focusing on developing officers towards an attitude of continuous improvement; and
- organisational review, focusing on structuring government agencies towards strategic improvements. [15]

   Most of these initiatives were already operating for several years. WITS, for example, started in the 1980s. Hence, PS21 was really "an extension of existing schemes and campaigns". [16] However, the combined

---

[12]Lim Siong Guan, Interview with Author, 20 November 2013.

[13]Quah (2010) 147. However, John Burns, "Explaining Civil Service Reforms in Asia," *The Civil Service in the 21st Century: Comparative Perspectives*, eds. Jos C. N. Raadschelders, Theo A. J. Toonen & Frits M. Von der Meer (Hampshire & New York: Palgrave Macmillan, 2007) 76 countered that PS21 "achieved few measurable results."

[14]In his interview for this study, Lim Siong Guan pointed out that PS21 cannot be taken in isolation; PS21 is tightly linked with two other initiatives: Scenario Planning and Currently Estimated Potential. Scenario Planning explores future challenges facing Singapore and capacities needed in the face of these scenarios. Currently Estimated Potential, apart from developing civil servants to their fullest potential, helps to identify talented officers and develop them in preparation for leadership positions. Lim Siong Guan, Interview with Author, 20 November 2013.

[15]A summary of the four areas is found in Saxena (2011) 89, and Commonwealth Secretariat, *Current Good Practices and New Developments in Public Service Management: A Profile of the Public Service of Singapore* (London: Commonwealth Secretariat, 1998) 21.

[16]Prime Minister's Office, 1995, p. 2, quoted in Quah (2010) 147.

effects of these concurrent efforts under the PS21 banner, and the main thrust of PS21, were to improve the quality of public services delivered to the citizenry.

A parallel emphasis of PS21 was in the area of training, which relates directly to this study. Training was recognised as a medium to improve the quality of public services: "Mr Lim Siong Guan . . . believed that people development was a very important part of raising the professionalism of the Public Service."[17] Lim himself, the architect of PS21, centred the subject of training within the context of the reforms in a fitting metaphor:

> . . . if you see the [civil servant] standing on a platform, around him are the demands of the public and . . . you need to serve them with quality service. At the same time, he's under continuous pressure from the top, from his bosses, on how to improve the organisation, and for want of a better word, we use the term, Organisational Review. So, you look at this guy, and he's being squashed, he's being squashed from the side, he's being squashed from the top.
>
> So, we say, 'How do we develop his muscles? How do we make him strong enough to be able to handle this?' And that idea was EXCEL — Excellence through Continuous Enterprise and Learning. The way to develop his muscles was to build up his competency, build up his skills-level, most of all, build up his confidence. And confidence is built up by doing stuff, and succeeding. That's why we have continuous enterprise. Try, learn, succeed.[18]

Lim Siong Guan, as Permanent Secretary in charge of the Public Service Division and hence responsible for personnel matters in the Public Service, set "the target of delivering 12.5 days of training per year for each employee by the year 2000, partly to improve the quality of public service, and partly to enhance the long term employability of public servants"[19] This 12.5 days, or 100 hours, of training was a five-fold increase in the commitment towards training, until then averaging 2.8 days.[20] Ms Lim Soo Hoon, who would play a critical part in the Public Service's use of training to introduce reforms, elaborated: "[W]hat to

---

[17]Lim Soo Hoon, Dean, Civil Service College, 1995–1998, Interview with Author, 15 June 2012

[18]Lim Siong Guan, Interview with Author, 20 November 2013.

[19]Lim Siong Guan (1996) 38.

[20]*ST* 28 February 1996: 23.

me was important about the policy was that, first, the signal that you believe in it, that it was an entitlement. That meant your boss cannot say: 'I can't spare you [to go for training].' Everyone has a right to go for training."[21]

As part of the PS21 reforms, a review of training was initiated. At that point in time, the two central training schools were the Civil Service Institute and the Civil Service College. The CSC, with Kishore Mahbubani as Dean, was responsible for training the Administrative Service leadership of the Public Service, as described in the preceding chapter. According to Ms Lim Soo Hoon, "the original CSC, was more like a think-tank. Whereas Mr Lim [Siong Guan's] was a more practise-oriented approach... introduce policy development, introduce training on policy." Around this time, Mahbubani was promoted to the position of Permanent Secretary at the Ministry of Foreign Affairs:

> Once I became Perm Sec, I really wanted to focus on MFA. It was very difficult to be Perm Sec and Dean at the same time.... And there was a new Head Civil Service [*sic*] Lim Siong Guan. Andrew Chew was prepared to leave the CSC alone and say: 'You do whatever you want to do.' He didn't bother me. Siong Guan had a much more clearly defined vision for Civil Service College. So he wanted a Dean that he could work with full time, not a part-time Dean. So he switched and got Soo Hoon."[22]

In March 1995, Ms Lim Soo Hoon was posted into the CSC as Deputy Dean, allowing incumbent Peter Ong to take up another assignment as part of his Administrative Service rotation. Within four months, Ms Lim succeeded Kishore Mahbubani as Dean. Almost immediately, Lim Soon Hoon began positioning the CSC "at the forefront of the efforts to create the Public Service for the 21st Century",[23] launched just two months earlier.

The other central institution at that time was the Civil Service Institute. In the 1990s, the CSI had more than 100 programmes annually

---

[21]Lim Soo Hoon, Interview with Author, 15 June 2012.
[22]Mahbubani, Interview with Author, 20 June 2012. Lim Siong Guan was appointed Head of the Civil Service in 1999; at that point in time in 1995, Lim Siong Guan was Permanent Secretary of the Public Service Division.
[23]Lim Soo Hoon, "Foreword," *Ethos*, Second Issue (1995): 2.

catering to 22% of the bureaucracy, as an earlier chapter detailed.[24] However, a predominantly rank-and-file clientele resulted in the CSI's image as a broad-based training school.[25] "Those who wanted a little bit more, I supposed a little bit more sophisticated, more branded training," Lim Soo Hoon remembered, "they would probably go outside CSI."[26]

Yet, for the Public Service to achieve its PS21 aim of providing every public officer with 100 hours of annual training, the bulk of these training would undoubtedly have to be undertaken by the CSI. Evidently, while PS21 was being conceptualised, plans were also underway to level up the training institutions to meet PS21 aspirations. Ms Lim recounted, "When I moved up, Mr Lim [Siong Guan] said he wanted to consolidate training. He gave me the task of merging the old CSI with the new animal called CSC... So when I joined, I was given the task of merging CSI and CSC." [27]

6.2 The New Civil Service College —'Diverge, Then Converge'

6.2.1 *Consolidation of training functions*

On 1 April 1996, a new Civil Service College was thus established under the Public Service Division, which in turn was within the purview of the Prime Minister's Office.[28] This reporting line, similar with those of preceding central training schools, continued to locate training and development as a subject within the personnel management portfolio, and a matter of high-level attention to the government.

The new CSC, with Ms Lim Soo Hoon as Dean, consolidated the existing training institutions under its ambit (*see* Table 6.1). The Institute of Policy Development continued with leadership development among

---

[24]The average Civil Service establishment in the 1990s was 90,245. *Training Programme 1990/91*: iii; *Training Programme 1991/92*: 1; *Training Programme 1994/95*: 1; *Budget FY1995/96*: 81; *Budget FY1997/98*: 66.
[25]John Ewing-Chow, Interview with Author, 11 June 2012; Tan Boon Huat, Interview with Author, 14 January 2013.
[26]Lim Soo Hoon, Interview with Author, 15 June 2012.
[27]*Ibid.*
[28]*Directory, July 1996*: 683–695; IPAM, *Training Directory 1997/98* (Singapore: IPAM, 1997) iii.

Table 6.1: Structure of the Civil Service College, 1996[29]

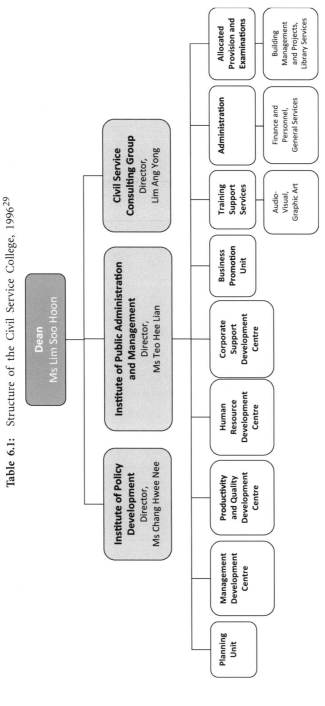

[29]*Directory, July 1996*: 690–695. Organisational units arranged left to right according to the sequence they were presented in the original documents.

the Administrative Service senior echelons of the Public Service. The Institute of Public Administration and Management, with Ms Teo Hee Lian remaining as Director, continued with the training of the broader Public Service. A Civil Service Consulting Group (CSCG) was created to provide training consultancy services to government agencies.

The restructuring appeared to have been well-thought through in advance. Lim Soo Hoon, the newly-appointed Dean, explained:

> ...the structure is important to support the policy... [because] you signalled to everyone, individuals as well as the bosses, that training was critical. And then we were very clear about different segments of people who needed to be trained. What were the capability-gaps that we needed to fill? So those were the early days, and the structure was important to make sure that you have people dedicated to focusing on different areas.[30]

However, before the newly-reorganised CSC could fully support PS21 reforms, some housekeeping was necessary — harmonising the various training institutes into a common CSC organisational culture. In particular, the IPAM staff were reeling from what they perceived as the relegation of their institute into the shadow of the IPD. Since the latter's establishment in 1993 as the then-Civil Service College, the IPAM in its earlier permutation as the CSI had to cede its leadership programmes and then its premises to the newer Civil Service College. Ms Teo Hee Lian, then-CSI Director, recalled: "we were seen as not compatible.... we were just told make way [for the new College]."[31] When the reorganisation was mooted, CSI staff did not understand why their institute with a longer history and larger staff complement should be subsumed under the name of a smaller Civil Service College. The rationale was not a deliberate favouring of the leadership centre, according to Lim Soo Hoon, who was tasked with the reorganisation:

> The real reason was because CSI had baggage.... CSI was doing all these broad-based training, the levels of people they were covering, Super-scale [apex grades] all the way to Division 4. There was a certain baggage, certain brand name.... If we still called it CSI, people would still have the perception

---

[30]Lim Soo Hoon, Interview with Author, 15 June 2012.
[31]Teo Hee Lian, Director, CSI and IPAM, 1989–1998, Interview with Author, 3 January 2012.

that it was the same thing. So, we had to refresh it, rebrand it. And we thought that CSC was a very good name.[32]

Looking back, more time to consult with staff could have generated wider acceptance for the changes. However, time was a luxury that Ms Lim could not afford:

> ...when I did this first merger, I mean, that was probably one of my first experiences doing something like that. Of course, on hindsight now, we can say, I could have handled it better, I could have done this, and I could have done that. But one of the problems I had then was there was no assurance how long I would be there for. And I think this is one of the biggest problems that AOs sometimes faced, we move from place to place. And sometimes people will be quite cynical: 'You guys come and shake up the place, change, change, change. And before the thing is over, you guys just disappear and leave the mess behind for other people to clear up.'[33]

Lim wanted to see through the changes, and to avoid leaving the CSC and its staff in a lurch.

In any case, the CSC's restructuring was not an end in itself but to get the training institutions ready to serve PS21 reforms. The reorganisation could be formalised overnight on 1 April 1996, but to realise the necessary changes — including training activities — required time. The inventory of courses disseminated among public officers that year continued to be issued in the name of the Civil Service Institute; *Training Programme 1996/97* contained no indications of the organisational changes concerning it.[34] A new section of courses, compared with previous years' training directory, made reference to PS21 but most were existing courses rearranged under the PS21 headline. In the one year since the launch of PS21, only two new dedicated PS21 courses were developed.[35]

6.2.2 *Aligning training for reforms*

The changes intended by the CSC's restructuring began to show a year later. While less apparent on the surface, changes in the Institute of

---

[32]Lim Soo Hoon, Interview with Author, 15 June 2012.
[33]*Ibid.*
[34]*Training Programme 1996/97.*
[35]*Ibid*: x, compared with *Training Programme 1994/95*: 6 and 8.

Policy Development were crucial. The IPD continued its "milestones programmes" for the Administrative Service but the curriculum had a new emphasis.[36] Lim Siong Guan, who as Permanent Secretary of the Public Service Division oversaw the bureaucracy's personnel and the CSC, saw the IPD playing a critical role beyond developing the leadership corps, in forging a 'Coordinated Vision' among the leaders of the Public Service:

> ... what we required is what I called 'Coordinated Vision'. As opposed to what people generally talked about 'Coordinated Action', to try to coordinate the activities of various ministries and all that. I didn't consider that to be the primary need; I considered the primary need to be 'Coordinated Vision'. In other words, can the people across all the ministries and stat [statutory] boards, do we have a common idea of the kind of challenges Singapore faces, the kinds of opportunities that we can use, and a vision therefore of what Singapore wants to get to and what we can be. And the Admin Service plays a primary role, not just the Admin Service, really the senior leadership of the public sector all across, the CEOs of statutory boards, everybody plays an important factor in this. And to me that was the critical goal of the IPD.[37]

The realignment of the Institute of Public Administration and Management with PS21 reforms was most pronounced. A new Director of the IPAM, David Ma, was appointed following the retirement of Ms Teo Hee Lian. However, what was more significant was his direct linkage with PS21 reforms: Ma was concurrently Head of the PS21 Office (PSO) at the Public Service Division. Overseeing PS21 initiatives across the bureaucracy in that capacity, Ma was posted into the CSC as part of the plans to align training with PS21:

> ... since I was familiar with PS21, because I was then ... Head of the PSO, Mr Lim [Siong Guan] said, 'Since we needed to make training to support PS21', I was put in as Deputy Head of the Civil Service Consulting ... when Hee Lian retired, I just took over. I supposed the reason why I was posted there, people expect that this fellow is going to take over. The whole idea was to support PS21.[38]

[36]"Courses Update," *Ethos* (January 1997): 17.
[37]Lim Siong Guan, Interview with Author, 20 November 2013.
[38]David Ma, Interview with Author, 8 March 2013. Also *Directory July 1996*: 689

Among the IPAM's adjustments to support PS21 was a Training Framework that mirrored the PS21 Training Initiative. More significant than offering relevant training to public officers at various stages of their careers were aims beyond officers' current work needs:

Induction: This is to introduce the officer to the job and his work environment upon joining the service.

Basic: This is training to enable the officer to perform his job adequately. It is given whenever an officer is recruited or given a new job.

Advanced: This is additional training to enable the officer to give superior performance on his current job.

Extended: This is further training to enable the officer to go beyond his current job to be able to handle related jobs on an incidental basis or higher-level jobs in due course.

Continuing: This is training that is not immediately related to the officer's current job but enhances his employability over the long-term.[39]

At every career stage, the IPAM developed "five groups of generic competence":

'**Managing service excellence**' courses help the individual understand the importance of quality management and service excellence and equip him with the tools and techniques to do an excellent job.

'**Managing change**' courses help the individual develop a positive attitude to change and equip him with the skills to manage it.

'**Managing/working with people**' courses develop the individual's ability to better gain the cooperation and commitment of his colleagues.

'**Managing operations and resources**' courses provide the individual with the necessary tools and techniques to manage his work unit effectively and efficiently.

'**Managing self**' courses help build the individual's confidence in himself and increase his effectiveness — both inside and outside his job functions.[40]

---

[39]Commonwealth Secretariat 39. Compare with *Training Directory, 1997–1998*: iv.

[40]*Training Directory, 1997–1998*: iv. This was the handiwork of Tina Tan, IPAM senior manager, and another IPAM staff. Tina Tan, Senior Manager, IPAM, circa 1997, Interview with Author, 31 October 2013.

The resultant matrix of lateral competencies cutting across every stage of the officers' career progression would thus guide the IPAM in drawing up programmes to support PS21.

6.2.3 *'Diverge, then converge': expansion of training programmes to meet PS21*

With a reforms-framework to guide course development, the training programmes began to align with PS21. As a benchmark, in 1996, the then-CSI only developed two PS21-related courses and rearranged some existing programmes under the PS21 tagline (*see* Table 6.2). A year after reorganisation into the IPAM, the number of PS21-linked courses increased slightly to 15 (*see* Table 6.3). Their proportion to the overall number of courses — including regular staples such as management and supervisory training, vocational and functional skills — remained the same. However, the IPAM had increased its total course-offerings by 17% to 177 courses, training 20,000 officers or about one-third of all civil servants.[41] Training Officer, Ms Ngiam Su Wei, remembered that the IPAM was "introducing many different training programmes,

Table 6.2: PS21 and Regular Courses offered by CSI, 1996[42]

1996	Division I	Division II	Division III	Division IV	Total	
Regular Courses	78	35	25	2	140	
Management Training	73	—	—	—		
Staff Training	—	30	20	2		
IT	5	5	5	—		
PS21 Courses	8	4	2	—	13	8.5%
Total					153	

---

[41] *Training Directory, 1997–1998*: i; *Budget FY1998/99*: 64. There were 62,963 civil servants at that time.

[42] Table computed from CSI, *Training Programme 1996/97*. Regular courses refer to those core training programmes pertaining to management training, supervisory training, vocational and functional skills, which were non-PS21 specific training. The total number of courses may be less than the sum of courses in each Division as some courses were targeted at officers across several Divisions.

Inception Point

Table 6.3: PS21 and Regular Courses offered by IPAM, 1997[43]

1997	Division I	Division II	Division III	Division IV	Total	
Regular Courses	**93**	**40**	**29**	**1**	**162**	
Managing Service Excellence	15	7	8			
Managing Change	10	2	1			
Managing People	34	15	6			
Managing Operations and Resources	14	3	3			
Managing Self	19	14	7			
COSEC			5			
Graduate Diploma	1					
PS21 Courses	**7**	**4**	**4**		**15**	**8.5%**
Total					**177**	

just to ramp up...I saw a surge in terms of the numbers [in order to cater to the PS21 target of] 100 training hours."[44] The IPAM also began framing its courses according to the competency-career stages matrix developed to support the PS21 goals of cultivating attitudes of service excellence and continuous change among public officers.

By 1998, PS21-courses increased to 25 (*see* Table 6.4). Although their proportion to the total IPAM courses dipped slightly to 7%, this actually highlighted the very substantial increase in the IPAM's regular programmes to 352 courses. The IPAM was also aiming to accommodate 45,000 trainees, or 69%, of the total 64,963 number of civil servants.[45] In 1999, the IPAM reported training 92,000 officers, technically reaching out to all 67,795 civil servants, with some returning as repeat customers.[46] By 2000, with the timeline for the PS21 goal of offering officers 100

---

[43] Table computed from *Training Directory, 1997–1998*.

[44] Ngiam Su Wei, Training Officer, IPAM, circa 1997, Interview with Author, 9 October 2013.

[45] *Training Directory, 1998:* ii; *Budget FY1998/99:* 64. With total number of civil servants rising slightly to 62,963, IPAM's 20,000 officers trained represented 32% of the Civil Service.

[46] *Training Directory, 2000:* ii; *Budget FY2000–2001:* 65.

Table 6.4: PS21 and Regular Courses offered by IPAM, 1998[47]

1998	Division I	Division II	Division III	Division IV	Total	
Regular Courses	131	109	73	14	327	
PS21 Courses	10	8	7		25	7.1%
Total					**352**	

Table 6.5: PS21 and Regular Courses offered by IPAM, 1999[48]

1999	Division I	Division II	Division III	Division IV	Total	
Regular Courses	**173**	**131**	**96**	**22**	**422**	
Managing Service Excellence	1					
Managing Change	14	5	3	2		
Leading/Working with People	75	51	39	3		
Managing Operations and Resources	48	45	28	12		
Managing Self	19	18	19	4		
PS21 Courses	**16**	**12**	**7**	**1.0**	**36**	**7.9%**
Total					**458**	

hours of annual training, the IPAM was able to increase the total number of course-offerings to 458 (*see* Table 6.5).

Indeed, these developments were in line with part of the broader strategy drawn up earlier. Mrs Tina Tan, an IPAM manager at that time, revealed that the spike in number of courses was planned out early in 1997:

> I had to write up the training paper where I had to project the training volume for five years, to 1.6 million training hours! I remember [asking], 'Huh! Mr Ma, how am I going to achieve 1.6 million!' Yeah, that was my target, to reach it in five years, from 1997.[49]

---

[47] Table computed from *Training Directory, 1998.*
[48] Table computed from *Training Directory, 2000.*
[49] Tina Tan, Interview with Author, 31 October 2013.

Presented with the opportunity, Mrs Tan quizzed the Permanent Secretary of the Public Service Division: "I had a conversation with Mr Lim Siong Guan. I said, 'We are doing all these things, don't know whether relevant or not.' Because we had to push up all these [training] hours!"[50] Once again, Lim's rather philosophical reply confirmed that these developments were a purposefully drawn-up plan in motion: "He [Lim Siong Guan] said, 'Never mind, now is the time to diverge, later we will converge.'"[51]

The tables of the IPAM courses between 1996 and 1999 above also highlighted the continued emphasis on senior levels of the hierarchy. Courses for Division 1 officers dominated the inventory. This was an extension of the long-standing policy since the inception of the Public Service of nurturing talented personnel. The weightier emphasis could also reflect the point-roles Division 1 officers were expected to play in leading PS21 reforms among staff across government agencies.

At the same time, the increase in course offerings was evident across all divisional levels, reflecting the efforts to be equitable in training opportunities. Courses for Division 2, for example, leapt to 109 in 1998 from 40 the previous year; while those for Division 3 jumped to 73 from 29. The exponential rise could be attributed to the small number of courses in earlier periods. However, it also pointed to new efforts to develop training opportunities for the broader rank-and-file of the Public Service hierarchy.

This exponential increase in the number of courses and capacity to accommodate so many officers in such a short period of three to four years was directly due to "12.5 [days of] annual training per [public] officer... reinforced upon us," according to one IPAM training officer at that time. In Rinkoo Ghosh's memories, "CSI to IPAM restructuring was pressure for us because LSG [Lim Siong Guan] said we need to offer training to ensure officers reach 12.5 days per year quota."[52] In other

---

[50] *Ibid.*

[51] *Ibid.*

[52] Rinkoo Ghosh, Training Officer, IPAM, circa 1997, email correspondence with Author, 15 September 2013.

words, PS21 reforms was the *raison d'être* for the rapid expansion in the IPAM's capacity to provide training across the Public Service.

6.2.4 *Injecting catalyst for change*

Amid the quantitative growth in programmes, David Ma, Director of IPAM, was conscious of the need to maintain the quality of the IPAM's training:

> The problem to me was, we can expand the courses but how do we know whether the courses are useful to people?...'How to make our courses more relevant, more useful?' So that when we expand, people would still say, 'I want to come because yours is useful to me.'[53]

Few options were available to monitor the standards of these courses, let alone improve their quality. Like many training institutions then, the IPAM was using course evaluations to gauge the quality of its courses.[54] Rather than objective measures, these were impressions by participants. To Donald Kirkpatrick, who researched the evaluation of training, this constituted "Reaction", which was the most basic of four levels of evaluation.[55] According to several training officers at that time, through end-of-course tests assessing whether learning had been internalised among participants, the IPAM could at most attain 'Level Two'.[56] Only in one programme was the IPAM able "to move from Smiles Sheet ['Level One', Reaction] to 'Level Three', Behaviour."[57] Examining the effects of training upon participants' behaviour at work and long-term job performance, 'Levels Three' and 'Four' were beyond the reach of the

---

[53] David Ma, Interview with Author, 8 March 2013.

[54] *Ibid.*

[55] These are Reaction, Learning, Behaviour and Results. Donald L. Kirkpatrick and James D. Kirkpatrick, *Evaluating Training Programmes: The Four Levels* (San Francisco: Berrett-Koehler Publishers, 2006) 21.

[56] Ghosh, email correspondence with Author, 15 September 2013; Ngiam Su Wei, email correspondence with Author, 14 October 2013.

[57] Level 1 evaluation, gauging the Reaction level of participants, are often referred to as 'Smiles Sheet', the implied reference was it seeks only to assess whether participants 'feel good'. IPAM was able to undertake Level 3 evaluation for a Learning Organisation programme because it spanned over a one-year period. Ghosh, email correspondence with Author, 15 September 2013.

IPAM.[58] With successive cohorts of public officers, the IPAM did not have the wherewithal to evaluate the large number of officers across government agencies three to six months after the end of their training. More important than the want of resources, the IPAM did not have the mandate to pursue a comprehensive evaluation across the bureaucracy.

In lieu of more practicable recourse, David Ma placed the IPAM on an Inter-Departmental Charging funding model (IDC). Until then, the central training schools — as departments within the bureaucracy — had always been funded by the government. With Inter-Departmental Charging, Ma was cutting off his own funding:

> I got the Ministry of Finance not to give us the money but to give that money to all the ministries...So instead of giving us the $10 million [for example, the Finance Ministry] would spread that $10 million among the civil servants.... we would organise courses, and we would charge the ministries for a fee.[59]

Transferring training budgets to the ministries also prodded them to be responsible for the training of their staff. Mylvaganam Logendran, a manager at the IPAM then, recalled that the previous practice left ministries and participants with the impression that training was 'free': "[P]eople when they felt like coming, they came; when they didn't feel like coming, they didn't come. That was not fair. You have a class here, you have to pay the trainers, you have the equipment, refreshment was based on the number of participants."[60] The Inter-Departmental Charging model, in contrast, made civil servants "understand that there's a cost to training."[61]

The risk while 'ring-fenced' was stark.[62] According to some IPAM officers at that time, although the central training budget was distributed among the ministries, the ministries' options were limited to spending the money for the IPAM courses or not to send their staff to the IPAM;

[58]David Ma, Interview with Author, 8 March 2013.
[59]*Ibid.* Also David Ma, email correspondence with Author, 16 September 2013.
[60]M. Logendran, Manager, IPAM, circa 1997, Interview with Author, 25 October 2013.
[61]Ngiam Su Wei, Interview with Author, 9 October 2013.
[62]Tina Tan, Interview with Author, 31 October 2013; Michelle Wong, Course Administrator, IPAM, circa 1997, Interview with Author, 24 October 2013; Ngiam Su Wei, Interview with Author, 9 October 2013.

ministries could not use the budget on training by external providers. The salaries of the IPAM officers, being civil servants, were also assured should the IPAM fail to attract anyone to its programmes. Yet, should government agencies decide not to subscribe to the IPAM's programmes, the IPAM could face relegation into obsolescence.

To complicate matters, economic outlook deteriorated dramatically in mid-1997 as currency crises spread across Southeast Asia. Empowered by a "decisive victory" at elections earlier that year, winning 81 of the 83 Parliamentary seats and 63.5% popular vote bettering its 1991 outing, the PAP government initiated a series of fiscal measures.[63] As events turned out, the Singapore economy managed "better-than-expected"[64] 7.8% growth.

For the IPAM, government agencies' subscription to its programmes did not dip. As it grew the number of courses in accordance to the PS21 goal, the number of civil servant-participants rose to soak up the supply. On reflection, Ms Ngiam thought:

> ...in a way, IDC would be a 'test' for us to see if public sector agencies would send their officers to CSC for training. If our programmes were good, we should be able to see better subscriptions to our programmes. So, in a way, IDC was one way to ensure that we offer quality training programmes to the Public Service.[65]

Meeting the needs of external government agencies cloaked the real subjects of this Inter-Departmental Charging model. Although IDC sought to maintain the quality of courses, Ma — by staking the IPAM's viability to the internal market — wanted to impress upon staff the imperative of delivering high-quality programmes. IDC was essentially an application of the New Public Management principle of injecting competition to improve services, though Ma said he was not influenced by it: "[W]ith competition, you made sure that your courses have to be useful. Otherwise, ministries don't have to come. They can go anywhere. They can go to the universities."[66] Hence, the real end-goal

---

[63] Lee Tsao Yuan, "Singapore in 1996: A Review," *SAR 1997*: 6.

[64] Patrick Daniel, "Singapore in 1997: A Review," *SAR 1998*: 2–6.

[65] Ngiam Su Wei, email correspondence with Author, 14 October 2013.

[66] David Ma, Interview with Author, 8 March 2013; David Ma, email correspondence with Author, 16 September 2013.

was to instil within the IPAM staff an attitude of service excellence. In all purposes, Inter-Departmental Charging triggered off PS21 reforms within the IPAM. For the training institution to be the point of introducing reforms into the bureaucracy, it first needed to undergo that reform.

6.3 Becoming a Statutory Board

6.3.1 *Market-competition to stimulate quality training*

Sometime in 1998, Brigadier-General Yam Ah Mee, who had just completed his service in the air force, was posted to the Public Service Division as part of his Administrative Service posting. As Deputy Secretary of Development to Permanent Secretary Lim Siong Guan, BG Yam oversaw the PS21 Office and Strategic Planning Office, and was concurrently Dean of the Civil Service College (*see* Table 6.6). One of his first tasks was to inject fresh impetus into the PS21 movement, suggesting an 'innovative and entrepreneurial Civil Service' as a new goal for the reform drive. Yam recalled that this was met with:

> . . . a lot of concerns, by some groups of people that the Civil Service, if it would to be entrepreneurial, it would tilt too much towards profit-driven. So eventually after many months, Eddie Teo was the Permanent Secretary by then, we managed to settle on the term, 'an innovative and enterprising Civil Service'.[67]

At the same time, the Scenario Planning 2020 exercise led by the Strategic Planning Office under his charge convinced Yam that "we needed to have a very innovative and enterprising Civil Service in order to be very nimble, very forward looking, future ready civil servants in order for us to position ourselves to deal with the challenges of the scenarios."[68]

The Civil Service College at that time included three units — (1) the IPAM, (2) the Institute of Policy Development, and (3) the Civil Service Consulting Group. BG Yam recalled that they "were operating like four [*sic*] different departments, each had a department director and they were

[67]Yam Ah Mee, Dean, CSC, 1998–2004, Interview with Author, 23 December 2011.
[68]*Ibid.*

Table 6.6: Public Service Division and Civil Service College, 1998[69]

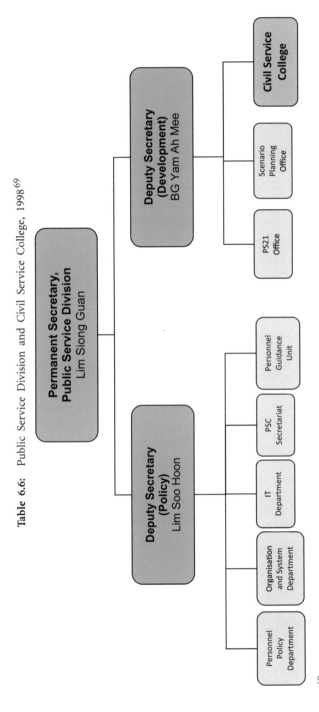

Permanent Secretary, Public Service Division — Lim Siong Guan

Deputy Secretary (Policy) — Lim Soo Hoon

Personnel Policy Department; Organisation and System Department; IT Department; PSC Secretariat; Personnel Guidance Unit

Deputy Secretary (Development) — BG Yam Ah Mee

PS21 Office; Scenario Planning Office; Civil Service College

[69] *Directory, July 1998:* 853–865; *Directory, January 1999:* 847–860.

all [receiving] Civil Service budgeting."[70] Earlier differences between staff of the IPAM and the IPD lingered, the physical distance between the two separately-sited institutes not bridged by any collaborative opportunities.[71] David Ma, Director of IPAM, remembered that:

> ...there was a bit of envy in a way that IPD's income was guaranteed. Because of the AOs. As long as you have the AOs, as long as the government says we are going to train the AOs, then IPD. But the future of IPAM, not sure. Because if you don't have money, then you're in trouble.[72]

IPAM Training Officer, Ngiam Su Wei, added that "It's a bit of a very strange situation, where it's two sister-departments — one sister department is the one that served the elite group and did all the high-profile things; and then IPAM, left with the run-of-the-mill programmes and the ordinary folks."[73] A CSC-commissioned survey also found some agencies were "not pleased or satisfied with IPAM's provision of training courses."[74]

To BG Yam Ah Mee, such a Civil Service College was not in synchrony with the PS21 goal:

> ...the training arm, the development arm of the Civil Service...cannot operate like this. Because if the directors, trainers, administrators operated in a Civil Service context, almost like an iron rice bowl, how did you make sure your programmes were up-to-date, totally relevant, high quality, and kept abreast of the needs of the Civil Service and forward looking. So, I felt that while we championed for PS21, scenario planning, we really needed to change the mentality.[75]

At this juncture, Permanent Secretary Lim Siong Guan broached an idea he had been mulling over for some time with BG Yam, which

---

[70]Yam remembered that there were four units in CSC at that time; in fact, there were three, as listed in records of Parliament. Yam Ah Mee, Interview with Author, 23 December 2011; Deputy Prime Minister, BG Lee Hsien Loong, "Civil Service College Bill", *Singapore Parliamentary Reports*, 25 July 2001, column. 1904.

[71]Michelle Wong, Interview with Author, 24 October 2013.

[72]David Ma, Interview with Author, 8 March 2013.

[73]Ngiam Su Wei, Interview with Author, 9 October 2013.

[74]This was a finding in the Gallup Organisational Poll Survey, 1996–1998. See Saravanan (2003) 42.

[75]Yam Ah Mee, Interview with Author, 23 December 2011.

was to replicate the IPAM's application of competition across the whole CSC. The motivation remained similar; compelling the CSC to produce high-quality and relevant training programmes by detaching it from the Public Service Division, effectively cutting it off from the ministry's funding. The risks between the two instances were different, though, as David Ma explained:

> ...with Inter-Departmental Charging, that means we were still a government department. If...we really couldn't survive, couldn't make the ends meet, we would still go back to our bosses and say, 'We have no money, help us.' And if you are part of a department, I think they can't say no to you. They may be very unhappy, but they will still have to bail you out, because you are a department.[76]

On the other hand, cutting the whole CSC adrift from PSD would effectively remove any last resort to the Civil Service for help. In plain words, the CSC would have to finance itself and pay for its staff and overheads from the courses it would sell.

At the same time, without being constrained by the strictures of Civil Service regulations, the CSC would have the flexibility to manage its own personnel according to its organisational needs. To allow the CSC to produce quality programmes, it must be empowered to recruit trainers and staff with the requisite competencies and capacities at the prevailing rates of remuneration. Correspondingly, in order to operate in a market environment, the CSC should have the leverage to let go of redundancies. Lim Siong Guan would elaborate afterwards:

> The only way the Civil Service College can keep up with all the developments in the training and work marketplace is to co-opt competencies wherever they are found.... If you have a trainer who has been with you for 30 years but carries the same set of skills, you can't bring in changes. So, you need a structure that can bring people in and out — something which public departments can't do.[77]

6.3.2 *Public sector remaining the focus*

Yam Ah Mee was prepared to give it a try, despite Lim Siong Guan mentioning that "he asked a few people but nobody wanted to take

---

[76]David Ma, Interview with Author, 8 March 2013.
[77]Lim Siong Guan, quoted in *ST* 12 July 2001: H7.

up this change."[78] Yam saw eye-to-eye with Lim that training played a critical role in supporting the PS21 reform:

> ...when Mr. Lim, two-three months after I came in, said that we should operate like this, where people pay to attend [training courses], and the four units [of CSC] should earn their rights, earn their positions in the way they deliver quality, I said, 'Yes, I was prepared to do this.'...That's where it got started, about two-three month after I came in, in 1998. Because I firmly believed that you really needed an innovative and enterprising Civil Service College in order to have an innovative and enterprising Public Service, so that we would be nimble enough for the future.[79]

While convinced that competition could draw out quality programmes from the CSC, questions remained over the model to structure the training institution. One option was to privatise the CSC, allowing market forces to ensure efficiency. However, Lim, Yam, and their senior management team were conscious that focusing on the lucrative private sector training market, which would necessarily result from privatisation, could lead to a void in the training of less profitable core public sector skills.[80] A corporatised CSC would also lose its links to the government.[81] Beyond the principles of competition and efficiency, the ultimate goal of the exercise was to align CSC to produce training relevant for the development of a stronger Public Service. Moreover, remaining within the public sector would allow the CSC to draw on some of the resources within the bureaucracy, such as senior civil servants as trainers. For these reasons, Lim, Yam, and their senior staff agreed, the CSC while separated from the Civil Service must still remain within the public sector.

The most optimal option, taking all into consideration, was to structure the CSC as a statutory board. As an agency enacted by legislation specifically with the mission to carry out training for the public sector, the CSC's focus would not be distracted from training the

---

[78]Yam Ah Mee, Interview with Author, 23 December 2011.

[79]*Ibid.*

[80]"An Interview with Chief Executive Officer and Dean, Civil Service College, BG(NS) Yam Ah Mee," *Ethos* (November 2001): 4.

[81]Jaime Teong, Director, Corporate Development, CSC, 2001–2007, quoted in Saravanan (2003) 42.

Public Service. At the same time, set adrift outside the financial resources of the Civil Service would compel the CSC to be market-driven, ensuring high standards in the development of its courses and programmes. The flexibility to operate at an arm's length from the Civil Service, conferring the CSC the flexibility to recruit the necessary competencies, would also boost its capacity to operate in an open market environment.

With the philosophical considerations worked out, Yam Ah Mee began plans to turn the CSC into a self-financing statutory board.[82] He convened an internal study into the CSC's financial situation; preliminary figures suggested that the Civil Service's annual training and development budget was around $40 million, almost all of which was spent in the CSC's programmes. To ensure objectivity and independence in assessment, Yam engaged an external consultancy to conduct a comprehensive viability study. The evaluation by Ernst and Young, after a six-month study, confirmed that the total training demands of the Civil Service indeed amounted to about $40 million. The overall conclusion was that, if the CSC could retain its existing customer base, proceeding with the self-financing model was feasible.

His confidence buoyed by empirical analyses, BG Yam proceeded with formal submissions. The exact justifications were still fresh in his mind a decade later:

> I wrote a paper to form a restructured self-funded statutory board. I remember that the first question that was asked was: do we need CSC to be a statutory board? . . . My arguments were: (1) we needed to be an innovative and enterprising Civil Service, therefore the training and development arm should first be innovative and enterprising; (2) if you really believe in being innovative and enterprising, then if the money came on a silver platter, you'll never be very innovative and enterprising. So its best that we operate as a self-funded statutory board, so that you would not think there's a grandfather behind, you have to earn the money.[83]

---

[82] An interviewee reported that original plans did not intend the CSC statutory board to be "self-financing". Though this could not be verified by other sources, Lim Siong Guan apparently laid Yam Ah Mee the challenge for CSC to be self-financing six months before October 2001. Jaime Teong, Human Resource Manager, PSD, 1997–2001, Interview with Author, 21 February 2014.

[83] Yam Ah Mee, Interview with Author, 23 December 2011.

6.3.3 *Finding the money*

Although BG Yam Ah Mee was fairly confident that the CSC's courses could finance its operations, this source of revenue could only be available after the courses were delivered and invoices paid. In the interim, which Yam and his management team assessed to range between six and seven months, the CSC needed an operating capital of $10.8 million.

While Singapore rebounded strongly from the 1998 regional financial crises, the economic outlook for the year 2001 was increasingly ominous. The September 11 attacks on the US worsened the already pessimistic sentiments; GDP contracted 2.2% and unemployment reached 6%.[84]

Against this outlook, BG Yam and his management team needed to convince bankers to extend a $10 million loan based on potential success of products yet to be sold, customers yet to be secured, and revenue that were still far from being clear. Approaching the DBS Bank, BG Yam recalled: "I had to show the bank the study we did with Ernst and Young: it's quite do-able, don't worry. These are my programmes, we know what we do. This is the strategy. I had to give them a value proposition. So the bank supported us, I signed this."[85]

Joining Yam in signing the loan instrument from the bank was Eddie Teo. Teo had by then succeeded Lim Siong Guan as Permanent Secretary at the Public Service Division and would become chairman of the board of directors governing the proposed autonomous CSC. Even with his boss joining him in undertaking the loan, BG Yam could not help but felt the gravity of that decision: "after I signed the $10.8 million, the first three nights I actually didn't sleep very well. This was the first time I borrowed $10.8 million and I knew that in six-and-a-half months, about seven months, it would run dry, unless we did well. I really didn't sleep well."[86]

---

[84]Zulkifli Baharudin, "Singapore 2001: The Remaking of Singapore," *SAR* 2002: 2.
[85]Yam Ah Mee, Interview with Author, 23 December 2011.
[86]*Ibid.*

6.4 CSC as Self-Financing Statutory Board

On 1 October 2001, the CSC formally became a self-financing statutory board under the purview of the Public Service Division, in the Prime Minister's Office (*see* Table 6.7).[87] In the debate leading to the Parliament's passing of the *Civil Service College Act,* two legislators while supporting the motion sought — and received — assurances that the CSC would keep civil servants across all levels of the personnel hierarchy abreast of professional developments.[88] Opposition Member of Parliament, Chiam See Tong, argued that placing the CSC under the PMO could subject it to undue political influence. To this, Deputy Prime Minister, Lee Hsien Loong, clarified that the Civil Service College was a "completely neutral outfit":

> It runs staff courses, courses for middle management, courses for senior management, courses on governance, courses on good English writing, courses on how to be a good civil servant... professional educational courses which need to be run for civil servants at all levels, from the top Permanent Secretary potential, all the way down to the clerical officer or the EO. So it is a completely neutral outfit.[89]

6.4.1 *Structure for oversight and control*

While the CSC was established as a statutory board outside of the Civil Service, its organisational structure positioned it firmly under the control of the Public Service Division. The CSC Act provided for a Board of Directors to exercise independent oversight over the College but the designation of the Permanent Secretary (PSD) as Chairman left no doubt that the predominant authority over the CSC would remain with the PSD. Up to 14 directors of the board could be appointed by the minister in-charge of the Civil Service,[90] but without provision for these

[87] *ST* 10 October 2001: H10.
[88] Hawazi Daipi, Loh Meng See and DPM BG Lee Hsien Loong, "Civil Service College Bill," *Parliamentary Reports* 25 July 2001, columns 1,907–1,911, and 1,913–1,914.
[89] DPM BG Lee Hsien Loong, "Civil Service College Bill," *Parliamentary Reports* 25 July 2001, column 1,913.
[90] DPM Lee, "Civil Service College Bill," *Parliamentary Reports* 25 July 2001, column. 1906; "Board of Directors," CSC, *Sharpening Minds, Beyond Public Service Excellence: Civil Service College 2001–03 (CSC 2001–2003)* (Singapore: CSC, 2004) 20–21.

Table 6.7: Civil Service College as a Statutory Board, circa 2001[91]

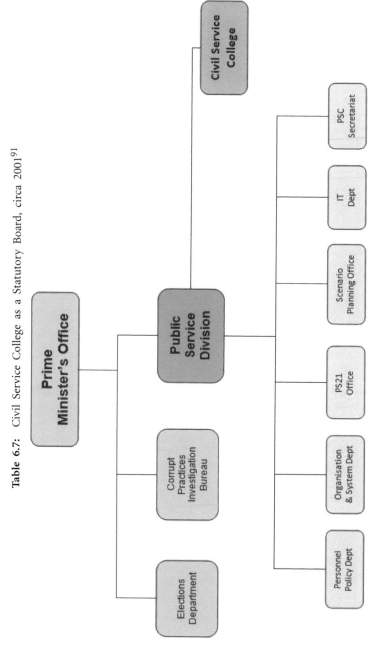

[91] *Directory, July 2002:* 1,137–1,151 and 1,159–1,165. Organisational units arranged left to right according to the sequence they were presented in the original documents.

positions to be advertised meant that the selection process was managed internally, most plausibly led by the senior officials within the PSD. The designated secretary of the board was the newly-established position of 'Dean and Chief Executive Officer' responsible for the College's daily operations.

With BG Yam Ah Mee, as Dean/CEO, concurrently Deputy Secretary at the PSD, reporting to the Permanent Secretary, the management structure effectively entrenched the Public Service Division's control over the CSC.

To offer additional guidance to the CSC management team, a high-level Advisory Panel was appointed, led by Lim Siong Guan, by now promoted to the position of Head of the Civil Service. The panel also included two heads of foreign bureaucracies: Joseph Wong, Secretary of Hong Kong's Civil Service, and Mdm Jocelyne Bourgon, President Emeritus of the Canadian School of Public Service and former Clerk of the Canadian Privy Council.[92]

The new CSC consisted of three main departments (*see* Table 6.8). The Institute of Policy Development remained focused on the development of the Administrative Service and leadership corps of the Public Service. The IPAM's programmes covered leadership, governance, public administration, and PS21 initiatives. The Civil Service Consulting Group and a Personnel Guidance Unit (PGU), transferred from PSD, merged to form the CSC Consultants.

The Personnel Guidance Unit was set up in 1996 when Lim Siong Guan was Permanent Secretary to provide PSD with psychometric assessment capacity in recruiting government scholars. According to Roger Tan, Assistant Head of PGU at that time, PGU also helped statutory boards and government-linked companies in the selection of job applicants, but these services were fee-paying for agencies outside of the civil service structure.[93] With all of its overheads funded from the PSD's budget, the charging of fees-for-services introduced the principle

---

[92]"CSC Advisory Panel," *CSC 2001–2003*: 18-19; Joseph Wong, Secretary for the Civil Service, Hong Kong, 2000–2006, Member of CSC Advisory Panel, 2001, Interview with Author, 6 September 2013.
[93]Roger Tan, Assistant Head, PGU, 1996–2000, Interview with Author, 18 October 2013.

Table 6.8: Civil Service College Organisational Structure, circa 2001[94]

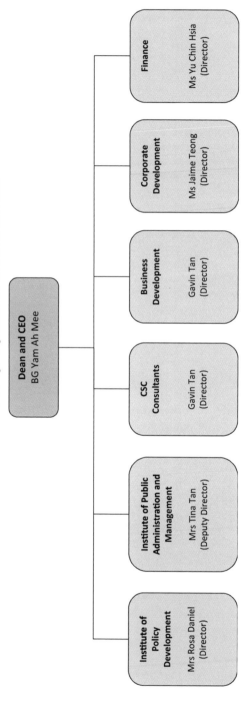

[94]"Speech by Mr Eddie Teo, Permanent Secretary (Prime Minister's Office), at the Launch of Civil Service College (CSC)," 8 October 2001, http://app.psd.gov.sg/data/Speech10Oct2001.pdf accessed on 18 September 2013; *Directory, July 2002*: 1,137–1,151 and 1,159–1,165. Organisational units arranged left to right according to the sequence they were presented in the original documents.

of costs in services into the PSD. Significantly, this predated the IPAM's introduction of Inter-Departmental Charging in 1997. Publicly, the PGU's inclusion into the CSC added psychological consultancy to allow the CSC to offer integrated services.[95] From the perspective of the PSD, Tan pointed out, merging the PGU with the IPAM, IPD, and CSC Consultants also separated the service-provision units to allow the PSD focus as a policymaking ministry.[96]

6.4.2 *Supporting departments*

A Business Development department was established to broaden the CSC's customer base. Even Yam Ah Mee, as Dean/CEO facing pressing matters, had to canvass for clients:

> ...the business development marketing group, I joined them going round to talk to permanent secretaries, talk to CEOs....And then we said we should also think about going overseas for the Civil Service, to position Singapore on the world map in the area of training and development. At that time, we were doing work in ASEAN countries, little bit in China. We should intensify and grow the ASEAN countries.[97]

While the initial aim was financial bottom-line, over time and with growing confidence, BG Yam seized the opportunity to use training for broader diplomatic goals:

> ...in 2001 when we started the restructured statutory board, I went to Dubai, Bahrain, Qatar — I went to many places — Canada, China, Vietnam, Cambodia, Australia, all over the place. I went to Dubai five times in one year, to make sure that all these things come through. I did a lot of travelling to engage....Why? For the purpose of positioning Singapore on the world map in the area of training and development, in the area of training quality.[98]

With the weight of financial viability weighing heavily over the CSC, a Finance Department was set up within the College to keep a constant watch over money matters. In order to instill real-world competition and

---

[95]DPM BG Lee Hsien Loong, "Civil Service College Bill," *Parliamentary Reports* 25 July 2001, column 1,906.
[96]Roger Tan, Interview with Author, 18 October 2013.
[97]Yam Ah Mee, Interview with Author, 23 December 2011.
[98]*Ibid.*

fiscal discipline into the organisation, Yam deliberately refrained from sourcing from within the public sector when selecting the personnel to oversee finances:

> I recruited a Director/Finance from outside, totally from the private sector. I said your role is to go through all these numbers, and make sure that from the finance angle, it's a doable thing. Although I had a consultant who provided me their views, Ernst and Young, internally, [I had] my Finance Director, who was also Director/HR concurrently.... bearing in mind that I only started with six to seven months of rolling capital, we were very tight with resources, tight with people.[99]

6.4.3 *Starting out*

Having laid out the preparations, the time came for the Civil Service College, modeled as a self-financing statutory board, to set forth into the market. The principal concern preoccupying BG Yam Ah Mee, who was Dean and Chief Executive Officer, and his senior management team and, in fact, all levels of staff in the CSC, was undoubtedly financial. Yam set up a system to monitor operations and the CSC's performance:

> ...we switched over. Every day when the courses finished, by the next day I already knew. I got my Finance, HR, and operations side. I already knew: yesterday, how many people came for programmes? What was the feedback of the course, of the trainer? If we went like this, how much were the earnings? How much were the costs? I was going day by day tracking of quality, delivery, results, bottom-line.[100]

This tight feedback loop allowed Yam and his management to make decisions on the fly — whether adjustments were needed, what improvements to be made, and so on.

Operating at such high intensity, especially after an emotional transition from government department to statutory board, was undoubtedly strenuous and exacting upon staff, from management to rank-and-file officers. Yam recalled that some CSC officers had chosen to remain as civil servants when given the option when the CSC restructured, rather than be faced with the uncertainty over the CSC's

---

[99] *Ibid.*
[100] *Ibid.*

viability and their livelihoods:

> Quite a number left on transition because they felt it was very tough to move from civil servant to restructured statutory board staff overnight. You now have to earn your income based on the quality of courses and programmes. The civil servants who [previously] must come to you now can go anywhere. You have to go and market, sell the product, convince the permanent secretaries, convince everyone, that my programmes were good. But everyone was looking at alternatives outside.[101]

After the CSC became a statutory board, the IPD and IPAM witnessed a reduction of 13 staff altogether, from 138 before October 2001 to 125.[102]

However, this was remembered differently by some at the staff level. Michelle Wong, a Course Administrator at the IPAM at that time, recalled:

> As one of the Division 1 graduates then, we weren't so much the affected ones, but I think it was the Division 2 and Division 3 officers, probably at that time more Division 3 officers, who felt it more. I think there was some unhappiness with how the transition was being communicated to them. Because it was basically something like, 'You go over [to CSC as a statutory board staff], then if you find that things are not suitable … you will be out of a job.' Somehow, maybe the way how the comms [communications] was handled, and I don't know whether it was deliberate or not. So, I think there was a feeling like job insecurity. And because of that, some people didn't want to go over, and even those who remained there was some residual unhappiness about how the whole thing was being handled.[103]

Indeed, those responsible for personnel matters leading up to the CSC's change into a statutory board agreed the subject required delicate handling. Mrs Jaime Teong, Human Resource Manager at the Public Service Division, recalled that management's preference was for all existing CSC staff to be "novated" into CSC statutory board officers when CSC changed its legal status.[104] Yet, earlier expansion to meet

---

[101] *Ibid.*

[102] Numbers calculated from *Directory, July 2001*:1122–1127; *Directory, July 2002*: 1160–1165.

[103] Michelle Wong, Interview with Author, 24 October 2013.

[104] Jaime Teong, Director, Corporate Development, CSC, 2001–2008, Interview with Author, 21 February 2014.

the PS21 training demands had resulted in rapid rise in CSC staff numbers. In particular, the IPAM had a substantial number of personnel on temporarily hired terms. With the prospects of a self-financing CSC less than crystal clear, apprehensions over job-security were real among some CSC staff, especially among those recently drafted into the IPAM or whose competencies might not survive open-market competition. At several town-hall style dialogues aimed at assuring staff, senior PSD officials promised staff choosing to remain as civil servants, i.e., not transferring into the CSC statutory board terms: they would not lose their jobs. However, the PSD, according to Jaime Teong, had difficulty securing positions in civil service agencies to emplace officers who chose not to transfer with the CSC into statutory board terms.

In other recollections, staff chose to leave the CSC not at the point of its becoming a statutory board but amid the intense atmosphere thereafter. Ngiam Su Wei, by this time promoted to manager in the IPAM, said:

> ... the reason why people left, from my perspective, was more like: they looked at the new place, it no longer resonated with them, and therefore they left. Can't blame Yam Ah Mee, he had to bring in private sector people, so he brought in private sector people, like Finance [director]. The way she [Director/Finance] operated was totally different from last time, maybe a more nurturing finance chief, or a more ministry way of doing things.[105]

In the memories of some working-level staff, a highly demanding environment within the CSC was emerging overnight: "We had to ramp up our capacity very quickly. It literally meant a sudden change of introducing different types of programmes."[106]

More exacting was the sudden emphasis on meeting performance targets. Ms Ngiam recalled: "We were suddenly given targets that we had to achieve, and it's in dollar amount ... you are accountable for your area, you have to grow your area, you have to bring in the targets ... Suddenly we swing to the extreme of becoming profit-driven."[107] Roger Tan,

---

[105]Ngiam Su Wei, Interview with Author, 9 October 2013.
[106]Interviewee A in Lim Peng Soon (2006) 96.
[107]Ngiam Su Wei, Interview with Author, 9 October 2013.

Deputy Director of CSC Consultants, added:

> ...when we became a stat-board, that time damn '*jialat*' ['very difficult' in Chinese colloquial vernacular] and it didn't help that the CFO [finance director] was so aggressive. Every meeting we were scolded upside down, kept being 'pressurised' to go for new money. So it was a culture shock for most.[108]

For some among the staff, the acuteness and magnitude of the series of sudden changes to their environment could be tough to bear. One informant revealed that:

> ...one of the staff passed away. Don't know whether [it was] because in the pursuit of numbers and profit, whether it causes the person to look at it, and then after that. I think it could be heart attack.... We heard his wife... [tapered off]. We heard that he every night would look at how to do better, how to bring in... [tapered off].[109]

Yam Ah Mee received "many nasty letters who said that: why were we doing this? How come this Director [of] Finance from the private sector? It's private sector penetrating into Civil Service! Why everything needed to do double fast time?"[110] Some complaints reached "Mr Lim Siong Guan [Head of the Civil Service], went to Mr. Eddie Teo [Permanent Secretary, PSD], went even beyond that."[111] The Minister in-charge of Civil Service then was Deputy Prime Minister Lee Hsien Loong, who would obviously be aware of these developments.[112]

Fortunately for Yam, the leadership — both the political leadership and the top echelons of the bureaucracy — were prepared to hear him out. Not that he looked forward to these meetings under the

---

[108] Roger Tan, Interview with Author, 18 October 2013.

[109] Informant 1, Interview with Author, 2013. Three other IPAM officers at that time pointed out that, notwithstanding the sentiments and grief felt by the wife of the deceased, the officer concerned had come from a high-pressure working environment previously, and he might have existing medical conditions leading to his succumbing to a heart attack. Tina Tan, Interview with Author, 31 October 2013; Logendran, Interview with Author, 25 October 2013; Jaime Teong, Director Interview with Author, 21 February 2014.

[110] Yam Ah Mee, Interview with Author, 23 December 2011.

[111] *Ibid.*

[112] This was confirmed by Jaime Teong, Interview with Author, 21 February 2014.

circumstances: "I had to explain to Mr Lim Siong Guan, Eddie Teo, many people: we were doing the right thing, it's moving well.... we were doing this, I'm moving this part, I'm moving this part, I needed to move this part like this, so we operated like this."[113] Yam and the CSC were allowed to continue, at least, for the time being.

Internally, Yam also had to manage CSC staff: "I had to tell my Director [of] Finance, 'Slow down a bit, I know you are doing the right thing, but the approach cannot be rough.'"[114] Yam did remove the personnel management duties from the finance director's portfolio. Also, according to Jaime Teong whom the Dean brought in to take over HR functions, Yam considered letting go of the Director/Finance.[115] While he retained the finance director for the time being, Yam had to devote a lot of time engaging staff:

> ... almost every month I had to do pep talk with our staff: 'Don't worry. We would show the results. Across, this was our overall performance; respective departments, this was your performance; this was feedback from our participants; this was our outreach to so many ministries and so many statutory boards; these were the new participants, local and overseas.'[116]

Officers who were more senior in the hierarchy appeared more able to appreciate the measures within the context of the CSC's drive for survival. Manager, M. Logendran, pointed out that there was a prevailing "fear of the unknown, we were going into [a] new area. Can we make it?" Hence, every avenue was sought to reduce cost and maximise revenue because "Survival was the word!... if your bottom-line was changed, breakeven was important, you must do 'x' number of courses... In fact, we used to rent out our auditorium for the evening classes. Not for us, but for the private sector, just to get the revenue."[117] There were at least some officers within CSC who had a greater level of confidence in the

---

[113]Yam Ah Mee, Interview with Author, 23 December 2011.

[114]*Ibid.*

[115]Teong's designation was Director of Corporate Development and included other functions. Jaime Teong, Interview with Author, 21 February 2014.

[116]Yam Ah Mee, Interview with Author, 23 December 2011.

[117]Logendran, Interview with Author, 25 October 2013.

leadership team. One manager said:

> We knew who the captain of the ship was and although we say there may be stormy waters, we were confident who the leader was, who was leading us. So, I think the leader is very important. If they believe in it and they are there, they stand by us, we will have the confident [sic] that it (the change) will work. So, I would say that there were risks involved, but I think if everyone put in their effort and everybody do [sic] their rowing and it means everybody has got to row and synchronise their rowing over the stormy days, at the end of the day we work as a team and that's important to achieve the target we have before us.[118]

As part of the autonomy vested in the CSC, Yam linked staff remuneration to their performance. Foregoing the Civil Service formula of pay increments with years of service, the CSC's new framework pegged remuneration to outcomes:

> First tier was how well Civil Service College overall performed? If we were in the red, I would say: so sorry I don't pay you, I have no money to pay you at all. We went bankrupt, then we went bankrupt. We had to operate such that we operated together. This level we make sure we do well.
> Tier 2 was by department. So even if we did very well, then I would break down into IPAM, IPD, CSCI. Because if your department did very well, I should recognise you even more compared to others.
> Tier 3 is you as an individual, how did you do? Maybe IPAM did very well but you as an individual didn't. Notice that all these three tiers were all tied to training development, mindset changes, delivery quality, training standards. But very line of sight — to individual, to team, to their department, overall.
> Then the last tier, Tier 4, I needed everyone to have the right mentality, Civil Service ethos and values, PS21, improvement, innovation, continuous improvement, WITS, SSS [Staff Suggestion Scheme]. So, Tier 4 was about other areas not just to your training and your delivery.
> So I had four tiers, every part of it was tied to how well we conceptualised, delivered, how innovative and enterprising, and what were our customers telling us, and the results.[119]

As an organisation in the training and development business, the CSC also built learning and development into its personnel development plan. Training was positioned as staff entitlement, and higher learning was

---

[118]Interviewee C in Lim Peng Soon (2006) 107–108.
[119]Yam Ah Mee, Interview with Author, 23 December 2011.

offered as incentives. From the organisation's perspective, well-trained staff would be able to expand its capacity.

6.4.4 *Taking stock*

Evaluating public sector organisations is difficult — their level of success cannot be simply derived from the amount of revenues generated from their activities. The problem with assessing public sector organisations is principally over the complexity involved in quantifying public service; what cannot be measured is difficult to evaluate. Perhaps one approach is to assess the CSC against the objective it set for itself.

When the Civil Service College transitioned into a self-financing statutory board, it aimed to provide high-quality training that was relevant to the Public Service. The Dean/CEO was determined that the CSC would succeed. The circumstances were far from conducive — the national economy contracted by 2% and global outlook was greatly undermined by the September 11 attacks.

Against this context, Yam Ah Mee recalled evaluating the CSC's performance after one year of operating as a self-financing statutory board:

> ...the first year, quite a number of ministries and statutory boards, assuming they used to come to IPAM so much, I saw that most of them, because they had a chance to try outside, they tried. Almost 50–60% they did with IPAM, the other 30–40%, some as much as 50% they tried outside in the first year.[120]

While the picture appeared grim on the one hand, CSC's efforts at broadening its customer base would prove rewarding. Following many rounds of canvassing, statutory boards which had previously not subscribed to the CSC's programmes and new government agencies were apparently won over by the CSC. These new training deals together with overseas projects would prove a lifeline to the CSC:

> So in my first year the total revenue brought in was $43 million [Financial Year 2002]. In fact, for the three years, it was about $43 million [FY2002], $39 million [FY2003], $43 million [FY2004]. Beyond expectations.

---

[120] *Ibid.*

The reason was that while we reached to the usual ministries, although they did lesser, we did more, we did local and overseas. And then I found that subsequent second year, they all came back. Because after they tried outside, then they said that outside not so customised, may not be so good. And the first year we had a net surplus of a couple of millions.[121]

Yam's greatest relief was the resolution of the cause of his many sleepless nights: "And within the first year I returned to DBS [Bank] $10.8 million, we paid back $10.8 million to DBS."[122] And with the remuneration framework pegged to financial outcomes, CSC staff were "rewarded for all the hard work." [123]

While CSC appeared to have achieved the fiscal independence aspect of its objective, Saravanan in his 2004 study questioned some of the financial figures:

When I thoroughly scrutinised the business resources of the CSC, I was informed that the CSC still receives funds from the PSO and the Managing for Excellence (MFE) office [both in the Public Service Division]. This funding amounts to about 15% to 20% of the total revenue of CSC. Thus, without the funding, the CSC's current financial viability would not be as sound as it has claimed to be.[124]

This, Senior Manager Logendran explained, was part of the initial measures designed to cushion CSC's migration to the full market; selected CSC programmes were "subsidised 50%, then 30%, 20% for five years."[125]

Saravanan also questioned the CSC's proposition as a public-sector organisation:

...operating on the middle of the private–public spectrum will affect the strategic focus of any organization. The tension created by the need to balance both of the functions can take a toll on the organization. Important public service values and ethics such as accountability, integrity, responsibility, and loyalty may be eroded by the competitive liberal private sector values. Thus, the durability of this model can only be seen with the passage of time.[126]

---

[121] *Ibid*; *CSC 2001–03*: 45; *CSC 2003–2004*: 20; *CSC 2004–2005*: 36.

[122] Yam Ah Mee, Interview with Author, 23 December 2011.

[123] Ngiam Su Wei, Interview with Author, 9 October 2013.

[124] Saravanan (2003) 58–59. Efforts to locate Saravanan to corroborate these were unsuccessful.

[125] Logendran, Interview with Author, 25 October 2013.

[126] Saravanan (2003) 60.

Saravanan might be right, except no empirical evidence was presented to substantiate these assertions. The difficulty in Saravanan's thesis lays in the principal problem of quantifying public-sector values and performance, as mentioned earlier.

Another approach is to evaluate the CSC's performance as a public-sector organisation against the rationale for retaining it within the public sector. For context, the key reason was to ensure that the CSC continued to provide training for the Public Service even as corporatisation set it up to chase after the more profitable segments of the market. In fact, the reason for injecting competition into the CSC was to compel it to develop high-quality and relevant training, with the ultimate aim of providing these for the Public Service.

In this regard, the CSC showed itself remaining focused on the public sector. Civil servants continued to attend the CSC's programmes, reflecting their ministries' approval of the CSC's courses. Statistics listed in the CSC's annual reports in the immediate period after its conversion into a statutory board did not appear to show a digression into the private sector — there were no records of participants from outside the Public Service.[127]

Further evidence of the CSC's continued focus on the Public Service could be found in its overseas ventures. Profit would be the obvious motivation for such international projects but these represented a small percentage in proportion to the CSC's overall more domestically-oriented programmes. In 2002, for example, the CSC undertook four foreign consulting projects while, apart from the already heavy focus on training local civil servants, being committed to 35 local projects.[128] Even so, part of the reason for pursuing these overseas projects was evidently driven

---

[127] In Financial Year 2002, for example, since all the participants for CSC courses were reported along their divisional strata, there were hence no indications of private sector participants. In FY2003, there were 1,700 "Others" among the rest of the 48,200 participants who were listed by divisional distribution. FY2004's report indicated 1,773 international participants; the rest of the participants were civil servants. *CSC 2001–2003*: 46; *CSC 2003–2004*: 18; *CSC 2004–2005*: 35.

[128] *CSC 2001–03*: 44. No available data for subsequent years: *CSC 2003–2004*; *CSC 2004–2005*.

to serve and advance the interests of the Singapore Public Service:

> We worked with UNDP [United Nations Development Programme], we
> worked with ADB [Asian Development Bank], we worked with CAPAM
> [Commonwealth Association of Public Administration and Management], we
> worked with ASTD [American Society of Training and Development]. Why?
> For the purpose of positioning Singapore on the world map in the area of
> training and development, in the area of training quality.[129]

A more valid evaluation of the CSC's transformation, achieving
financial self-sufficiency and remaining rooted in its Public Service-focus,
was the high 'cost' upon its staff. Evidently, most staff were fatigued
by the rapid ramping up of programmes and stressed by the sudden
preoccupation with performance targets. The organisational culture,
already far from cohesive with lingering differences between the IPAM
and IPD officers, became even more competitive and adversarial under
the circumstances. Yet, this 'cost' might be inevitable in order to 'unlock'
the full potential of the organisation and its staff. Pointing to the
doubling in output of some departments before and after the CSC's
'stat-boardisation', Roger Tan, reflected:

> ...if you look at it from the not-so-good point of view, it increased the
> workload tremendously. But if you look at it from another point of view, you
> might wonder how much spare capacity we had been harbouring in the old
> set-up, that there was hidden capacity there that we didn't unleash....The
> moment you turned it the other way around and say, 'I'm going to pay
> you based on performance, I'm going to pay you based on whether you
> meet your KPIs, the more you earn, the more bonus you get.' Straight
> away, human behavior changes and you can unleash, almost doubling. It's
> quite a good illustration of how market forces can unleash all these sleepy
> government performance.[130]

Several managers who had served longer stints in the central training
school of the Public Service took a longer view of the CSC's circumstances
transitioning into a statutory board. Logendran, a manager who joined
during the CSI period, said:

> If you ask me, now looking back at it, I think sometimes you have to do
> some things which were not pleasant at the time, but it was the right thing

---

[129]Yam Ah Mee, Interview with Author, 23 December 2011.
[130]Roger Tan, Interview with Author, 18 October 2013.

to do.... if you are already given this mandate, you have to go ahead and do it. What were the options?[131]

Mrs Tina Tan, who started her career with the CSI, addressed criticisms that the focus on financial viability led the CSC to lose its public-sector focus:

> People on hindsight said that, 'We lost our way.' But I don't think so. ... You asked me to start a stat board [statutory board], you don't give me the capital, I must make sure that everything can be paid for, including my staff's salaries, I have to pay rental. So I must make sure that the 'business' is viable. But I don't think we have deviated from the mission. We also did programmes that were needed by the people at that time.... to say that we had lost our way, I don't think that was correct.[132]

Logendran continued:

> ... if we had remained there [within the civil service structure], then honestly I think we may not be where we are now. Having gone through it, to me there is a very good lesson for us. Baptism of fire or whatever you can call it. I thought that having gone through it, it made us wiser and stronger, than if we continued to remain there, I'm not sure we will be where we are now. Because we have gone through it, we understood what we needed to do, what we needed to focus on.[133]

All other CSC officers interviewed for this study were in agreement that the intense focus on survivability at that time was necessary despite the strain on the staff, and it laid the foundation for today's Civil Service College.[134]

6.5 Conclusion: A Stand-Alone College

From its establishment in 1996 to its transition into a statutory board in 2001, the transformation of the Civil Service College was a remarkably purposeful and well-planned alignment of training functions to support PS21 reforms in the Singapore Public Service. The eventual CSC

---

[131] Logendran, Interview with Author, 25 October 2013.
[132] Tina Tan, Interview with Author, 31 October 2013.
[133] Logendran, Interview with Author, 25 October 2013.
[134] Michelle Wong, Interview with Author, 24 October 2013; Ngiam Su Wei, Interview with Author, 9 October 2013.

was the result of decades of tinkering, rebadging, and organisational restructurings — all representing attempts by the senior echelons of the Public Service to get the model they wanted. The decision to detach it from the Civil Service, from where the previous generations of training schools had all originated and been subsidiaries of, was effectively an implicit criticism of the erstwhile structure. However, the training schools' long-standing position as subsidiaries within the Civil Service meant that the task of detaching them would require deep deliberation and careful planning.

Seen in context, the promulgation of PS21 and the centrality of executive development and training in that reforms-drive did arise from within the bureaucracy. Already efficient and operating at high-performance level, the Singapore Public Service was seeking to leap for even higher bounds.

Yet, the state in the broader context continued to loom large. An even more efficient and effective Public Service would certainly help the electoral fortunes of the ruling PAP government, amid much talk of development–democratisation theories at that time. Ultimately, even though Lim Siong Guan might not have cleared the 'reforms-through-training' agenda with the political leadership and the political masters, by withholding any objections for it, by tacitly endorsing it, and by approving budgetary allocations for it, the political leadership was instrumental in supporting PS21 and the CSC.

In retrospect, the eventual emergence of the CSC as a self-financing statutory board as the ultimate end-state of a series of restructuring was clearly already conceived alongside the promulgation of the PS21 reforms. Between 1996 and 2001, each phase of the CSC's transition was an incremental but progressive step towards that final permutation. The two existing central training institutions were first merged into one central CSC to consolidate control over the bureaucracy's training functions, in preparation of the subsequent phase of reorganisation. This was the introduction of competition into the IPAM, to push its staff to rapidly expand capacity, in order for the Public Service to realise the PS21 goal of offering public officers with 100 hours of annual training. On hindsight, this was clearly a trial, or a controlled experiment, for the follow-on replication of market competition across the CSC. Cutting the CSC adrift from government funding and 'empowering' it with the autonomy to be responsible for its own finances was the ultimate measure in compelling staff to produce or perish. Yet, by making it a statutory board anchored within the public sector ensured that the CSC would continue to focus on relevance towards the Public Service. The emergence of the CSC as a self-financing statutory board was thus the unfolding of a well-laid plan that was five years in the making, like the coming-together of a patiently assembled set-piece on a chess-board.

Lim Siong Guan, the Permanent Secretary in the Prime Minister's Office and the architect of PS21, affirmed that the CSC's restructuring was a purposeful alignment of the training institution to support the Public Service's reforms. In an interview for this study, Lim recounted the strategy that was unfolding at that time:

> The whole idea is very plain: Civil Service College is a critical node, it is a critical agency, for doing good for the whole Civil Service, on both counts, about the vision for the future of the country, and about knowledge and building experience and shaping the culture of the Service. I considered CSC as a critical instrument in shaping the culture and values of the Service. And therefore, if there is any big change that you want to make in the Service, I consider the Civil Service College as the instrument for this.[135]

Drawing on the CSC as that instrument for PS21 might have been convenient for Lim, since he was overseeing the CSC. However, more significantly, Lim recognised the importance of the Civil Service College as a dedicated agency to shape the bureaucracy through training:

> Certainly, this feeling that we needed an agency which saw its task as shaping the Civil Service. Any time you wanted to make a change, we could get people to go through the Civil Service College to imbibe these new ideas and approaches.[136]

Another indication of this purposefully planned-out transition was the careful pre-staging of key personnel. The appointment of Ms Lim Soo Hoon into the original Civil Service College by Lim Siong Guan, ostensibly to fill a routine vacancy of Deputy Dean, was really to position her for plans that were already charted out. Lim Siong Guan,

---

[135] Lim Siong Guan, Interview with Author, 20 November 2013.
[136] *Ibid.*

as Permanent Secretary at the Public Service Division, was responsible for the movements of senior personnel across the bureaucracy. More significantly, Lim was the architect of the PS21 reforms movement. Within four months of her 'deputising', Ms Lim Soo Hoon would become Dean, succeeding Kishore Mahbubani who was 'coincidentally' promoted at this time. This allowed Ms Lim to consolidate the two central training schools into a new Civil Service College within a year. David Ma was another example of well-crafted personnel plans to facilitate organisational change. As head of the PS21 Office before taking over the IPAM, Ma would naturally forge coherence between the training functions and the reforms movement. Brigadier-General Yam Ah Mee further amplified this positioning of key personnel into positions of influence, ready to carry out the respective phases of moves on the chess board. Critically, all these leaders, from Ms Lim Soo Hoon to David Ma to Yam Ah Mee, shared Lim Siong Guan's conviction on the role of training in supporting PS21.

When asked how he was able to spot the right people to carry out the particularly fitting tasks, Lim Siong Guan responded:

> I'm not so sure that I spotted the right people. I tell you, fundamentally, my approach is not about spotting the right people. I think I have more strength taking the people that are available and bringing them to the point where they say, 'This makes good sense! It's exciting stuff to do! Let's go get it done well!'
>
> By and large, when we talk about Yam Ah Mee, David Ma, remember they are members of the Admin Service, they start with the intellectual capacity. What we need to draw upon is the emotional dimension, the sense of engagement of what I'm trying to do, which I find, no matter where I go, that if it's an exciting idea, people are drawn in. And if you make them part of it and say, 'I'm not giving you directions on this, but do you all agree this is where we want to go and this is what we want to become? If you agree, then carry on, what are your ideas? Let's talk about it.' And I find every place I go, people are motivated by this.[137]

This highlights the importance of organisational leadership amid this aligning of training for reforms, especially in defining and articulating the vision to the secondary layer of key personnel. Lim Siong Guan was evidently able to communicate his idea of PS21 to a large cross-section of the Public Service; the conviction manifesting through Lim Soo Hoon,

---

[137] *Ibid.*

David Ma, and Yam Ah Mee as they carried out each of their phases of change demonstrated the success of Lim Siong Guan — not only in articulating — but also in securing a deep identification with the vision. As it appeared in the case of the CSC's reorganisation, the challenge laid in these secondary leaders breaking up the grand-strategic intellect of the vision into concrete clarity, in order to assure rank-and-file staff preoccupied with actual operations and very real subsistence motivation. The case of the CSC's transformation amply demonstrated that leadership is key in order to carry through implementation, not just at the broad strategic apex, but at each and every level of the hierarchy.

Another notable feature of this alignment of training functions for reforms was the lack of reference to any foreign models. In the preceding years, the training schools had drawn on expatriate expertise to run programmes or studied overseas institutions like the British Civil Service College, France's École Nationale d'Administration, and the Canadian Centre for Management in starting up training centres. The travails in Britain to keep the UK Civil Service College relevant and viable might have marked out the pitfalls to be avoided rather than offer lessons to be replicated.[138] The distinct absence of any foreign influence in the restructuring of Singapore's Civil Service College pointed to a progressive level of institutional maturity. The CSC had plausibly ventured into uncharted waters — no foreign training institutions had attempted such an alignment of training functions to directly facilitate administrative reforms.

In fact, the CSC's transformation was rather inspiring for Hong Kong's Secretary for the Civil Service. Joseph Wong, a top civil servant in Hong Kong overseeing the territory's bureaucracy and invited to sit on the CSC's Advisory Panel during this time, was impressed by the CSC. He recalled that although the CSC lost the monopoly over civil service training and had to compete with the private sector, it was able to finance itself. In Wong's mind, this was because the CSC had "very clear targets" working towards financial self-sufficiency.[139] The statutory

---

[138]Efforts to keep the UK Civil Service College viable saw its evolution into the National School of Government (2004) but this did not save it from closure in 2012. National School of Government, *Annual Report & Resource Accounts, 2006–2007* (London: Stationary Office, 2007) 5; Cabinet Office, *Annual Report & Accounts, 2011–2012* (London: Stationary Office, 2012) 37.

board-status also helped by freeing up the CSC from unnecessary red-tape and cumbersome regulations.

In contrast, Hong Kong's Civil Service Training Institute (CSTI) — having evolved from its earlier nominal permutations — was not conducting many courses of its own at that time. Instead, by contracting out most of the training services to vendors in the private sector, the CSTI was effectively a course secretariat or training broker for the Hong Kong bureaucracy. Joseph Wong, the most senior official responsible for Hong Kong's civil service, while sufficiently impressed by Singapore's CSC to consider modeling Hong Kong's CSTI after Singapore's CSC, nevertheless intimated that these options were constrained by Hong Kong's particular context. Financial pressures within the bureaucracy resulted in the CSTI eventually being absorbed into the Civil Service Bureau. In any case, Wong pointed out that Hong Kong's political context at that time meant that the government of the day, while having jurisdiction over the bureaucracy, did not have sufficient control over the legislature to extend to the CSTI the statutory autonomy similar to the CSC. In comparison, while Singapore's CSC was granted autonomy to grow out of the civil service, in the same period, Hong Kong's CSTI lost much of its autonomy to become a smaller subordinate entity under its larger parent department. Joseph Wong analysed that the political and bureaucratic context divided the training institutions of Hong Kong and Singapore down different paths.

Finally, in evaluating the Civil Service College as a self-financing statutory board, the original objective had been achieved, challenging as it may have been when faced with the complexity of quantifying and measuring public services. The CSC managed to remain financially solvent amid competition from the private sector training market. More significantly, this fiscal viability attested to the relevance of its training products, and a relevance that was focused upon the bureaucracy, with the overwhelming majority of its clientele being government agencies. With PS21 positioned as a continuous long-term reform movement, the Civil Service College has truly become a focal point for introducing reforms into the Singapore Public Service.

---

[139]Joseph Wong, Interview with Author, 6 September 2013.

Chapter 7

Conclusion: Training and Development as Inception Point of Reforms

"The public sector for the new Singapore must be a catalyst for change, a pace setter in change, and a standard bearer on change.... the pursuit of the best of standards...demands first-class training, extensive sharing of experience and a whole work environment conducive to the generation and experimentation of ideas. The Civil Service College plays a critical role in this."

Lim Siong Guan, Head of the Civil Service, 2001[1]

7.1 Summing Up: Training and Development as Inception Point of Reforms

The study began by posing the key research questions — why did the Singapore Public Service invest so heavily and consistently in executive development and training? How did the Singapore bureaucracy undertake training and development over the years? What were the defining features and characteristics of Singapore's approach in institutionalising training and development in its Public Service?

The principal argument of this book is that *executive development and training served as inception point through which reforms were driven in the Singapore Public Service, over the course of 40 years.*

At self-government, Singapore's recently-elected local leadership inherited a Public Service in dire need for reforms. As recounted in Chapter 1, the colonial bureaucracy was driven by the metropole's

---

[1]Lim Siong Guan, Head of the Civil Service, Speech at the launch of the Civil Service College Statutory Board, 8 October 2001.

directive to exploit Singapore's location as a base for Britain's Far Eastern empire at minimum operating cost. Not only was it consequently small, the colonial bureaucracy was bifurcated into a small British elite directing a broad swathe of locally-recruited manpower to staff the rank-and-file appointments to keep costs low. With a singular focus on safeguarding the British military bases and unconcerned with local socioeconomic development, the colonial bureaucracy's leadership was disconnected from the population and street-level bureaucrats largely indulged in petty corruption.

To reform the Singapore Public Service, the PAP set up the Political Study Centre, to socialise the leadership of the bureaucracy through the guise of training, into a new appreciation of the nation-building milieu, as described in Chapter 2. Against the broader context of state-formation, the emerging political elite — i.e., the People's Action Party leadership — sought to consolidate their authority. Yet, the colonial-era bureaucracy was not conducive for the PAP's delivery of public services, the platform through which the PAP needed to secure electoral votes and its viability. The local population continued to see civil servants as aloof and rent-seeking. Using training as a medium, the Political Study Centre was able to reorient the leadership of the bureaucracy for the tasks of nation-building. As senior civil servants enjoined their political masters in shared interests, a symbiotic relationship emerged between the political leadership and the bureaucracy. Discipline across the bureaucracy improved as newly-socialised superiors tightened supervision. The survival of the PAP government through internecine party struggles, Singapore's merger with Malaysia, Singapore's sudden independence, and several elections, was in no small part due to the Public Service's ability to translate the PAP's political visions into actual public services. That turn-around of the bureaucracy, from its politically disconnected and self-serving image to one that was dependable to the regime, can be traced to the reforms introduced through the Political Study Centre.

The priority accorded to training the leadership elite arose from their role as spearheads of reforms across the bureaucracy. Chapter 3 pointed out that, with the bureaucracy pressed into an "economic general staff" to direct the capitalist developmental state in the 1970s, senior civil servants needed to quickly pick up management skills. Evidently, the focus in every training initiative, whether the Political Study Centre, the Staff Training Institute or later, the Civil Service Institute, started with the elite Administrative Service leadership corps in mind. This emphasis on the elite was not a random or personal choice by this author. Rather, this study reported the reality of the highly-selective Administrative Service cadre as a longstanding focus of the Public Service and the government. In reality, this leadership cadre did indeed play a highly influential role that was disproportionate to their small number. Training was focused on 'training the leaders' and cultivating leadership. Although the HR structure of a leadership apex presiding over all other staff across the base of the hierarchy was a colonial legacy, it was allowed to continue after independence (*see* Tables 7.1 and 7.2). The bureaucracy's

Table 7.1:   Personnel Structure of the Singapore Public Service, 1959[2]

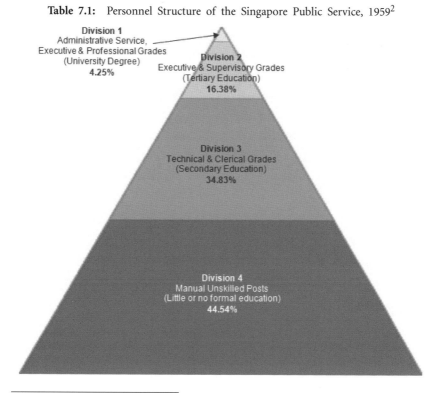

Division 1
Administrative Service,
Executive & Professional Grades
(University Degree)
4.25%

Division 2
Executive & Supervisory Grades
(Tertiary Education)
16.38%

Division 3
Technical & Clerical Grades
(Secondary Education)
34.83%

Division 4
Manual Unskilled Posts
(Little or no formal education)
44.54%

---

[2]*PSC Report* 1959–1960: 4.

Table 7.2: Proportion of Civil Servants in each Division (Actual Numbers and Percentage), 1959–1969[3]

	Total	Division 1	Division 2	Division 3	Division 4
1959	28,253	1,200	4,628	9,841	12,584
		4.25%	16.38%	34.83%	44.54%
1969	57,650	3,794	16,327	16,257	21,272
		6.58%	28.32%	28.20%	36.90%

personnel structure remained pyramidal — a small Division 1 presiding over the supervisory, technical, and manual grades that formed the base of the hierarchy. Correspondingly, executive development and training took on a bifurcated character.

The purpose in prioritising the leadership elite was apparently to employ them, post-training, as vanguards of reforms across the bureaucracy. The productivity movement and computerisation drive in the 1980s demonstrated this *modus operandi* in action, as recounted in Chapter 4. In each instance, the Administrative Service officers were first trained in order for them, upon returning to their respective posts across the bureaucracy, to introduce and lead these reforms among the staff under their supervision. In this process, reforms were quickly cascaded down and across the depth and breadth of the whole hierarchy. Hence, while every training initiative first targeted the leadership elite, this prioritisation sought to equip them as spearheads to introduce and disseminate reforms across the whole Public Service.

Despite the leadership-priority, the dilemma between elite and broad-based training did tend to preoccupy the Singapore bureaucracy. As the training schools grew and began to institutionalise their presence, training programmes for all personnel across the hierarchy expanded amid the prioritisation accorded the Administrative Service corps. So significant was the growth of broad-based programmes in the early 1980s that some among the Public Service leadership saw the Civil Service Institute becoming a school for the rank-and-file. Perhaps, the lack of headway in parallel efforts to set up a staff college for the AOs sharpened

[3] *Ibid*; SAR 1969: 228.

the debate — should resources be concentrated on developing talented leaders with pivotal roles over the bureaucracy, or should attention be evenly distributed among all officers to skill up the whole bureaucracy? The establishment of the Civil Service College in 1993 institutionalised the emphasis on executive development, as addressed in Chapter 5. However, the hurry to transfer leadership programmes from the CSI caused staff in the latter organisation to see a hollowing out of their *raison d'être*. Although unintended, such angst as an organisation nevertheless had the effect of constantly engaging the bureaucracy — including its leadership — in contemplating the subject of training, and its use as a point of introducing reforms into the Public Service.

The Public Service for the 21st Century (PS21) movement launched in 1995 was the epitome in harnessing the use of training to introduce reforms across the bureaucracy. As described in Chapter 6, this drive in the 1990s to improve public services was envisioned with training playing a pivotal role. Yet, skilling up public officers in functional competencies belied the more ambitious goal of PS21, which was to imbibe in public officers a lifelong quest for excellence and learning. For training institutions to lead this attitudinal socialisation, they had to undergo their own reforms of sorts. Key personnel were appointed to the training institutions to consolidate executive development and vocational training under a new Civil Service College in 1996. The injection of competition thereafter compelled CSC staff to attune themselves to the market and ensure that programmes were relevant to their public officer-clientele. The Civil Service College was thus oriented into a constant quest for relevance, becoming a fitting agent to lead the introduction of PS21 reforms of continuous change across the Singapore Public Service.

In sum, training and executive development was employed as a medium to introduce reforms into and across the Singapore Public Service. The use of training to socialise the leadership of the Public Service broke the bureaucracy from 140 years of colonial-era organisational culture and mindset. The priority in training and grooming the leadership elite, a continuity in the 40 years under investigation, was a function of its role in spearheading change and adaptation across the bureaucracy, another constant in the period. Above all, amid the changes in various training initiatives in the course of these four decades — whether these

be renaming the training institutions or changing their organisational
structures — the enduring constant was to ensure that executive
development and training remained relevant to the operating milieu of
the bureaucracy.

7.2 Framework for 'Reforms-Through-Training'

Taking stock of this 40-year period, hence, what are the factors facilitating
the use of training in reforming the Public Service? The political
leadership's consistently strong support was the most crucial factor in
Singapore's use of training to spearhead reforms in the bureaucracy.
Upon their election to government in 1959, the People's Action Party
leadership first started using training as a platform to socialise the
senior officers of the bureaucracy. Subsequent training initiatives might
arise from within the bureaucracy, from management training in the
1970s to productivity in the 1980s, but they owed their existence to
the acquiescence of the political leadership. As projects financed by
public money, they required the prior approval of the Cabinet — not
just the ministers overseeing the bureaucracy, but also the ministers
whose portfolios sought funding from the same budget. Even when Lim
Siong Guan attested that the PS21 initiative "was never cleared with
the political leadership, because I saw the improvement of productivity
and efficiency in the civil service as the responsibility of the civil
service leadership",[4] the location of the Civil Service College and Public
Service Division within the Prime Minister's Office meant that the
'reforms-through-training' programme must have received the prior
blessing of the most senior-ranking political master. Consistently strong
support of the political leadership provided the authorisation and budget,
which then sustained these reform-through-training initiatives.

High economic growth over the years provided the necessary
wherewithal to finance executive development and training as recourse
for reforming the bureaucracy. To be sure, the budget for civil service
training was never extravagant in relation to the overall expenditure of
the state. However, as the country's coffers deepened following years

---

[4]Lim Siong Guan, Interview with Author, 20 November 2013.

Table 7.3: Training Expenditure in relation to National Budget, 1959–2000[5]

Years	Total National Government Expenditure	Total Civil Service Establishment	Training Expenditure Total	per officer
1960	$274,314,430	29,900	$53,920	$1.80
1969	$1,024,893,580	64,229	$238,190	$3.71
1980	$7,635,000,000	69,226	$1,135,700	$16.41
1990	$14,135,000,000	108,939	$4,699,000	$43.13
2000	$28,994,000,000	121,637	$28,536,700	$234.61

of sustained economic growth, the amount of money devoted to the bureaucracy's training in absolute terms increased exponentially. Hence, while the training expenditure remained less than 0.1% of the national budget between 1959 and 2001, the actual dollar value of the training budget grew from a mere S$53,920 to S$28.5 million during the same period. This meant that, even as the size of the bureaucracy increased, the amount of money invested in training each individual public officer grew from S$1.80 in 1959 to S$3.71 a decade later, to S$16.41 in 1980, to S$43.13 in 1990. By 2000, the training dollar per public officer had reached S$235 (US$158) (*see* Table 7.3).

In comparison, the training budgets of other bureaucracies were much lower. In 2000, the Australian Commonwealth government set aside just A$3.9 million (US$2.9 million) for the development and training of all 113,322 officers of the Australian Public Service.[6] This amounted to a

---

[5]Budgetary allocations for the respective training institutions (Political Study Centre, Civil Service Institute and Civil Service College) during each period, except for the year 1969. For 1969, budgetary allocation was for the Training and Organisation Division comprising the Political Study Centre, Staff Training Centre and the Organisation and Methods Branch; data excluded allocations for O&M. Data drawn from *SAR* and *Budget 1960–2001*. Table tracks training expenditure every 10 years, where information is available. USD = S$1.4848 in 2000.

[6]Australian Government, "Prime Minister and Cabinet, Portfolio Budget Statements, 2000–2001," 161, Table 2.1, Output 2, Web, 3 February 2014, http://www.dpmc.gov.au/accountability/budget/1998-2003/docs/pbs_2000-01.pdf.; Public Service & Merit Protection Commission, Australia, *State of the Service, Australian Public Service Statistical Bulletin, 2000–2001* (Canberra: Commonwealth of Australia, 2001) 9, Web 2 February 2014, https://resources.apsc.gov.au/pre2005/SOSR0001.pdf. USD = A$1.3439 in 2000

Table 7.4:   Civil Service Training Expenditure in Selected Jurisdictions, 2000*

Jurisdiction	Total Establishment	Training Expenditure			
		Total		per staff	
Singapore	121,637	SG$28,536,700	US$19,219,221	SG$235	US$158
Australia	113,322	AU$3,938,000	US$2,930,277	AU$35	US$26
Hong Kong	198,605	HK$160,058,000	US$20,672,651	HK$806	US$104

*Malaysian data is available in the Malay language; UK data is not available.

training budget of A$35 (US$26.92) per officer (*see* Table 7.4). In Hong Kong, HK$160 million (US$20.7 million) was allocated for the training and development of a total establishment of 198,605 civil servants.[7] This translated to a training budget of HK$806 (US$104) per officer. Although this was three times that of the Australian figure, this is still half the budget committed to training the Singaporean public officer.

Social development, also benefitting from the rapid economic growth, further facilitated training through reforms. Improvements to general standards of living inevitably raised the quality of human capital available to the Public Service. Specifically, rising educational levels altered the traditional structure of the personnel hierarchy — the proportion of Division 4 posts (manual, and unskilled grades requiring little or no formal education) shrank from 45% of the establishment in 1959 to 37% a decade later (*see* Table 7.5; compare Table 7.6 with Table 7.1). In contrast, the number of Divisions 1 and 2 tertiary-educated executive and professional staff increased from 20% in 1959 to 35% in 1969. By 1976, the proportion of Divisions 1 and 2 officers had grown to 44% of the civil service workforce, while Division 4 officers constituted only 23%.[8] Today, highly-educated administrative and executive Division 1

---

[7]Hong Kong Government, "Head 29, Civil Service Training and Development Institute," *2000–2001 Budget Draft Estimates*, Web, 3 February 2014, http://www.budget.gov.hk/2000/estimates/pdf/english/head029.pdf; Hong Kong Government, "Summary of Establishment," *2000–01 Budget Draft Estimates*, Web, 3 February 2014, http://www.budget.gov.hk/2000/estimates/pdf/english/sum_est_e.pdf. USD = HK$7.7425 in 2000

[8]*SESL* 1976: 7. Records ceased to breakdown the staff numbers according to Divisions from 1976.

Table 7.5: Proportion of Civil Servants in each Division, 1959 and 2013[9]

	Total	Division 1	Division 2	Division 3	Division 4
1959	28,253	1,200	4,628	9,841	12,584
		4.25%	16.38%	34.83%	44.54%
2013	80,128	44,631	26,202	5,689	3,606
		55.70%	32.70%	7.10%	4.50%

Table 7.6: Personnel Structure of the Singapore Public Service, 2013

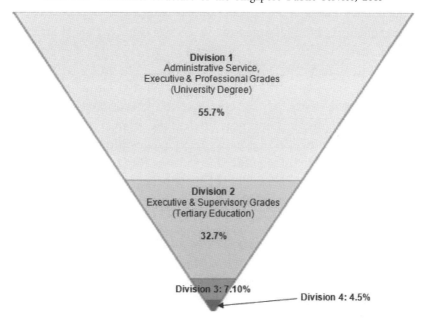

officers constitute more than 50% of the total establishment, while only a small 4.5% remains in Division 4. Rising educational levels among the Singaporean population, funded by a steadily growing economy over the years, allowed the bureaucracy to expand its executive and professional staff, and develop its leadership and long-term strategic capacity. With

[9] *PSC Report* 1959–1960: 4; Civil Service College, "Professionalising Adult Educators," Web, 4 February 2014, http://www.wda.gov.sg/content/dam/wda/pdf/L325B/WS1a_Rinkoo%20Ghosh.pdf.

most public officers thus able to access knowledge and learning, the 'reforms-through-training' agenda could be pursued with greater ease, a shorter timeline, and possibly more effective outcomes.

Finally, the bureaucracy's ability to inspire confidence as an institution of the state allowed it to pursue its reforms agenda through executive development and training. Reforms through the Political Study Centre were initiated by the PAP government at self-government, largely to change the colonial era organisational culture of the bureaucracy, but also to show civil servants 'who is boss'. However, the political masters' initial distrust for the bureaucracy gradually ebbed and, over time, turned into confidence as the reformed Public Service delivered the policies and services that strengthened the PAP's credibility with the electorate. By the time the Civil Service College was marshalled to introduce PS21, the bureaucracy was demonstrating a growing sophistication in training and reforms beyond its capacity for efficiency and effectiveness in delivering public services. More significantly, the latitude granted the bureaucracy to pursue its 'reforms-through-training' agenda, without having to clear the PS21 initiative with the political leadership, for example, reflected the political master's trust in the Public Service as an institution of the state.

7.2.1 *Training-reform-modernisation trajectory?*

Did training result in reforms of the Public Service which, in turn, led to Singapore's modernisation? The empirical data lined up in this book points out that executive development and training did contribute towards the reforms of the Singapore Public Service, but the study also showed that training was only one of the contributory factors. In the state-formation period, for example, the reorientation of the bureaucracy from the colonial organisational culture was pursued — apart from socialising the leadership — by a combination of measures: a campaign against corruption, the tightening of disciplinary regulations, and bridging civil servants' disconnect with citizens by compelling them to undertake public work. Efficiency drives such as productivity and computerisation, while aided by training, were in themselves measures that improved the reliability and performance of the Public Service. At the same time, adjusting the remuneration of civil servants in the face of heightening competition for manpower in the booming economy helped retained talented officers to lead and implement reforms across the Public Service.

Similarly, although a more efficient and high-performing Public Service contributed towards the modernisation of Singapore, the bureaucracy was one among many factors in Singapore's success. The political vision of Lee Kuan Yew and the PAP leadership, while needing implementation by the bureaucracy, was certainly critical in laying out the strategic goal of transforming the colonial outpost into the vibrant city-state that is today's Singapore. The political will in pressing the citizens together in pursuit of economic development, and overcoming dissent and opposition helped provided Singapore with the resources to finance comprehensive social development and reinvestment in further economic development.

These are all factors the study refrained from belabouring in light of limitations in time and space, and with the focus of the book on executive development and training. In sum, executive development and training certainly contributed to the reforms of the Public Service, and a more efficient and high-performing Public Service with high integrity helped the modernisation of Singapore, but there are other contributory factors at the same time.

*   *   *

The defining features of the Singapore development model underscore the positive effects of executive development and training upon the bureaucracy and Singapore's modernisation. Key among these was the importance of strong political initiation and support for the bureaucracy and its reform agenda. Consistently strong support from the political leadership throughout the 40-year period provided the political authorisation necessary to engage in ambitious training exercises, as well as the resource commitments and budgetary allocations to finance the Public Service's training and reforms initiatives. Secondly, an economy-first imperative generated the resources to fund the bureaucracy's programmes. The high-performing Singapore Public Service today had very modest origins and budgetary allocations at the time of self-government. The fruits of prioritising economic development, while taking some time to materialise, provided the wherewithal for the bureaucracy to develop, including growing its training initiatives, and to pursue reforms. At the same time, growth from an economy-first imperative also financed comprehensive social development, which in turn availed higher capacity human capital to staff the Public Service.

7.3 A Template for Cross-Jurisdictional Replication?

The evolution of the Singapore Public Service charts out a trajectory of development for bureaucracies in nascent states. As an almost amateurish bureaucracy in the beginning and alienated from the public it was meant to serve, the Singapore Public Service attracted the intervention and guidance of the political masters to gain a new appreciation of the electoral constituency that was its clientele. By the time it was technically proficient in its primary role of delivering public policies and services in the 1980s, the direct hands of the political masters were no longer as conspicuous and the Public Service was allowed to grow and it developed according to the courses senior civil servants charted for the bureaucracy. When the Public Service embarked upon reforms to prepare itself for the future, with the PS21 movement anticipating change and preparing for change, the bureaucracy had clearly come into its own, confidently charting its own course without the need of political intervention and, many would argue, without fear of upsetting the political leadership.

Amid the background of Singapore's successful modernisation and high-performance reputation of its bureaucracy, distilling these defining features and identifying the Singapore model leads to the inevitable question — can the Singapore model of executive development and training offer a template for countries aspiring reforms?

This book does not seek to prescribe a template for replication in other jurisdictions, but offers some features for consideration. Singapore's use of training to reform its Public Service and, in turn, modernise the country, hinged upon its particular islandwide context. Indeed, the background of this account highlights the exceptional context of Singapore — its small physical size aiding governance, an extended one-party rule providing political continuity, a steady economic growth financing wide-ranging development, and a highly-educated workforce facilitating learning and development. It bears highlighting that these circumstances did not remain static but instead, evolved and changed rapidly over the course of time. Accordingly, the strategy of using training and development to reform the bureaucracy also had to adjust and be adapted to the changing circumstances and context to remain relevant.

The harnessing of executive development and training as a catalyst to reform the bureaucracy offers, at one level, an example that has helped modernise a colonial outpost into a developed state and high-performing economy. Hopefully, this can inspire other jurisdictions — particularly developing countries seeking to reform — an exemplar of the possible despite seemingly implausible odds.

On a deeper level, specific aspects in Singapore's approach towards 'reforms-through-training' in this study can be decontextualised. In other words, these features are not specific to the Singapore jurisdiction alone, and can be explored across other jurisdictional contexts. Hence, these jurisdictional-neutral features offer some themes for consideration, at the very least, some food for reflection for any reform-aspirant.

Consistently strong political support features prominently in Singapore's case. For any initiative to take off within the bureaucracy, the task of securing the necessary political authorisation and approval for funding from the limited budget will be challenging. Yet, as pointed out by Lim Siong Guan, who headed the PS21 reforms in Singapore, training and reforms improve the bureaucracy's capacity to deliver public services: "[Y]ou are doing something intended to raise the capabilities of the Public Service and raise the standard as well as the achievements and capabilities of Singapore."[10] Politicians whose careers depended on electoral votes can be persuaded that any improvement in public services ultimately ingratiates them with the electorate, as the government of the day. Even in countries where different political parties are elected to power at each election, enhanced public services from improved training and reforms will strengthen the electoral position of the political leadership in government. Hence, consistent support from the political masters will provide the authorisation that will kickstart

---

[10]Lim Siong Guan, Interview with Author, 20 November 2013.

and sustain the drive to reform the bureaucracy through training and development.

A strong fiscal position, arising from steady economic growth over the years, certainly provided the fiscal wherewithal to drive and sustain the training-for-reforms initiative in the Singapore Public Service. Economic growth and fiscal largess may not be readily available to most countries, especially developing economies most in need of reforming their bureaucracies. Hence, the reality is the importance of an economy-first imperative, especially for the foundational years, in order to accrue sufficient resources to finance developmental projects.

Improving the population's standards of living often stands out as an obvious and urgent developmental priority, but setting aside budgetary allocations to improve the bureaucracy has the consequential advantage of injecting efficiency in social reforms. Indeed, social development contributes to the reform of the civil service, since its personnel are drawn from the population. The knowledge and skills that are the foundational basis for post-recruitment training and development have their genesis in the educational system. The well-being of civil servants that constitute the bureaucracy's human capital is a function of the population's healthcare and standards of living. The values of civil servants — whether professing high levels of integrity or rent-seeking, service excellence or self-serving behaviour — are shaped by the years of social norms as well as their induction into the bureaucracy. With citizens constituting the vote-banks of the politicians, allocating the yields of an economy-first imperative on social development needs no belabouring. However, focusing solely on social development and neglecting the bureaucracy can undo any progress in development. The key is drawing up a fine balance between investing in social development, wide-ranging as it may be, and executive development and training to reform the bureaucracy.

These features stand out as factors that facilitated Singapore's 'reforms-through-training' experience. As mentioned, they are by no means a definitive solution towards bringing efficiency and effectiveness to all bureaucracies. These are mere factors for consideration, in any reform-venture and — it bears reiteration — their relevance hinges upon the context for their application.

7.4 Starting a Conversation, Areas for Further Study

This book does not aim to provide a prescriptive template as research outcome; rather, it seeks to start a conversation, particularly on the current scholarship in the fields of the history and political science applied to developing nations. By drawing up an administrative history of training and executive development in the Singapore Public Service between 1959 and 2001, this study has filled a gap in current literature on the Singapore bureaucracy, training, and executive development *vis-à-vis* reforms in public administration, and the role played by the Public Service in the historical narratives of Singapore's modernisation.

More significantly, this study wants to raise for discussion, by contextualising the evolution of the Singapore Public Service against the country's economic and social development, whether Singapore's transformation from colonial outpost to modern city-state can completely depend upon the political leadership or, indeed, just *one* man? By tracing the impact of training institutions upon the Singapore bureaucracy, it surfaces for discussion whether training, learning, and executive development have a broader scope in public administration beyond the current bounds of personnel management? Can the bureaucracy and training, learning, and executive development be designed with a more significant and precise role in drawing up state-formation and nation-building strategies for developing countries?

This book is designed with a time distance from the scope in order to desensitise the sources and ease access to information. This approach has worked well indeed, as demonstrated by the availability of crucial information, and can well be the basis for approaching future similar studies. When I began the study, I feared that I would be denied the cooperation of the key actors over the decades and not benefit from their observations and explanations; but this was not the case.[11] A historical orientation (and distance from current politics) proved to be a successful strategy to get key officials to talk of their experiences and observations.

---

[11]All the officials approached for this study agreed to be interviewed or answered my questions through email correspondences.

Be that as it may, events in Singapore affecting the Public Service and the Civil Service College since the period examined for this study have evolved rapidly that an update will soon be timely. The Civil Service College witnessed numerous changes since 2001. The CSC underwent a few leadership successions of Deans. A visioning exercise around 2006 tempered the performance-driven orientation with a greater emphasis on staff well-being. A broadening in the definition of talents by the Public Service Division, beyond the traditional bounds of the Administrative Service, led the CSC to expand its stable of executive development programmes. This is a significant development given the longstanding emphasis on grooming *only* the Administrative Service elite, and the constant dilemma between leadership development and broad-based training.

Structurally, the CSC underwent several organisational changes since 2001, as its programmes and personnel strength grew to meet the new environment. Its main internal departments at the time when the CSC became a statutory board have been renamed a decade later — the Institute of Policy Development has since become the Institute of Public Sector Leadership, and the CSC Consultants evolved into the Institute of Leadership and Organisational Development, although the IPAM has retained its name. A new research centre had also been set up as the Institute of Governance and Policy. These are not mere changes in nomenclature but signal significant repositioning in the role and importance of executive training in Singapore.

Changes in the operating milieu of the Public Service, particularly after the 2011 General Elections, are also requiring the CSC to adjust itself in relation to the bureaucracy. The 2011 election has sharpened the impact of citizens upon politics, especially with the access to Internet technologies and new media, and the proliferation of views and the rapid snowballing of opinions on social media, compressing the time and space for policy responses. As the government continues to grapple with the complexity of emerging issues, such as an ageing population, healthcare financing, remaining economically competitive, transnational terrorism and non-traditional security threats, just to name a few, it has to set aside additional attention to engage with the citizenry.

How the Civil Service College will respond to the inevitable changes expected from the present Public Service in this newly-emerging operating milieu should be the focus of an update to this administrative history or even a dedicated study. Indeed, with the tetra-speed of Internet media compressing policymaking and response timeline, the 'new normal' will probably soon be succeeded, if not already, by a 'newer normal'. The time-lapse needed to facilitate access to data can well be shortened in order for a timelier review. There is much scope for future research to follow up from this study.

Bibliography

Unpublished Sources

Civil Service College, Singapore
Civil Service College Records

National Archives of Singapore

AR 8 & 49	Ministry of Culture
MF 267	Ministry of Finance
PRO 17 & 24	Public Relations Office

Public Records Office, Hong Kong

Civil Service Training Division. Internal Circular No. 15/79. 12 June 1979.
HKRS 822-1-3

The National Archives, Kew, Great Britain

JY 3	Civil Service College: Working Papers
CO 877	Colonial Office: Appointments Department
CO 1017	Colonial Office and successors: Colonial Service Division
CO 1022	Colonial Office: South East Asia Department: Original Correspondence
CO 1030	Colonial Office and Commonwealth Office: Far Eastern Department.

Personal Records

John Ewing-Chow's Papers (JEC)

Published Official Sources

Australia

Australian Government. "Prime Minister and Cabinet, Portfolio Budget Statements, 2000–2001." Web, 3 February 2014, http://www.dpmc.gov.au/accountability/budget/1998-2003/docs/pbs_2000-01.pdf.

Public Service & Merit Protection Commission, Australia. *State of the Service, Australian Public Service Statistical Bulletin, 2000–2001.* Canberra: Commonwealth of Australia, 2001. Web, 2 February 2014, https://resources.apsc.gov.au/pre2005/SOSR0001.pdf.

Great Britain

Cabinet Office. *Annual Report and Accounts, 2011–2012.* London: Stationary Office, 2012.

Colonial Office. *Organisation of the Colonial Service Command paper No. 197.* London, His Majesty's Stationery Office, 1946.

———. *Post-War Training for the Colonial Service: Report of a Committee appointed by the Secretary of State for the Colonies, Colonial No. 198.* London: His Majesty's Stationary Office, 1946.

Commonwealth Secretariat. *Current Good Practices and New Developments in Public Service Management: A Profile of the Public Service of Singapore.* London: Commonwealth Secretariat, 1998.

National School of Government. *Annual Report and Resource Accounts, 2006–2007.* London: Stationary Office, 2007.

Hong Kong

Civil Service Training Centre. *Prospectus 1983–1984.* Hong Kong: Civil Service Training Centre, 1983.

Hong Kong. *Report on the Public Service (1965–1971).*

Hong Kong Government. *2000–2001 Budget Draft Estimates.* Web, 3 February 2014, http://www.budget.gov.hk/2000/estimates/pdf/english/head029.pdf.

———. *Report on Training of Government Servants 1952–1958.* Hong Kong: Establishment Branch, Colonial Secretariat, Hong Kong, 1958.

——— "The Facts." Web, 4 August 2011, http://www.gov.hk/en/about/abouthk/facts.htm.

Hong Kong Government Records Service. "Public Records Office." Web, 6 October 2011, http://www.grs.gov.hk/ws/english/org_pro.htm.

Malaysia

Malayan Union. *Report of the Asiatics in Senior Posts Committee.* Kuala Lumpur, Malayan Union Government Press, 1946.

Malaysia, National Institute of Public Administration. "INTAN in Brief." Web, 5 October 2011, http://www.intanbk.intan.my/i-portal/en/about-intan/intan-in-brief.html.

Singapore

Alpha Soc Newsletter (1986–1993).

ASAS Newsletter (1977).

Bakti: Journal of the Political Study Centre 1 (July 1960) – 4.1 (November 1966).

Civil Service College. *Civil Service College Annual Reports (CSC) (2001/03–2004/05)*. Singapore: CSC.

———. "Milestone Programmes." Web, 6 June 2011, http://www.cscollege.gov.sg/page.asp?id=55&pf-=1.

———. "Writing Reports and Proposals." Web, 28 January 2013, http://www.cscollege.gov.sg/programmes/pages/display%20programme.aspx?PID=2590;

———. "Written Dynamics." Web, 28 January 2013, http://www.cscollege.gov.sg/programmes/Pages/Display%20Programme.aspx?PID=2579.

———. "Professionalising Adult Educators." Web, 4 February 2014, http://www.wda.gov.sg/content/dam/wda/pdf/L325B/WS1a_Rinkoo%20Ghosh.pdf.

Civil Service Institute *Civil Service Institute Training Programme (1980–1996)*. Singapore: CSI.

Civil Service Staff Development Institute. *Training Programme (1976–1979)*. Singapore: CSSDI.

Colony of Singapore. *Report of the Singapore Constitutional Commission*. Singapore: Government Printing Office, 1953.

Colony of Singapore Annual Report, 1954–1958. (continued as *State of Singapore Annual Report, 1959*).

———Department of Statistics. *Economic and Social Statistics: Singapore 1960–1982* Singapore: Department of Statistics, 1983.

———. "Latest Data." Web, 8 April 2014, http://www.singstat.gov.sg/statistics/latest_data.html#1.

Ethos (1994–2001)

Institute of Public Administration and Management, CSC. *Training Directory (1997/98–2000)*. Singapore: IPAM.

Language Section, CSI. *Handbook on Written Communication*. Singapore: CSI, undated.

Management Development (1973–1984).

Ministry of Culture. *One year of peaceful revolution, June 3, 1959 to June 3, 1960*. Singapore: Ministry of Culture, 1960.

———. *Singapore Government Directory (Govt Directory) (1977–2002)*. Singapore: Ministry of Culture.

———. *What you should know about (Ministries and Departments)*. Singapore: Government Printing Office, 1959.

————. *Year of fulfilment, June 1961–June 1962.* Singapore: Ministry of Culture, 1962.

————. *Year of progress, June 1960–June 1961.* Singapore: Ministry of Culture, 1960.

Ministry of Finance. *The Budget for the Financial Year (Budget) (1960–2001).* Singapore: Ministry of Finance.

Ministry of Manpower. "Unemployment." Web, 8 April 2014, http://stats.mom. gov.sg/Pages/Unemployment-Summary-Table.aspx.

National Archives of Singapore. "Speech by the Prime Minister, Mr Goh Chok Tong, at the Third Administrative Service Dinner, 5 July 1991" Web, 22 June 2014, http://www.nas.gov.sg/archivesonline/data/pdfdoc/gct19910705.pdf.

————. "The Civil Service — A Retrospective." Web, 7 December 2011, http://www.a2o.com.sg/a2o/public/html/findoutmore/accq01_06.jsp.

————. *The Papers of Lee Kuan Yew: Speeches, Interviews and Dialogues.* Singapore: National Archives of Singapore, 2012.

National Computer Board. *Connected Government — Using IT in the Singapore Civil* Service. Singapore: NCB, 1998.

Parliament of Singapore *Parliamentary Debates Republic of Singapore, Official Report* (1965–2001).

Public Service Commission. *Annual Report (1959–1981).* Singapore: PSC.

Singapore. *Directory (1961–1975).* Singapore: Government Printing Office.

————. *Establishment List for the Financial Year (Estab List) (1974–1976).* Singapore: Government Printing Office.

————. *Malayanisation, Statement of policy.* Singapore, Government Printing Office, 1956.

————. "National Heritage Board Act, 1993." *Government Gazette, Acts Supplement,* 14 May 1993.

————. *Report of the Public Service Commission (PSC Report) (1959–1962).* Singapore: Government Printer, 1962.

————. *Reprint of the Constitution of the Republic of Singapore.* Prepared by the Attorney-General, Singapore, with the authority of the President, 31 March 1980.

————. *Towards a more just society.* Singapore: Government Printing Office, 1959.

Singapore, 1969–2001.

Singapore Year Book, 1966–1968 (continued as *Singapore, 1969*).

Singapore Department of Statistics *Economic and Social Statistics: Singapore 1960–1982.* Singapore: Department of Statistics, 1983.

————. *Singapore in Figures 2011,* Web, 8 August 2011, http://www.singstat.gov. sg/pubn/reference/sif2011.pdf.

Singapore Establishment Staff List (1955–1976).

Singapore Legislative Assembly Debates (1959–1963) (continued as *Parliamentary Debates, Republic of Singapore 1965*).

Singapore Horizon Scanning Centre. "The RAHS Programme." Web, 4 August 2011, http://app.hsc.gov.sg/public/www/content.aspx?sid=5.
Singapore Public Service Division "Organisation Chart." Web, 4 August 2011, http://www.psd.gov.sg/AboutUs/OrganisationChart/.
———. "Speech by Mr Eddie Teo, Permanent Secretary (Prime Minister's Office), at the Launch of Civil Service College (CSC)." 8 October 2001. Web, 18 September 2013, http://app.psd.gov.sg/data/Speech10Oct2001.pdf.
Staff Training Institute. *Report of Activities, July–December 1972.*
Staff Training Institute, Ministry of Finance. *Training Programme 1975*, January 1975.
State of Singapore. Annual Report, 1959–1964 (continued as *Singapore Year Book, 1966*).

Newspapers

Business Times. 11 July 1992, 20 April 1993, 28 February 1996.
The Singapore Standard. 14 November 1957.
The Straits Times. 1959–2001.

Oral History Interviews

Goh Koh Pui. Oral interview transcript. NAS, Accession no. 288, Reel 11.
Goh Sin Tub. Oral interview transcript. NAS, Accession no. 1422, Reels 4–5.
Vernon Palmer. Oral interview transcript. NAS, Accession no. 1423, Reel 9.
Tan Chok Kian. Oral interview transcript. NAS, Accession no. 1400, Reel 3.
Teo Kah Leong. Oral interview transcript. NAS, Accession no. 1431, Reel 4.

Interviews and Email Correspondences

Anonymous by request of Interviewee. Interview with Author, 20 June 2012.
Chew, Evelyn. Email correspondence with Author, 12 April 2013.
Ewing-Chow, John. Interview with Author, 28 December 2011.
Ghosh, Rinkoo. Email correspondence with Author, 15 September 2013.
Hochstadt, Herman R. Interview with Author, 21 August 2012.
Jeyamalar, Ayadurai. Interview with Author, 25 June 2012.
Lam, Patricia. Email correspondence with author, 27 March 2013.
Lim Ang Yong. Interview with Author, 21 June 2012.
Lim Hsiu Mei. Interview with Author, 21 August 2012.
Lim Siong Guan. Interview with Author, 20 November 2013.
Lim Soo Hoon. Interview with Author, 15 June 2012.
Logendran, Mylvaganam. Interview with Author, 25 October 2013.
Ma Kwok Leung David. Interview with Author, 8 March 2013.
Mahbubani, Kishore. Interview with Author, 20 June 2012.
Ngiam Su Wei. Interview with Author, 9 October 2013.
Ngiam Tong Dow. Interview with Author, 10 January 2013.

Ong Boon Kwee Peter. Interview with Author, 6 June 2012.
Tan Boon Huat. Interview with Author, 14 January 2013.
Tan Saw Tin Tina. Interview with Author, 31 October 2013.
Tan Thiam Soon. Interview with Author, 21 November 2012.
Tan Tian Hong Roger. Interview with Author, 18 October 2013.
Teo Hee Lian. Interview with Author, 3 January 2012.
Teong, Jaime. Interview with Author, 21 February 2014.
Vij, Kirpa Ram. Interview with Author, 22 January 2013.
Wong Mei Ching Michelle. Interview with Author, 24 October 2013.
Wong Wing Ping Joseph. Interview with Author, 6 September 2013.
Yeo Yong Boon George. Email correspondence with Author, 21 June 2012.

Dissertations and Theses

Ghosh, Rinkoo. "An Empirical Study on a Customer-focused Strategy for a Singapore Government Training Organisation," Doctor of Business Administration dissertation, Graduate School of Business, Southern Cross University, 2008.
Lai, Tony. "Administrative training in the Singapore civil service: an evaluation of recent changes." B.Soc.Sci.(Hons) academic exercise, National University of Singapore, 1995.
Lee Ah Chai. "Singapore under the Japanese, 1942–1945." B.A.(Hons) academic exercise, Department of History, University of Malaya, Singapore, 1956.
Lee Boon Hiok. "The Singapore civil service and its perceptions of time." PhD thesis, University of Hawaii, 1976.
Lim Peng Soon. "Organisational Change and the Impact on the Individual: A Phenomenological Study in the Transitory Experience of Employees in the Context of Transformational Change in Organisations." D.Ed. dissertation, George Washington University, 2006.
Quah, Jon S. T. "Administrative Reform and Development Administration in Singapore: a comparative study of the Singapore Improvement Trust and the Housing and Development Board." PhD thesis, Florida State University, 1975.
_____. "The Public Service Commission in Singapore: a comparative study of its evolution and its recruitment and selection procedures *vis-à-vis* the Public Service Commissions in Ceylon, India and Malaysia." M.Soc.Sci. Thesis, Dept. of Political Science, University of Singapore, 1971.
Sangiah, Saravanan s/o. "Transformation of the Civil Service College into a Statutory Board: Causes and Implications." B.Soc.Sci.(Hons) academic exercise, Department of Political Science, National University of Singapore, 2003.

Seah Chee Meow. "Bureaucratic evolution and political change in an emerging nation: a case study of Singapore." PhD thesis, Manchester: Victoria University of Manchester, 1971.

Sim Sock Hoon. "Training in the Singapore Administrative Service." B.Soc.Sci. (Hons) academic exercise, National University of Singapore, 1985.

Siow, Viola. "Training in the Singapore civil service: the way forward." B.Soc.Sci.(Hons) academic exercise, National University of Singapore, 1998.

Tan Kang Uei Anthony. "Meritocracy in the Singapore Civil Service: recruitment and promotion of Administrative Service officers." B.Soc.Sci.(Hons) academic exercise, National University of Singapore, 1997.

Books and Articles

Abdul Manaf, Noor Hazilah. "Civil service system in Malaysia" *Public Administration in Southeast Asia: Thailand, Philippines, Hong Kong and Macao.* Ed. Evan Berman. London: Routledge, 2011. 211–235.

Abdullah, Wan Mansor. *Service Par Excellence.* Kuala Lumpur: PNMB, 2004.

Anek Laothamatas, "Development and Democratisation: A Theoretical Introduction with Reference to the Southeast Asian and East Asian Cases." *Democratisation in Southeast and East Asia,* ed., Anek Laothamatas. Singapore: Institute of Southeast Asian Studies, 1997. 1–20.

――――. Ed. *Democratisation in Southeast and East Asia* Singapore: Institute of Southeast Asian Studies, 1997.

Ang Cheng Guan. "Writing Diplomatic History: A Personal Journey." *The Makers & Keepers of Singapore History.* Eds. Loh Kah Seng and Liew Kai Khiun. Singapore: Ethos Books and Singapore Heritage Society, 2010. 171–180.

Michael Armstrong. *A Handbook of Personnel Management Practice.* London: Kogan Page Limited, 1996.

――――. *Armstrong's Handbook of Strategic Human Resource Management.* London: Kogan Page, 2011.

Asmerom, Haile K. and Reis, Elisa P. Eds. *Democratization and bureaucratic neutrality,* New York: St. Martin's Press, 1996.

Australia New Zealand School of Government. "Who We Are." Web, 5 October 2011, http://www.anzsog.edu.au/content.asp?pageId=106.

Baharudin, Zulkifli. "Singapore 2002: The Remaking of Singapore." *Singapore 2002.* Singapore: Ministry of Information and the Arts, 2002. 2–12.

Baumgartner, Frank and Jones, Bryan. *Agendas and Instability in American Politics.* Chicago: University of Chicago Press, 2009.

Bellows, Thomas J. "Bureaucracy and Development in Singapore." *Asian Journal of Public Administration* 7.1 (June 1985): 55–69.

――――. "Meritocracy and the Singapore Political System." *Asian Journal of Political Science* 17.1 (April 2009): 24–44.

Berman, Evan. Ed. *Public Administration in Southeast Asia: Thailand, Philippines, Hong Kong and Macao.* London: Routledge, 2011.

———, James S. Bowman, Jonathon P. West, Montgomery R. Van Wart, *Human Resource Management in Public Service: Paradoxes, Processes and Problems.* Los Angeles: SAGE, 2010.

Bird, Dennis L. "Training Civil Servants: Some Reflections after 17 Years." *Public Policy and Administration,* 7.2 (Summer 1992): 70–79.

Bloodworth, Dennis *The Tiger and the Trojan Horse.* Singapore: Times Books International, 1984.

Blunt, Edward. *The Indian Civil Service.* London: Faber and Faber Ltd., 1937.

Bogaars, George "Public Services" *Towards Tomorrow: Essays on Development and Social Transformation in Singapore.* Singapore: National Trade Unions Congress, 1973. 72–83.

Burns, John "Explaining Civil Service Reforms in Asia." *The Civil Service in the 21st Century: Comparative Perspectives* Eds. Jos C.N. Raadschelders, Theo A.J. Toonen and Frits M. Von der Meer. Hampshire & New York: Palgrave Macmillan, 2007. 65–81.

———. Ed. *Asian civil service systems: improving efficiency and productivity.* Singapore: Times Academic Press, 1994.

——— and Scott, Ian. Eds. *The Hong Kong Civil Service: Personnel Policies and Practices.* Hong Kong: Oxford University Press, 1988.

Caldwell, Lynton K. *Improving the Public Service through Training.* Washington, DC: Agency for International Development, 1962.

———. "The relevance of administrative history." *International Review of Administrative Sciences,* 21.3 (1955): 453–466.

Chaidhry, Shahid, Reid, Gary and Malik, Waleed. Eds. Washington, D.C.: The World Bank, 1994.

Chan Heng Chee. *A sensation of independence: a political biography of David Marshall.* Singapore: Oxford University Press, 1984.

———. "Politics in an administrative state: Where had the politics gone?" *Trends in Singapore.* Ed. C.M. Seah. Singapore: Institute of Southeast Asian Studies, 1975. 51–68.

———. "Political Developments, 1965–1979." *History of Singapore.* Eds. Ernest Chew and Edwin Lee. Oxford University Press, 1991. 157–181.

———. "The PAP and the Structuring of the Political System." *Management of Success: The Moulding of Modern Singapore.* Eds. Kernial Singh Sandhu, and Paul Wheatley. Singapore: Institute of Southeast Asian Studies, 1990. 70–89.

Cheong Yip Seng. *OB Markers: My Straits Times Story.* Singapore: Straits Times Press, 2013.

Cheng Siok Hwa. "Economic change and industrialization." *History of Singapore.* Eds. Ernest Chew and Edwin Lee. Oxford University Press, 1991. 182–215.

Chew, Ernest and Lee, Edwin. Eds. *History of Singapore*. Oxford University Press, 1991.

Chin, James. "History and Context of Public Administration in Malaysia." *Public Administration in Southeast Asia: Thailand, Philippines, Malaysia, Hong Kong and Macau*. Ed. Evan Berman. London: Routledge, 2011. 141–154.

Chu, Yun-han. "State structure and economic adjustment of the East Asian newly industrialising countries." *International Organisation* 43.4 (Autumn 1989): 647–672.

Chua Mui Hoong. *Pioneers once more: the Singapore Public Service, 1959–2009*. Singapore: Straits Times Press and Public Service Division, 2010.

Clague, Christopher. "Bureaucracy and Economic Development." *Structural Change and Economic Dynamics*, 5.2 (1994): 273–291.

Clutterbuck, Richard. *Conflict and Violence in Singapore and Malaysia, 1945–1983*. Colorado: Westview, 1985.

Cotton, James. Ed. *Korea under Roh Taewoo*. New South Wales: Allen and Unwin, 1993.

Daniel, Patrick. "Singapore in 1997: A Review." *Singapore 1998*. Singapore: Ministry of Information and the Arts, 1998. 1–13.

Davies, Jonathan S. and Imbroscio, David L. Eds. *Critical urban studies: new directions*. Albany: State University of New York Press, 2010.

de Cruz, Gerald. *Rojak Rebel: Memoirs of a Singapore Maverick*. Singapore: Times, 1993.

Dean, Peter. Ed. *Government Budgeting in Developing Countries*. London and New York: Routledge, 1989.

Dowding, Keith. *The Civil Service* London: Routledge, 1995.

Drysdale, John. *Singapore: Struggle for success*. Singapore: Times Books International, 1984.

Dzafir, Ridzwan. *Ridzwan Dzafir: From Pondok boy to Singapore's Mr ASEAN: an autobiography*. Singapore, Didier Millet, 2009.

Eddy, J.J. and Nethercote, J.R. Eds. *From Colony to Coloniser*. Sydney: Hale & Iremonger, 1987.

ESCAP, "History." Web, 27 December 2012, http://www.unescap.org/about/history.

Evans, Peter "Transferable lessons? Re-examining the institutional prerequisites of East Asian economic policies." *Journal of Development Studies*, 34.6 (August 1998): 66–86.

Fischer, Frank, Miller, Gerald and Sidney, Mara. Eds. *Handbook of Public Policy Analysis: Theory, Politics and Methods*. Boca Raton: CRC Press, 2006.

Flora, Peter. Ed. *State formation, nation-building and mass politics in Europe: the theory of Stein Rokkan*. Oxford: Oxford University Press, 1999.

Fong, Peter K.W. "Training as an Instrument of Organisational Change in Public Administration in Hong Kong." *Handbook of Comparative Public*

Administration in the Asia-Pacific Basin. Eds. Hoi-kwok Wong and Hon S. Chan. New York: Mercel Dekker, 1999. 253–277.

Fry, Geoffrey. *Statesmen in disguise: The changing role of the administrative class of the British Home Civil Service, 1853–1966.* London: Macmillan, 1969.

Ghesquiere, Henri. *Singapore's success: engineering economic growth.* Singapore: Thomson Learning, 2007.

Gladden, E.N. *A history of public administration.* London: Frank Cass, 1972.

Grebenik, E. "The Civil Service College: The First Year." *Public Administration* 50(1972): 127–138.

Han Fook Kwang, Fernandez, Warren and Tan, Sumiko. *Lee Kuan Yew: The man and his ideas.* Singapore: Times Editions, 1998.

Hanaoka, Keiso. Ed. *Comparative Study on the Local Public Administration in Asian and Pacific Countries.* Tokyo: EROPA Local Government Centre, 1984.

Harris, Peter. *Foundations of Public Administration.* Hong Kong: Hong Kong University Press, 1991.

Heng Hiang Khng. "Economic Development and Political Change: The Democratisation Process in Singapore." *Democratisation in Southeast and East Asia* ed. Anek Laothamatas. Singapore: Institute of Southeast Asian Studies, 1997. 113–140.

Hewison, Kevin, Rodan, Garry and Robison, Richard. Eds. *Southeast Asia in the 1990s: Authoritarianism, democracy and capitalism.* Australia: Allen & Unwin Pty Ltd, 1993.

Heussler, Robert. *British Rule in Malaya: The Malayan Civil Service and Its Predecessors, 1867–1942.* Oxford: Clio Press, 1981.

_____. *Yesterday's Rulers: The Making of the British Colonial Service.* London: Oxford University Press, 1963.

Ho Khai Leong. *The politics of policy-making in Singapore.* Singapore: Oxford University Press, 2000.

Haque, Ahmed Shafiqul Lee, Grace O.M. and Cheung, Anthony B.L. *The civil service in Hong Kong: continuity and change.* Hong Kong: Hong Kong University Press, 1998.

_____ and Vyas, Lina. *Public service in a globalized world: central training institutes in India and Hong Kong.* Aldershot: Ashgate Publishing, 2004.

_____, Lam, Jermain T.M. and Lee, Jane C.Y. Eds. *Public Administration in the NICs: Challenges and Accomplishments.* London: Macmillan Press, 1996.

Johnson, Chalmers. *MITI and the Japan Miracle.* California: Stanford University Press, 1982.

_____. "South Korean Democratisation: The Role of Economic Development." *Korea under Roh Taewoo.* Ed. James Cotton. New South Wales: Allen and Unwin, 1993. 1–10.

_____. "The Developmental State: Odyssey of a Concept." *The developmental state*. Ed. Meredith Woo-Cummings. New York: Cornell University Press, 1999. 32–60.

_____. "The nonsocialist NICs: East Asia." *International Organisation* 40.2 (March 1986): 557–565.

Jones, David Seth. "Public Service for the 21st Century – PS21." *Everyday Life, Everyday People*. Eds. Chua Fook Kee and Thana Luxshme Thaver. Singapore: Ministry of Education and National University of Education, 1997. 76–80.

_____. "Recent reforms in Singapore's administrative elite: Responding to the challenges of a rapidly changing economy and society." *Asian Journal of Political Science* 10.2 (2002): 70–93.

Jones, Ray. *The Nineteenth Century Foreign Office: An Administrative History*. London: Weidenfeld and Nicolson, 1971.

Keeling, Desmond. "The Development of Central Training in the Civil Service, 1963–1970." *Public Administration*, 49 (1971): 51–71.

Kernaghan, Kenneth and Langford, John W. *The Responsible Public Servant*. Nova Scotia: Institute for Research on Public Policy, 1991.

Kirk-Greene, Anthony *On Crown Service: A History of HM Colonial and Overseas Civil Services, 1837–1997*. London: I.B. Taurius & Co., 1999.

Kirkpatrick, Donald L. and Kirkpatrick, James D. *Evaluating Training Programmes: The Four Levels*. San Francisco: Berrett-Koehler Publishers, 2006.

Klinger, Donald E. and Nalbandian, John. *Public Personnel Management: Contexts and Strategies*. New Jersey: Prentice Hall, 2003.

Koh, Gillian. "Bureaucratic rationality in an evolving developmental state: Challenges to governance in Singapore." *Asian Journal of Political Science*, 5.2 (1997): 114–141.

Kratoska, Paul. *Japanese Occupation, The Japanese Occupation of Malaya: A Social and Economic History*. London: Hurst & Co., 1998.

Kurosawa, Susumu, Fujiwara, Toshihiro and Reforma, Mila A. Eds. *New trends in public administration for the Asia-Pacific region: decentralization*. Tokyo: Local Autonomy College, Ministry of Home Affairs, 1996.

Kurosawa, Susumu, Fujiwara, Toshihiro and Reforma, Mila A. Eds. *Corruption and Governance in Asia*. Basingstoke: Palgrave Macmillan, 2003.

Kwa Chong Guan and Ho Chi Tim. "Archival Records in the Writing of Singapore History: A Perspective from the Archives." *The Makers & Keepers of Singapore History*. Eds. Loh Kah Seng and Liew Kai Khiun. Singapore: Ethos Books and Singapore Heritage Society, 2010. 48–64.

Koh Buck Song. Ed. *Heartwork: Stories of how EDB steered the Singapore economy from 1961 into the 21st century*. Singapore: Economic Development Board and EDB Society, 2002.

Tommy Koh and Chang Li Lin. Eds. *The Little Red Dot: reflections by Singapore's diplomats* Singapore: World Scientific, 2005.

Lam Peng Er and Tan, Kevin Y.L. Eds. *Lee's Lieutenants: Singapore's Old Guard.* Australia: Allen & Unwin, 1999.

Latif, Asad *Lim Kim San: A builder of Singapore.* Singapore: ISEAS, 2009.

Lau, Albert *A Moment of Anguish: Singapore in Malaysia and the Politics of Disengagement.* Singapore: Times Academic Press, 1998.

_____. *The Malayan Union controversy, 1942–1948.* Singapore: Oxford University Press, 1991.

Lee Boon Hiok *Statutory boards in Singapore.* Singapore: University of Singapore, 1975.

_____. "The Bureaucracy." *Management of Success: The Moulding of Modern Singapore.* Eds. Kernial Singh Sandhu and Paul Wheatley. Singapore: Institute of Southeast Asian Studies, 1990. 90–101.

_____. "The Public Personnel System in Singapore." *Asian Civil Services: Developments and Trends.* Eds. Amara Raksasataya and Heindrich Siedentopf. Kuala Lumpur: Asian and Pacific Development and Administrative Centre, 1980. 431–479.

Lee, Edwin. "The Colonial Legacy," *Management of Success: The Moulding of Modern Singapore.* Eds. in Kernial Singh Sandhu and Paul Wheatley. Singapore: Institute of Southeast Asian Studies, 1990. 3–50.

Lee Geok Boi. *The Syonan Years: Singapore under Japanese rule, 1942–1945.* Singapore: National Archives of Singapore, 2005.

Lee, Jane C.Y. "Transformation of Public Administration in Hong Kong: Managing an Expanding Economy in the Process of Political Transition." *Public Administration in the NICs: Challenges and Accomplishments.* Eds. Ahmed Shafiqul Huque, Jermain T.M. Lam and Jane C.Y. Lee. London: Macmillan Press, 1996. 33–58.

Lee Kuan Yew. *From Third World to First: The Singapore Story, 1965–2000, Memoirs of Lee Kuan Yew.* Singapore: Singapore Press Holdings and Times Editions, 2000.

_____. *The Singapore Story: Memoirs of Lee Kuan Yew.* Singapore: Singapore Press Holdings and Times Editions, 1998.

Lee Tsao Yuan. Ed. *Singapore: The Year in Review 1991* Singapore: Institute of Policy Studies, 1992.

_____. "Singapore in 1996: A Review." *Singapore 1997.* Singapore: Ministry of Information and the Arts, 1998. 1–12.

Lim Siong Guan. "The Public Service." *Singapore: The Year in Review 1995.* Ed. Yeo Lay Hwee. Singapore: Institute of Policy Studies, 1996. 35–48.

Loh Kah Seng and Liew Kai Khiun. Eds. *The Makers & Keepers of Singapore History.* Singapore: Ethos Books and Singapore Heritage Society, 2010.

Long, S.R. Joey. "Making and Keeping the History of the US Involvement in Singapore." *The Makers & Keepers of Singapore History*, Eds. Loh Kah Seng and Liew Kai Khiun. Singapore: Ethos Books and Singapore Heritage Society, 2010. 147–157.

Low, James. "Kept in position: the Labour Front-Alliance Government of Chief Minister David Marshall in Singapore, April 1955–June 1956." *Journal of Southeast Asia Studies*, 35.1 (2004): 41–64.

Low, Linda. Ed. *Developmental States: Relevancy, Redundancy or Reconfiguration?* New York: Nova Science Publishers, 2004.

———. *Rethinking Singapore Inc. and GLCs*. Singapore: NUS Business School Research Paper Series, 2002.

———. "Singapore's Developmental State between a Rock and a Hard Place." *Developmental States: Relevancy, Redundancy or Reconfiguration?* Ed. Linda Low. New York: Nova Science Publishers, 2004. 161–178.

———. Ed. *Singapore towards a developed status*. Singapore: Oxford University Press, 1999.

———. "The Singapore developmental state in the new economy and polity." *The Pacific Review*, 14.3 (2001): 411–441.

Lowe, Rodney. *The official history of the British Civil Service: Reforming the Civil Service, Volume 1: The Fulton Years, 1966–1991*. London and New York: Routledge, 2011.

Marican, Y. Mansoor. *Public Personnel Administration in Malaysia*, Research Notes and Discussions Paper No. 12, 1979. Singapore: Institute of Southeast Asian Studies, 1979.

Maslow, A.H. "A Theory of Human Motivation." *Psychological Review* 50 (1943): 370–396. Web 15 July 2014, http://psychclassics.yorku.ca/Maslow/motivation.htm.

Mauzy, Diane K. and Milne, R.S. *Singapore Politics Under the People's Action Party*. London and New York: Routledge, 2002.

Mbabazi, Pamela and Taylor, Ian. Eds. *The Potentiality of 'Developmental States' in Africa: Botswana and Uganda Compared*. Dakar: Codesria, 2005.

McNabb, David. *Research Methods in Political Science: Quantitative and Qualitative Approaches*. New York: M.E. Sharpe Inc., 2010.

Mills, Lennox *British Malaya, 1824–1867*. Kuala Lumpur: Oxford University Press, 1961.

Mercer "2011 Quality of Living worldwide city rankings — Mercer Survey." Web, 7 December 2011, http://www.mercer.com/print.htm;jsessionid=572919tE3ThHq07ITSvbsA**mercer04?indContentType=100&idContent=1173105&indBodyType=D&reference=#Asia-Pac.

Mercer. "Quality of Living worldwide city rankings 2010." 26 May 2010, Web, 17 August 2011, http://www.mercer.com/press-releases/quality-of-living-report-2010.

Mutalib, Hussin. "Domestic Politics." *Singapore: The Year in Review 1991*. Ed. Lee Tsao Yuan. Singapore: Institute of Policy Studies, 1992. 69–106.

Mushkat, Miron. "Staffing the Administrative Class." *The Hong Kong Civil Service: Personnel Policies and Practices*. Eds. John P. Burns & Ian Scott. Hong Kong: Oxford University Press, 1988. 96–117.

Nathan, S. R. *An Unexpected Journey: Path to the Presidency*. Singapore: Editions Didier Millet, 2011.

Ng, Irene. *The Singapore Lion: A biography of S. Rajaratnam*. Singapore: Institute of South East Asian Studies, 2010.

Ngiam Tong Dow. *A Mandarin and the Making of Public Policy: Reflections of Ngiam Tong Dow*. Singapore: NUS Press, 2006.

Ooi Jin-Bee and Chiang Hai Ding. Eds. *Modern Singapore*. Singapore: University of Singapore, 1969.

Omar, Elyas bin. "The Civil Service Systems in Malaysia." Amara Raksasataya and Heindrich Siedentopf. Eds. *Asian Civil Services: Developments and Trends*. Kuala Lumpur: Asian and Pacific Development aresund Administrative Centre, 1980. 249–299.

Ong Teng Cheong. "Bridging the perception gap." *Petir* (August 1992): 9–19

O'Toole, Barry. *The Ideal of Public Service: Reflections on the higher civil service in Britain*. London and New York: Routledge, 2006.

Political & Economic Risk Consultancy Ltd. "Bureaucracy: Asia's Best and Worst." *Asian Intelligence*, No. 885, 16 October 2013: 3.

Pugh, Cedric. "Budget Innovation in Singapore." *Government Budgeting in Developing Countries*. Ed. Peter Dean. London and New York: Routledge, 1989. 91–103.

Pyper, Robert. *The British Civil Service*. Hertfordshire: Prentice Hall/Harvester Wheatsheaf, 1995.

Quah, Jon S. T. *Administrative and legal measures for combating bureaucratic corruption in Singapore*. Singapore: Chopmen, 1978.

―――. "Culture change in the Singapore Civil Service." *Civil service reform in Latin America and the Caribbean*. Eds. Shahid Chaidhry, Gary Reid and Waleed Malik. Washington, D.C.: The World Bank, 1994. 205–216.

―――. "Decentralizing public personnel management: the case of the public sector in Singapore." *New trends in public administration for the Asia-Pacific region: decentralization*. Eds. Susumu Kurosawa, Toshihiro Fujiwara and Mila A. Reforma. Tokyo: Local Autonomy College, Ministry of Home Affairs, 1996. 492–506.

―――. "Improving the efficiency and productivity of the Singapore civil service." *Asian civil service systems: improving efficiency and productivity*. Ed. John P. Burns. Singapore: Times Academic Press, 1994. 152–185.

―――. "Public Administration in a City-State: The Singapore Case." *Comparative Study on the Local Public Administration in Asian and Pacific Countries*.

Ed. Keiso Hanaoka. Tokyo: EROPA Local Government Centre, 1984. 206–216.

―――. *Public Administration Singapore Style.* Singapore: Talisman Publishing, 2010.

―――. "Public bureaucracy and policy implementation in Singapore." *Southeast Asian Journal of Social Science,* 15(2)1987: 77–95.

―――. "Singapore in 1988: Safeguarding the future." *Singapore 1989.* Singapore: Ministry of Communication and Information, 1989. 1–24.

―――. "Singapore's Anti-Corruption." *Corruption and Governance in Asia.* Eds. Susumu Kurosawa, Toshihiro Fujiwara and Mila A. Reforma. Basingstoke: Palgrave Macmillan, 2003. 180–197.

―――. "Statutory Boards." *Government and Politics of Singapore.* Eds. Jon S.T. Quah, Chan Heng Chee and Seah Chee Meow. Singapore: Oxford University Press, 1987. 120–145.

―――. "The Study of Public Administration in the ASEAN Countries." *International Review of Administrative Sciences,* 46 (1980): 354–360.

―――. "Transforming the Singapore civil service for national development." *Democratization and bureaucratic neutrality.* Eds. Haile K. Asmerom and Elisa P. Reis. New York: St. Martin's Press, 1996. 294–312.

―――. "Study of Public Administration in the ASEAN Countries," *International Review of Administrative Sciences,* 46 (1980): 354–360.

―――, Chan Heng Chee and Seah Chee Meow. Eds. *Government and Politics of Singapore.* Singapore: Oxford University Press, 1987.

Raadschelders, Jos C. N. "Administrative History as a Core Dimension of Public Administration." 2008. Web, 6 July 2011, http://www.aspanet.org/scriptcontent/pdfs/FPA-AH-Article.pdf, 2.

―――. *Handbook of Administrative History.* New Brunswick, London: Transaction Publishers, 1998.

―――, Toonen, Theo A. J. and Von der Meer, Frits M. Eds. *The Civil Service in the 21ˢᵗ Century: Comparative Perspectives.* Hampshire & New York: Palgrave Macmillan, 2007.

Raksasataya, Amara and Siedentopf, Heindrich. Eds. *Asian Civil Services: Developments and Trends.* Kuala Lumpur: Asian and Pacific Development and Administrative Centre, 1980.

Rhodes, R. A. W. "Frank Stacey Memorial Lecture 2008: Scenes from the Departmental Court", *Public Policy and Administration,* 24.2 (2009): 437–454.

―――. Ed. *Training in the Civil Service.* London: Joint University Council for Social and Public Administration, 1977.

―――, Wanna, John and Weller, Patrick. *Comparing Westminster.* Oxford: Oxford University Press, 2009.

Rodan, Garry. Ed. *Singapore Changes Guard: Social, Political and Economic Directions in the 1990s.* New York: St. Martin's Press, 1993.

———. "The Growth of Singapore's Middle Class and its Political Significance." *Singapore Changes Guard: Social, Political and Economic Directions in the 1990s.* Ed. Garry Rodan. New York: St. Martin's Press, 1993. 52–71.

Rokkan, Stein. "The Basic Model." *State formation, nation-building and mass politics in Europe: the theory of Stein Rokkan.* Ed. Peter Flora. Oxford: Oxford University Press, 1999. 122–134.

Sandhu, Kernial Singh and Wheatley, Paul. Eds. *Management of Success: The Moulding of Modern Singapore.* Singapore: Institute of Southeast Asian Studies, 1990.

Saxena, N. C. *Virtuous cycles: The Singapore Public Service and national development.* Singapore: United Nations Development Programme, 2011.

Scott, Ian and Burns, John P. "Training." *The Hong Kong Civil Service: Personnel Policies and Practices.* Eds. John P. Burns and Ian Scott. Hong Kong: Oxford University Press, 1988. 118–143.

Scott, Joanne and Wanna, John. "Trajectories of public administration and administrative history in Australia: Rectifying 'a curious blight'?" *Australian Journal of Public Administration,* 64.1 (2005): 11–24.

Seah Chee Meow. "The Administrative State: Quo Vadis?" *Singapore towards a developed status.* Ed. Linda Low. Singapore: Oxford University Press, 1999. 250–270.

———. *The Singapore Bureaucracy and Issues of Transition.* Singapore: University of Singapore, 1975.

———. "The Civil Service." Jon S. T. Quah, Chan Heng Chee and Seah Chee Meow. Eds. *Government and Politics of Singapore.* Singapore: Oxford University Press, 1987. 92–119.

———. Ed. *Trends in Singapore.* Singapore: Institute of Southeast Asian Studies, 1975.

Sidney, Mara S. "Critical perspectives on the city: constructivist, interpretive analysis of urban politics." *Critical urban studies: new directions.* Eds. Jonathan S. Davies and David L. Imbroscio. Albany: State University of New York Press, 2010. 23–39.

Simon, Herbert A. *Administrative Behaviour: A study of Decision-Making Processes in Administrative Organisation.* New York: The Free Press, 1976.

Singh, Bilveer. *Whither PAP's Dominance? An Analysis of Singapore's 1991 General Elections.* Malaysia: Pelanduk Publications, 1992.

Skocpol, Theda. "Bringing the State Back In: Strategies of Analysis in Current Research." *Bringing the State Back In.* Eds. Peter B. Evans, Dietrich Rueschemeyer and Theda Skocpol. Cambridge: Cambridge University Press, 1985. 3–37.

Spann, R. N. *Government Administration in Australia.* Sydney: George Allen and Unwin, 1979.

————. *Public Administration in Australia.* New South Wales: V. C. N. Blight, 1973.

Tan, Lily. "Archival Strategies for Oral Sources in Southeast Asia: Southeast Asia's Forgotten History." Oral History Centre, National Archives of Singapore. *Reflections and Interpretations.* Singapore: National Archives of Singapore, 2005. 32–49.

Tan Siok Sun. *Goh Keng Swee: A portrait.* Singapore: Editions Didier Millet, 2007.

Tan Tai Yong. *Creating 'Greater Malaysia': Decolonization and the Politics of Merger.* Singapore: Institute of Southeast Asian Studies, 2008.

Taylor, Ian. "The Developmental State in Africa: The Case of Botswana." *The Potentiality of 'Developmental States' in Africa: Botswana and Uganda Compared.* Eds. Pamela Mbabazi and Ian Taylor. Dakar: Codesria, 2005. 44–56.

Theakston, Kevin. *The Civil Service since 1945.* Oxford: Blackwell, 1995.

Tilly, Charles. "Reflections on the history of European state-making." *The Formation of National States in Western Europe.* Ed. Charles Tilly. Princeton: Princeton University Press, 1975. 3–83.

————. Ed. *The Formation of National States in Western Europe.* Princeton: Princeton University Press, 1975.

Tilman, Robert. *Bureaucratic Transition in Malaya.* Durham: Duke University Press, 1964.

Torpey, William G. *Public Personnel Management.* Canada: D. Van Nostrand Company, 1953.

Transparency International. "Corruption Perception Index, 2011." Web, 7 December 2011, http://cpi.transparency.org/cpi2011/results/#Country Results.

Trocki, Carl. *Singapore: Wealth, Power and the Culture of Control.* Routledge, 2006.

Turnbull, C. M. *A History of Modern Singapore, 1819–2005.* Singapore: National University of Singapore Press, 2009.

————. "Constitutional Development, 1819–1968." *Modern Singapore.* Eds. Ooi Jin-Bee and Chiang Hai Ding. Singapore: University of Singapore, 1969. 181–196.

————. *The Straits Settlements, 1826–1867: Indian Presidency to Crown Colony.* London: University of London, 1972.

United Nations. "Republic of Singapore: Public Administration Country Profile." November 2005. Web, 2 August 2011, http://unpan1.un.org/intradoc/groups/public/documents/un/unpan023321.pdf.

Van de Walle, Steven and Scott, Zoe. "The Role of Public Services in State- And Nation-Building: Exploring Lessons from European History for Fragile States." Governance and Social Development Resource Centre Research Paper, 2009.

Wade, Robert. *Governing the Market: Economic Theory and the Role of Government in East Asian Industrialisation.* Princeton: Princeton University Press, 1990.

Waldner, David. *State building and late development.* Ithaca: Cornell University Press, 1999.

Wanna, John, Ryan, Christine and Ng, Chew. *From Accounting to Accountability: A Centenary History of the Australian National Audit Office.* Sydney: Allen & Unwin, 2001.

Weiss, Robert S. *Learning from Strangers: The Art and Method of Qualitative Interview Studies.* New York and Toronto: Free Press, 1994.

Wettenhall, R. L. "The challenge of administrative history: an Australian perspective." *Colony to Coloniser.* Eds. J. J. Eddy and J. R. Nethercote. Sydney: Hale & Iremonger, 1987. 14–22.

Wong Hoi-kwok and Chan, Hon S. Eds. *Handbook of Comparative Public Administration in the Asia-Pacific Basin.* New York: Mercel Dekker, 1999.

Woo-Cummings, Meredith. Ed. *The developmental state.* New York: Cornell University Press, 1999.

World Economic Forum. *The Global Competitiveness Report 2010–2011.* Web, 2 August 2011, http://www3.weforum.org/docs/WEF_GlobalCompetitivenessReport_2009-10.pdf.

Worthington, Ross. *Governance in Singapore.* London: Routledge Curzon, 2003.

Yanow, Dvora. "Qualitative-Interpretive Methods in Policy Research." *Handbook of Public Policy Analysis: Theory, Politics and Methods.* Eds. Frank Fischer, Gerald Miller and Mara Sidney. Boca Raton: CRC Press, 2006. 405–415.

Yap, Sonny Lim Richard and Leong Weng Kam. *Men in White: The untold story of Singapore's ruling political party.* Singapore: Singapore Press Holdings, 2009.

Yeo Kim Wah and Lau, Albert. "From colonialism to independence." *History of Singapore.* Eds. Ernest Chew and Edwin Lee. Oxford University Press, 1991. 117–153.

Yeo Lay Hwee. Ed. *Singapore: The Year in Review 1995.* Singapore: Institute of Policy Studies, 1996.

Zhang Zhibin. Ed. *Dynamics of the Singapore Success Story: Insights by Ngiam Tong Dow.* Singapore: Cengage Learning Asia Pte Ltd, 2011.

Zheng Yongnian, *The Chinese Communist Party and Organisational Emperor.* London: Routledge, 2010.

———— and Lye Liang Fook. "China's Central Party School: Adapting to Changes (II)." EAI Background Brief No. 182 (2004).